PRAISE FOR
HAPPY DOG

Illustrated by Justin Graham

Photographs by Michael Vistia

BILLY RAFFERTY AND JILL CAHR

HAPPY
DOG

Caring for Your Dog's Body,
Mind and Spirit

NEW AMERICAN LIBRARY

New American Library
Published by New American Library, a division of Penguin Group (USA) Inc., 375 Hudson Street, New York,
New York 10014, USA • Penguin Group (Canada), 90 Eglinton Avenue East, Suite 700, Toronto, Ontario
M4P 2Y3, Canada (a division of Pearson Penguin Canada Inc.) • Penguin Books Ltd., 80 Strand, London
WC2R 0RL, England • Penguin Ireland, 25 St. Stephen's Green, Dublin 2, Ireland (a division of Penguin
Books Ltd.) • Penguin Group (Australia), 250 Camberwell Road, Camberwell, Victoria 3124, Australia
(a division of Pearson Australia Group Pty. Ltd.) • Penguin Books India Pvt. Ltd., 11 Community Centre,
Panchsheel Park, New Delhi - 110 017, India • Penguin Group (NZ), 67 Apollo Drive, Rosedale, North Shore
0632, New Zealand (a division of Pearson New Zealand Ltd.) • Penguin Books (South Africa) (Pty.) Ltd., 24
Sturdee Avenue, Rosebank, Johannesburg 2196, South Africa

Penguin Books Ltd., Registered Offices: 80 Strand, London WC2R 0RL, England

First published by New American Library, a division of Penguin Group (USA) Inc.

First Printing, September 2009
10 9 8 7 6 5 4 3 2 1

The author gratefully acknowledges permission to reprint Chef Art Smith's
Puppy Biscuit recipe on peges 82–83.

 REGISTERED TRADEMARK—MARCA REGISTRADA

LIBRARY OF CONGRESS CATALOGING-IN-PUBLICATION DATA:

Rafferty, Billy.
Happy dog: caring for your dog's body, mind, and spirit/Billy Rafferty and Jill Cahr;
illustrated by Justin Graham; photographs by Michael Vistia.
p. cm.
ISBN 978-0-451-22786-7
1. Dogs-Health. I. Cahr, Jill. II. Title.
SF991.R34 2009
636.7'0893-dc22   2009004760

Set in Scala
Designed by Kate Nicholas

Printed in the United States of America

BILLY

For my mom and dad, Bridget and Thomas Rafferty,

my brothers and sister, my beloved Portie, Gabriel Rafferty,

and all of my wonderful four-legged companions

who have shared my life and inspired me.

. . . .

JILL

For my husband, Darren, and my son, Ian,

and all the dogs that have shared my life

and made me happy—

especially Shadow, Zelda, Inky, Farina and Filbert, my forever dog.

Acknowledgments

Many people had a role in the creation of this book. First of all, this book would never have happened without Ms. Oprah Winfrey, who has inspired us personally and professionally. Billy is grateful that he had the opportunity to help care for Solomon and Sophie for almost fourteen years. Billy sends thanks and hugs to Sheri Salata, Lisa Erspamer, Novona Cruz, Libby Moore, Chris Hill, Carla Bird, Danita Ruiz and Louise Price at Harpo for their friendship and support over the years. We thank Art Smith, who graciously provided us with a recipe, advice and wonderful dogs to photograph. Tremendous thanks to our photographers, Michael and Tracy Vistia and Sheri Berliner, and our illustrator, Justin Graham, for their undying creativity and patience, even in the face of multiple revisions. For their assistance with technical review, thanks to Dr. Sheldon Rubin and Dr. John Kasmersky, who were extremely helpful and insightful. A special thanks and big hugs to all the owners and their beautiful dogs who endured long photo shoots full of crazy canines, and a shout-out to Brenda Holdren—the Portie Porter. Thanks also to Guadalupe Rodriguez of Estée Lauder, makeup artist extraordinaire, for making us look like a million bucks; and to Molly Boren of Simplicity Works, for introducing us to our fabulous agent, Rebecca Oliver, at Endeavor, the ultimate master at managing freshman expectations. Truly, there are not enough words in the English language to express our gratitude to Becka for her assistance and willingness to talk us in off the ledge on countless occasions. Mindy Malkin and Emily Cappo read and reread this book until their eyes hurt; their comments and advice were invaluable and helped us keep only the things that truly mattered. A robust thank you to our production, publicity and sales crew at NAL. We appreciate all your hard work and attention to detail. Enormous thanks, hugs and kisses to the ladies at Goldberg McDuffie Communications, Inc.: Lynn C. Goldberg, Angela Hayes and Megan Underwood Beatie. We could not have asked for more skilled or delightful publicists! Thank you and big hugs to Carol Bell, Jill Katz and Lara Shiffman of the Patton Group for their outstanding work on our events and publicity. Thanks also to Billy's assistant, Alfred Laurie. Others who helped, supported and guided us on our journey include Mark Mitten, Lisa Ross, Blythe Mendelson, Joan Cusack, Jackie Petree, Lori Ovitz, Jacky Ferro, Meredith Cusick, Elaine Moss, Julie Mora, Paul Payton, Richard and Beverly Bernstein, Michael and Naoma Cahr, Jim and Erin Kaese, Jennifer Berman, Rob, Davida, Sammy and Rachel Pesick, Tom, Patrick, Jim, David and Ray Rafferty and Joann Rafferty-Reed, Eric Arnson, Randy Stearns, Stacey Bashara, Cheryl Russell-Miller, Tamron Hall, John J. Lanzendorf, Rolli Grayson, Lynn Brezina, Judi Feiger, Michael Povsher, Sue Naiden, Alice Lerman, David McMillan, Grace and Tom Woodford, Paul Bryant, Pam and Chuck Lauritzen and Mary and Susan, from Billy's early years.

We offer our deepest gratitude and biggest hugs to our editor, Tracy Bernstein, a wonderful and caring book mom whose counsel and advice shaped and nurtured our baby and allowed it to blossom and shine; and to Darren and Ian Cahr, who were supportive when not complaining, and always willing to help us with a joke, editing or an idea.

Finally, Jill also wants to thank Bob and Barb Malina of Small Dog Adoption in Plantation, Florida, for giving me and my family Shadow when our hearts needed mending; kisses to Shadow who served as my canine model and foot-warmer while I hovered over my computer; and HUGE hugs to Billy, my coauthor and dear friend, whose astounding expertise and passion made this book possible and who was especially hilarious at two o'clock in the morning. Billy also wants to thank Tiger, my first paying client, for being a trooper, and his owner for actually paying me. Thanks to all my wonderful clients over the years for allowing me to take care of their special four-legged furry angels, high-fives to Michael Vistia for being the best personal trainer I've ever had and I want to thank my coauthor Jill for giving me the kick to get up and do this book that needed to be done. Her persistence and attention to detail have helped make this book a beautiful thing.

"The greatness of a nation and its moral progress can be judged by the way its animals are treated."
—Mahatma Gandhi

. . . .

"Heaven goes by favor; if it went by merit, you would stay out and your dog would go in."
—Mark Twain

Contents

1.

Please Allow Me to Introduce Myself

So who am I, and why should you listen to me, a nice guy from the burbs south of Chicago? Let's just say that I know a few things about dogs. OK, maybe more than a few. But before we get into the details, perhaps you should know a bit about your guide and how my background has shaped my opinions. As you'll see, you and your dog are in good hands, indeed.

Some people are born knowing that they want to be doctors or lawyers when they grow up. Well, fate revealed my professional destiny when I was a young child too. At the ripe old age of eight, I was incited by a mysterious drive to steal into my sister's room to cut her dolls' hair. She never actually caught me red-handed, but that hardly stopped her from going ballistic when she discovered my handiwork. While my sister did not approve of me bobbing Chatty Cathy's hair, the experience was transcendent. Right then and there, as I was holding Chatty Cathy, something clicked inside me. I knew that I yearned to do something creative and artistic—I wanted to *style*.

But something else was inside me as well—a love for animals. Animals provided a safe refuge from my childhood, which was tumultuous, to say the least. I was a sensitive child in an emotionally complex environment. Unlike many people I encountered, animals always responded positively to me. They loved and understood me even though I was different from other kids. Animals, and dogs in particular, brought happiness into my otherwise gloomy childhood. I longed to return the favor and bring joy into their lives. Later on, when I discovered that I had a flair for the creative, I realized that I could pamper animals and make them look and feel fabulous using my artistic talents. Deep in my heart, I understood that animals were my true love, and I knew that I wanted to be surrounded by them, help them and work with them.

While I was growing up, our family always had a dog. Unfortunately for me, the budding groomer, not one of our family dogs had a long coat. So I abandoned Chatty Cathy and got busy with my sister's stuffed animals. I trimmed and primped every teddy bear and stuffed animal I could get my hands on. No one was safe, not even Snoopy! At one point he had a lopsided Lion Cut, a bald tail and a pink bow on his left ear. Woodstock was mortified.

At age ten, I spotted a small home-grooming kit in a mail-order catalog. I begged and begged my mom to buy it for me. This was a *gen-u-ine* kit, not a toy, and it was expensive—thirty dollars way back in the 1970s. While everyone else was disdainful of my grooming aspirations, my mom always encouraged me. Of course, she bought me the kit, and again, I went to town on the teddy bears.

As the years passed, I continued to follow my grooming dreams. I saved up every cent of my allowance to purchase any grooming book that I could find. The only books available back then were of the "how to groom your Poodle with fancy and ridiculous haircuts" variety. These books were absolutely awful but, *sigh*, they were a start.

After I had *fabulously* coiffed all the teddy bears and other stuffed animals in my house (my sister *still* hasn't forgiven me), I began crafting my own. I bought furry fabric and attached it to a ceramic Poodle my mom had given me. I'd put that ceramic dog up on a table and pretend I was a groomer. Other kids spent their money on candy at the corner store, while I spent every dime I had on ersatz fur at Minnesota Fabrics.

When I wasn't "grooming" stuffed animals, I was walking neighborhood dogs for free. I just loved dogs and I couldn't get enough of them. The more time I spent with dogs, the happier and more accepted I felt, and I wanted to make these generous pooches happy too.

One of my favorite dogs was a Poodle named Tiger. I used to visit Tiger and his owner frequently. One day, I told Tiger's owner that I was a licensed dog groomer and she actually believed me. Clearly, the fact that I was not quite eleven years old, stood less than four feet tall and arrived on a bicycle with a sparkly banana seat and purple streamers had no bearing on her reality. Thus, I booked my first appointment as a "professional" groomer. The pressure was on and I knew that all my study and practice was about to be put to the ultimate test.

Poor Tiger! His haircut gave the term "plucked chicken" a new canine meaning. I only knew what I had read in my grooming books and Tiger looked nothing like the dogs in those books. At the end of the session, Tiger had bald patches and I had a bloody finger. The neighbor paid five dollars, but she never called me again. In fact, I retired from grooming for a year.

Still, throughout my teenage years, my love for dogs grew as they continued to bring me unconditional love, and unlike my peers, they accepted me for who I was. Let's just say that in my working-class suburb, there were not many kids, especially boy kids, who had dreams of becoming a professional dog groomer! While the neighborhood kids played baseball or hockey, I was curled up with *How to Groom a Hungarian Puli*.

After high school, I worked full-time at a kennel that raised show dogs. The owner was wonderful and she taught me how to *actually* groom. At first, I just watched her groom for hours and hours. Finally, she let me pick up my first pair of professional scissors. From the start, I felt like I had been doing it for years. All the reading and the practice with the teddy bears and that faux-fur-sheathed ceramic Poodle had paid off at long last. The exceptionally low wages notwithstanding, I was overjoyed because I was finally doing what I loved and my career took off faster than a figure skater on Crisco!

|||||||||||||||||||||||||||||||||||||||||||||||||||||||||||||||||||||||||||||||||||||||||||||||||||||||||||||||||||||||||

Why I Don't Groom Cats and Neither Should You

It's nothing personal—I love cats and grew up with Totsie, a beautiful feline who slept in my bed—but as any cat lover knows, cats suffer no fools, especially fools wielding grooming tools. I learned this lesson early in my grooming career.

One morning a woman brought in Sunny, her stunning Flame Point Himalayan. As she set Sunny's kennel on my grooming table, she touted his relaxed and easygoing temperament. "Sunny doesn't bite. He's gentle as a lamb!" I peeked my head into the kennel and chirped, "Hi, Sunny!" Sunny responded with a deep, guttural growl. As if she'd heard a quaint meow, the owner continued, "Sunny is so sweet! He always loves being groomed, so he won't bite."

Having grown up with cats, I knew that Sunny's growl was not a friendly overture but a declaration of war. Moreover, experience had taught me that cats do not cooperate unless they believe that grooming is *their* idea and clearly it hadn't crossed *Sunny's* mind.

Knowing this, I asked the woman to stay and hold Sunny while I groomed him. She dutifully held him as I started gently brushing. Almost instantly, Sunny turned around and swatted the woman's left hand, drawing blood. She seemed unfazed. I continued to brush Sunny and almost immediately he became agitated again. He began to swing his tail ominously back and forth, which I took as a sign of imminent danger. Sunny's owner, however, interpreted the tail wagging as a sign of his fondness for grooming. The fragile détente between Sunny and my brush held for a few minutes until I found a mat. At that point, Sunny reared back, grabbed the woman's hand with both front paws and chomped down like Jaws. Within thirty seconds her hand had doubled in size. I threw down my brush and ran for peroxide. While Sunny's owner examined her swelling mitt, he cleverly turned around and bit her other hand. At that point, I declared the grooming session officially over and I retired from cat grooming on the spot.

The moral of this story: if your cat needs grooming, take him to a professional who specializes in cats—and works in a salon that's not filled with barking dogs.

||||||||||||||||||||||||||||||||||||||||||||||||||||||||||||||||||||||||||||||||||||||||||||||||||||||||||||

Grooming is not *just* about "styling" a dog. Rather, it involves a variety of activities that are crucial to canine health and happiness. If done incorrectly or carelessly, these activities can cause serious physical and emotional injury. For that reason, I began to study the science of grooming and animal cosmetology. Just for the record, this is no easy task.

An outrageous number of states have no licensing or training requirements for groomers. I find this shocking and I think most pet owners would too. With this in mind, I've devoted countless hours and many years to expanding my knowledge and honing my skills, including attending numerous symposia, studying complex material and passing difficult tests on a wide variety of formidable topics (skin and coat, first aid, CPR, animal behavior and anatomy, advanced scissoring techniques, geometry and canine design and topical conditioning). I learned to make a dog appear perfect despite (and in some cases because of) his natural imperfections. For example, by using complex geometric principles, I can take a short, stubby dog and trim him so that he appears taller and slimmer. (Don't you wish I could do this for people too?)

All the hard work paid off and in 1996 I became a Certified Master

Groomer. Several years later, I earned a prestigious and rare DermaTech Specialist Certification from the esteemed International Society of Canine Cosmetologists. That same year, I earned the World Wide Pet Supply Association's Certification for Companion Animal Hygienist.

In 1997, I started competing at grooming competitions. I made a name for myself by transforming household pets into show-dog divas. Since this is *my* book, I *will* toot my own horn: I've won so many grooming awards and accolades that I've run out of display space. I do, however, appreciate each one!

I loved competing, but in the back of my mind, I was disturbed by some of the work presented. Frankly, some of the groomers were so awful that I was embarrassed for everyone, especially the dogs. I knew that I wanted to help transform grooming into a respected profession. To that end, I started judging grooming competitions in 2003, and two years later I officially retired from competition to pursue judging. The United Showmanagers Alliance has since designated me a sanctioned grooming-show judge. Now I frequently judge at prestigious grooming competitions across the country.

I firmly believe in sharing my knowledge and experience. I regularly lecture and speak all over the country at grooming conventions. And I'm thrilled to write this book so that I can share what I know with the countless dog owners out there and help dogs lead healthier, happier and more beautiful lives.

Owning my own salon had always been a significant aspect of my grooming dreams, and eventually I did it—I opened Doggy Dooz Pet Styling Salon in 2001. Doggy Dooz is an awful lot of work, but I truly love it. I now have a waiting list several hundred dogs long. Realizing my dream took me on a roller-coaster path and some days I'm busier than a three-legged man at a butt-kicking contest. Because I'm pursuing my dream, however, I smile every morning when I walk into my own salon. Truly, who wouldn't be happy surrounded by furry faces and waggy tails all day!

The most important thing to realize from my history is that I'm a dyed-in-the-wool dog person. Currently, I share my home with Zeke, a rambunctious Portuguese Water Dog, and Arthur, a sweet, friendly black-and-white Cocker Spaniel. These dogs are *my family*, and yes, they're impeccably groomed at all times!

I've been a professional groomer for over two decades; I've worked with thousands of dogs and I've seen or played with thousands more. I can tell you with authority that way too many dogs out there look and feel terrible. Some can't see because their fur is so long that it covers their eyes. Other dogs have white coats that look gray or black coats that are covered in a layer of dust from infrequent washing. I see dogs whose coats are peppered with mats, burs and other uncomfortable debris. Many dogs are too fat or too thin and some clearly need to visit a veterinarian because they're limping or suffering from skin ailments. And whose fault is it? *Ours*, people! Dogs cannot purchase or read the latest self-help book. They look to us for answers and we have a responsibility to provide them.

Dogs give us so much: unconditional love, happiness, loyalty and an excuse to have fun. In return, we must safeguard their physical and emotional health. This means more than just providing the basics, like food and shelter. Many other necessities, such as grooming (of course), good nutrition, exercise and play, veterinary care, love, attention, socialization, security and safety, also play key roles. In my book, I teach you not only how to groom your pooch at home but how to be a caring and responsible owner. Simply put, my goal is to help *you* improve your dog's life. Besides, it feels good to take care of someone else, so properly caring for your pooch will improve your life too.

|||||||||||||||||||||||||||||||||||||||||||||||||||||||||||||||||||||||||||||||||||||||||||||||||||||||||||||

Community-Service Kudos

In the process of writing this book, my coauthor and I talked about how shelter dogs are often unkempt, rarely brushed or even bathed. It occurred to us that these poor dogs would have an easier time finding a home if they were groomed. To test this theory, we brought a little white Poodle mix from New Leash on Life, a Chicago dog rescue, to my shop. He was grimy and covered in mats, and his nails had probably never been cut. I groomed him and he was adopted the very next day! This experience motivated me to raise money for New Leash by running the Chicago Marathon, and I raised over five thousand dollars! I hope this book will inspire you to use your new skills to groom shelter dogs in addition to your own pets (or simply to make a donation to a local animal rescue or shelter).

|||||||||||||||||||||||||||||||||||||||||||||||||||||||||||||||||||||||||||||||||||||||||||||||||||||||||||||

My life has been shaped by my belief that it's our duty to take care of little (and sometimes big) creatures. They don't have a voice so we must make sure they're happy, comfortable and safe. I hope my book will enhance your relationship with your canine pal and introduce you to the best ways to maintain the whole dog: body, mind and spirit.

2.

Getting to Know Your Pooch

Think you know enough about your dog to keep her healthy, wealthy (in spirit) and wise? Let's play a game to test your knowledge. You may think that common sense is all you need to answer my questions, and I agree that it's a good guide. In my experience, however, people seem to lose all sense of common sense when it comes to their dogs. For example, I have one former client who has stored her beloved dead Poodle, Ralphie, in her kitchen freezer next to the ice cream for years. She takes Ralphie out on his birthday, enjoys a bottle of whiskey with him and then puts him back in for another year in the deep freeze. This lady is an otherwise perfectly normal person; it's just that her logic departed with Ralphie's soul.

Now, let's roll the theme music while I move my podium into position. I've slipped into something more appropriate: a dark wool suit with a subtle windowpane pattern complemented by a serious and subdued maroon tie. In my best Canadian accent, I look at the camera and announce, "Hello and welcome to *Canine Jeopardy*. I'm your host, Billy Trebek." You smile nervously and request, "Canine Anatomy for $500."

In our game, you won't have to worry about being put in double jeopardy because you'll find all the answers here. To nurture your dog's body, mind and spirit, you must first learn the basics, which I conveniently discuss in this chapter. With this background in place, you'll be able to help your pooch lead a longer and healthier life.

What the Hock Is That? An Overview of Canine Anatomy

Before you can properly care for your dog, you must be comfortable touching and manipulating him—head, rear and everywhere in between—and part of getting comfortable comes from understanding basic canine anatomy. Long, technical tomes have been written about the subject, but I'm going to forgo

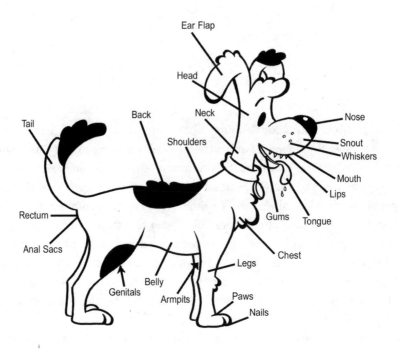

scientific language and concentrate only on what we need to know to care for and nurture our dogs. Besides, I'd feel terrible if you tumbled to the ground while retrieving your dusty two-volume *Oxford English Dictionary* from the top shelf of your library. For everyone's convenience, then, I will use everyday language and cleverly exclude superfluous body parts. For instance, rather than dissecting a leg into the forearm, elbow, wrist, pastern, stifle joint, rear pastern, lower thigh and hock, I just refer to the leg as, well, "the leg." It's simple and to the point. Besides, for home dog care this is all you need to know. If I've left you craving polysyllabic scientific terms, feel free to acquire a library card at the nearest college of veterinary medicine or enroll in grooming school. We can talk technicalities over coffee.

Skin

The skin is Fido's largest organ and it performs a variety of critical functions. For instance, skin shields and protects the body and internal organs from external hazards. Additionally, skin stores a variety of essential nutrients and substances, such as protein, fat, water, vitamins and minerals. For this reason, the skin's condition and appearance are helpful indicators of canine health. Dogs can develop dry, flaky, scaly, crusty, stinky or thickened skin, rashes and infections due to poor diet, parasites or systemic illnesses. Regularly inspecting Fido's skin allows you to discover and treat these conditions.

Healthy skin is pliable, supple, clean and relatively odor free. If your dog's skin smells, he should smell only like the substance he rolled in, not musty or rancid. To remain healthy, skin must be exposed to air, which allows it to breathe and regenerate. Thus, we see why routine brushing is important: accumulated dead fur and mats block airflow to the skin.

Coat

"I'll take 'From Hair to Eternity' for $300 Billy."
"The answer is 'Blowing coat.'"
A. What is illegal in thirteen states?
B. What happens when a canine spy is discovered by the enemy?
C. What happens when a dog loses his fur quickly or all at once?

All dogs, other than the absolutely hairless breeds, are covered in a coat of hair/fur.* As a loving and responsible owner, you'll tend to Fido's coat for aesthetic *and* health reasons. Like you, Fido feels good when his coat is clean, tidy and tangle free. In addition, medical problems often manifest in a dog's coat. A healthy coat is full, bright, shiny, supple and not smelly (unless Fido has rolled in something gross). If you notice that your pooch's coat is dry, brittle, dull, sparse or musty, breaks off easily or is suddenly different, you have cause for concern. The change could be due to a nutritional deficiency, a parasite or an underlying illness. Severe medical conditions, extreme stress (including giving birth), trauma or abuse may cause a dog to "blow coat," which means losing a large amount of fur quickly or all at once.

---

*For all you purists and grooming buffs out there, I'll note that anything growing out of a follicle is *technically* called "hair." Getting caught up in technicalities, however, will not help you care for the stuff you see covering your pooch. Most pet owners use "hair" and "fur" interchangeably, and in the book I will too.

Regular inspecting, brushing and washing allow you to spot obvious and subtle coat changes that require veterinary attention.

Head and Face

To many people, grooming a dog's head and face is somewhat intimidating. No one wants to accidentally deposit soap in a dog's eyes, spray water up his nose or leave brush burns on his noggin. Once you understand what's there, though, your fear will melt away. For our purposes, the head is made up of many basic, easy-to-understand parts: the nose, snout, whiskers, mouth, lips, folds, tongue, teeth, gums, eyes, eyelashes and ears. Much of your dog-care time and effort will be spent here.

Nose

Staring at the front tip of the dog, you'll find a cartilage ball with two nostrils that lead into a nasal cavity. The "ball" comes in all sorts of sizes, shapes and colors. The noses on some dogs, like Labrador Retrievers, actually change from black to pink in the summer. When you're grooming, keep the brush away from the delicate cartilage and try to avoid shooting water inside.

Snout

The snout (or more technically the muzzle) starts between the eyes and ends at the nose. Snouts come in an assortment of shapes and sizes, each one having a fancy, flowery name. For our purposes, we'll just label them long, medium and short. Compare the long pointy snout of a Collie with the medium snout on a Labrador Retriever and the short snout of a Pug or a Bulldog.

All snouts must be washed, brushed and petted on a regular basis. The skin folds on short-snouted dogs, however, need extra attention to keep them clean, dry and healthy.

Whiskers

Most dogs have whiskers, which are long, thick hairs protruding around the nose and snout. The amount, texture and length of whiskers differ by breed and individual genetics. Some look sparse, while others could have been borrowed from Rutherford B. Hayes. Whiskers help dogs sense their physical surroundings. For example, Terriers and other hunting dogs use their whiskers to judge the width of a hollow tree trunk or hole while chasing prey.

Whiskers are like any other fur and have no feeling. So feel free to trim or shave them unless your pooch is a fox hunter. Depending on a dog's preferred haircut, I sometimes shave off the whiskers, like on a Poodle's snout. I trim Zeke's and Arthur's whiskers only if they grow longer than their facial hair.

Some people pluck whiskers, which is something I would never do—ouch! Anyone who suggests plucking whiskers should be forcibly subjected to a full body waxing and then named in a restraining order forbidding him from coming within five hundred feet of your pooch.

Mouth, Lips, Folds, Tongue, Teeth and Gums

"I'll take 'Farcical Facial Folds' for $300, Billy."
"The answer is 'Flews, dewlaps and jowls.'"
A. *What is the name of a prestigious East Coast patent-law firm?*
B. *What were the most commonly used fireplace tools in medieval Europe?*
C. *What are the various folds found in a dog's mouth and lip area?*

A dog's mouth is usually easy to spot—just follow the drool. Once there, you'll see lips, which open to reveal teeth, gums and a floppy tongue. Fido's oral area is a hoppin' place and must be cleaned and inspected often.

Lips vary in color and thickness. On many dogs, the lips and surrounding area are full of flaps and folds. For example, Mastiffs, Saint Bernards and hounds have fleshy, pendulous upper lips called "flews" (I know that's a technical term, but it's so fun to say that I couldn't resist including it). Beagles, Bulldogs and Cocker Spaniels and many other breeds also have "jowls," which are heavy, droopy lower lips or folds hanging off the lower jaw. Other dogs, such as Bloodhounds and Basset Hounds, have loose pendulous skin folds on their chin, throat or neck called "dewlaps." All these areas are highly effective drool slingers and food catchers and, if your dog has them, require a bit of extra hygienic attention.

Carefully part Fido's lovely lips to reveal a tongue, teeth and gums. The tongue is one of Fido's most useful organs. In fact, it's all muscle and a major-league anatomy all-star. On the HVAC team, it plays the hot corner (third base), where it specializes in heat regulation and cooling by hanging loose and panting. It bats cleanup for the Health and Wellness team, where it licks wounds and self-cleans the body. The tongue is the designated hitter for Sustenance, since it's crucial to chewing, swallowing and drinking. The tongue also plays center field for Environmental Monitoring, as it's central to taste, smell and touch. Like all stars, the tongue always has time to meet and greet its fans with big wet kisses.

On most dogs, healthy tongues are pink. Chow Chows and several other breeds have blue-black tongues and many breeds and mixes have dark spots on the top and/or bottom. Tongues are relatively maintenance free, but can be injured if Fido bites something sharp or brittle.

If left to his own devices, Fido won't brush his teeth. As a result, the entire area, gums and all, becomes a veritable Garden of Eden for germs, bacteria and disease. Brushing Fido's teeth and gums not only keeps his breath steak-y fresh (dogs don't like mint) but also helps him remain healthy, as dental disease can contribute to serious systemic illnesses.

Many dogs have a beard on the bottom and a mustache on the top of their mouths. Food and other debris cling here and spawn dog breath. Careful grooming and spot washing prevent the area from smelling awful like offal.

Eyes

It's perfectly fine to work in the eye *area* as long as you exercise caution when using a brush, scissors, fingers and grooming products. In case I'm being too subtle, let me put it this way, and yes, I'm yelling: **NEVER TOUCH YOUR DOG'S EYEBALLS!** Certain breeds, such as Pugs, Shih Tzus and others with bulging eyes, are particularly prone to eye injuries. Some breeds, such as Poodles, can have overly active tear ducts, which tend to clog and produce brownish tearstains. Congenital eye problems, including cherry eye, inverted eyelids or ingrown lashes, are also common with some breeds. If you suspect these conditions, talk to your veterinarian.

Regardless of their appearance, all eyes require daily attention and any long hair in the area must be trimmed, preferably by a professional groomer.

Eyelashes

Dogs have eyelashes, but thankfully no one has yet invented canine mascara. Eyelashes are protective shields that catch dust and other minute particles before they can enter the eyes. Eyelashes on many dogs, such as Spaniels and Doodles, grow quite long and must be trimmed for hygienic purposes. If Fido's lashes are too long, bring him to your professional groomer for a trim. Do not try this at home—it's too dangerous!

If your dog's eyes produce a lot of goo (yes, that's another fancy, technical term), her eyelashes can become glued shut overnight and require daily cleaning.

Ears

Canine ears come in an assortment of sizes and shapes, but they all function like an antenna to catch sound waves. In general, ears are categorized by the shape and position of the flap, the fur-covered skin that protrudes from the head: (1) Erect,* where the flaps are in a fully upright and locked position like on a German Shepherd or Siberian Husky, (2) Drop, where long and often pendulous flaps fold over and cover the ear opening like Snoopy's or a Labrador Retriever's, and (3) Semi-drop, where the flap is upright but the tippy-top folds over, as on a Collie, an English Bulldog and some terriers. A dog's ear flap is covered on the outside with fur, which must be brushed, washed and inspected as part of regular wellness care.

All dogs have an L-shaped ear canal, which is an ideal breeding ground for dirt, fungi, yeast and bacteria. Allergies, excess moisture, foreign objects, genetics and parasites also cause internal ear disease. All dogs are at risk for ear problems, but dogs with Drop ears are especially prone because the folded flaps inhibit internal air circulation. This is especially true for

---

*Many breed standards still require surgical alteration, or "cropping," of the ears to make them Erect. The United States is woefully behind most of Europe, where ear cropping, tail docking, dewclaw removal and other such procedures are barred when done for purely cosmetic reasons.

canine swimmers. With ears, cleanliness *is* next to godliness. Thus, you must monitor your dog's ears weekly and clean inside as needed. If you're lax, she can develop serious and painful ear conditions that require drugs or even surgery.

Some dogs grow hair inside their ears. As you might expect, the ear hair traps moisture, wax and debris, which can cause infections and other problems. The jury is still out on whether this hair should be removed and we'll discuss it further in chapter 15, "Dirty Deeds Done Dirt Cheap . . . at Home." Suffice it to say that it's difficult to remove ear hair safely and painlessly. This procedure is best left to professionals.

Neck

Like yours, Fido's neck is located between his head and his body. Fido's neck is covered in fur and must therefore be groomed on a regular basis. The front of the neck is delicate, especially near the throat, so be careful when you brush, wash and inspect this area. A gentle touch is also important when using restraints like leashes and nooses.

Back

The back is that long straightaway on top of your dog's body that starts at the base of the back of the neck and ends at the tail. If you want to get technical, this area can be broken into multiple subparts, but who needs technicality when you've got me to guide you? The shape of a canine back is primarily a function of breed, age, activity level, musculature and genetics. All backs, however, must be washed, brushed and inspected in the same manner. Bear in mind, however, that older or arthritic dogs may have sensitive backs and you must adjust your grooming routine according to their physical condition and pain tolerance. Your veterinarian and professional groomer can help develop a suitable plan to accommodate special needs.

For the record, the shoulders are located a few inches below the back of the neck. If your dog is not overweight, you should be able to feel his shoulder blades. Many parasite preventatives and other topical medicines are applied here.

The Rhodesian Ridgeback, the more obscure Thai Ridgeback and a few other breeds have a stripe of longer fur growing down the middle of their backs. Although beautiful and exotic, this ridge is merely fur that grows in the opposite direction from the rest of the coat and is groomed in the same manner as the rest of the body.

Chest

For our purposes, the chest is the front half of your dog's undercarriage. The chest starts at the front of the neck and ends where the belly and genital area begin. The rib cage is located here, along with many important internal organs. I like to put my ear to Zeke's or Arthur's chest and listen to his heart beating. I find this enormously relaxing and they enjoy the cuddling time. As a rudimentary test to determine if your pooch is overweight, periodically rub your dog's chest and try to feel her ribs. If you stroke nothing but flesh, Fido probably needs to sign up for Weight Watchers.

Many dogs, such as Dachshunds and Basset Hounds, sport the short leg–low chest combination that attracts dirt and debris like flies on honey. Similarly, Cocker Spaniels, Lhasa Apsos and others have long belly hair, which is in almost constant contact with the ground. These dogs require bathing and brushing more frequently than long-legged, high-chested models like the Dalmatian or Greyhound.

Belly and Accoutrements

"I'll take 'Understanding Undercarriages' for $200, Billy."
"The answer is 'Six to ten.'"
A. What is the average jail term for people who brush a wet dog?
B. What is the number of hours it takes a person who has not read Billy's book to wash her dog?
C. What is the typical number of nipples on a canine?

Your dog's belly is the hind part of his undercarriage. The belly begins at the bottom of the chest (about the middle of the dog) and runs to the end, right between the back legs. Belly fur is usually thin and the skin is exposed, so exercise care when brushing. Wash and inspect this area the same as the rest of the dog, just more gently.

If Fido weren't fixed, this is where the magic would have happened. Mind you, absolutely no magic should *ever* happen here. Your dog is much better off both physically and mentally when spayed or neutered as soon as your veterinarian says it's safe. If you haven't done this already, stop reading and make an appointment immediately!

We're all adults here, so I'll assume I don't have to talk at length about genitalia, their function and appearance. This is not *that* type of book and I'm not *that* type of guy.

Along with the expected collection of internal reproductive organs, tubes and glands, a male dog, of course, has a visible penis. If he's neutered (and he should be), his scrotum is out of sight. People frequently ask me why their recently neutered dog's scrotal sac is missing. Like it or not, removing the inside of the scrotum is the whole point of neutering: no sperm-production equipment means no unwanted puppies! After neutering, the empty sac shrinks away and is barely visible.

Not surprisingly, females have the usual reproductive organs too. On the outside, you'll see her vulva. Her vagina is internal and neither you nor any other dog has any business being anywhere near it. Spaying doesn't change the outward appearance of a female's genitals. It does, however, afford your female a healthier and safer life.

Both males and females have raised, frecklelike bumps on their bellies. I have one client who rushed her new Poodle puppy to the veterinarian for an emergency appointment after discovering a "suspicious" black bump on his belly. She felt sheepish when the veterinarian said, "That's a nipple—the dog has eight of them." Indeed, all canines, regardless of sex, have six to ten nipples. They are clearly visible on some dogs (especially females that have given birth) and merely specks on others. Many people mistake canine nipples for fleas or ticks.

Armpits

This is the area where the body and legs meet, so maybe "*legpits*" is a more precise term. Luckily for Fido, hairy armpits are the height of canine fashion.

This area is difficult to reach and a high-friction zone. As a result, debris often finds its way in but not out, and mats and tangles rapidly sprout up here. While grooming, ensure that you are making contact with each of Fido's armpits, and use caution—the blood vessels are close to the skin here.

Legs

The canine leg begins at the armpit and ends at the floor (well, actually the paw, but that wasn't as droll). These important appendages are critical for mobility, scratching an itch, poking your leg to beg for food and a host of other vital canine activities. Canine legs come in all sorts of shapes, sizes and thicknesses. No matter their appearance, all legs require regular inspecting, brushing and washing.

||||||||||||||||||||||||||||||||||||||||||||||||||||||||||||||||||||||||||||||||||||||||||||||||||||||||||||||||||||||||

Why Is My Dog Wearing Fur Pants?

Some dogs have longer fur on the backs of their legs or on their bellies, chests or tails. The texture of this fur is often lighter and fluffier than on the rest of the dog. Fancy dog people refer to this phenomenon as "furnishings," "feathering" or "fringing." A few breeds, like Border Collies and Papillons, also have furnishings on their ears.

Many otherwise short-haired dogs sport furnishings. Picture an Irish Setter, Border Collie or Golden Retriever.

||||||||||||||||||||||||||||||||||||||||||||||||||||||||||||||||||||||||||||||||||||||||||||||||||||||||||||||||||||||||

Paws

"I'll take 'Pause for Paws' for $500, Billy."
"The answer is 'Communal pad.'"
A. What is the 1970s slang term for a house rented by multiple bachelors?
B. What is a lumpy seat cushion issued to the members of a Soviet farming collective?
C. What is the largest paw pad on a dog?

Show-dog people and other dog fanciers have myriad names to describe the enormous diversity of canine paws. For us regular folk, however, we'll keep it simple and just call them all plain old "paws." Take a moment to delicately feel in and around your pooch's paws. You'll be surprised at what's going on in there.

On the front of each paw, Fido has four separate toes, each with a nail sprouting from the end. On the bottom of each toe, you'll find four pads situated above a larger "communal" pad. Pads are actually made up of fatty tissue that becomes callused with age and use.

The pads and toes are joined together by fleshy skinlike webbing, which is an ideal hiding spot for small pebbles, mud, dirt and other debris. On some dogs, the fur growing here requires regular trimming, and mats can form too.

Dogs have another pad located a few inches above each paw on the back of the front legs called a "stopper" pad. It's a canine shock absorber useful for climbing or sprawling out on the floor. None of Fido's pads require special grooming other than cleaning, inspecting and occasional moisturizing. Try to keep the brush away from all paw pads to prevent scrapes.

Nails

Each canine toe ends in a nail. The color of the skin and fur surrounding the nail determines its color, so many dogs have multicolored nails, which saves money on canine polish. The "quick" is the fancy name for the veins and nerves that grow through the center of each nail. The quick is responsible for the blood you see during a faulty canine pedicure. The tip of the nail has no nerves or vessels and is safe to cut. It's impossible to distinguish the quick on dark nails.

Dewclaws

"I'll take 'How Do You Dew' for $400, Billy."
"The answer is 'Dewclaws.'"
A. *What is the portion of a financial contract articulating moneys owed?*

B. *What is the moisture that collects on the feet of birds each morning?*

C. *What is the superfluous toe found on some dogs?*

Dewclaws resemble an extra toe with a nail. They are loosely attached to the inside of the leg a few inches above the front and/or back paws. Like your appendix, dewclaws are evolutionary stragglers with no purpose, and many dogs have them only on their front paws or are born without them. A few breeds, like the Saint Bernard, Briard, Great Pyrenees and Norwegian Lundehund, have double dewclaws on their paws.

The dewclaws on many dogs are removed shortly after birth (hopefully by an experienced professional using proper procedures) for cosmetic reasons or to prevent tearing injuries. Removing dewclaws on an older dog is major surgery. Many countries outside the U.S. now ban *cosmetic* dewclaw removal. Eventually dewclaws will go the way of Neanderthal man and we won't have to worry about them.

Because dewclaws never make contact with the ground, they aren't worn down and require more frequent trimming to prevent painful ingrown nails.

We're at the End of Our Story: Rear, Tail, and Anal Sacs

"I'll take 'Righteous Rears' for $200, Billy."

"The answer is 'Anal sacs.'"

A. *What is the latest couture handbag from Paris worn low on the derriere?*

B. *What is the name of the bundles loaded onto members of the* Equus asinus *species?*

C. *What is the gland that produces a foul-smelling liquid used for marking territory?*

The aft section of a dog is one of nature's most perfect debris magnets, since it spends so much time on the ground. If anything gross gets within five feet of your dog, odds are that it will end up stuck to her rear end. Indeed, much of that stuff emanated from the area in the first place. As stated in the fine print of your Canine Guardianship Contract, *you* are obligated to keep close tabs on Fido's caboose so that dirt can't accumulate and cause odor, mats or infections. Fido can't wipe his own butt (technically his "rectum"). Luckily for you, your thumbs are opposable, so that's *your* job. Unscented baby wipes are useful for a quick cleanup here.

The tail, which is the last part of a dog's spine, is conveniently located at the tail end of your dog. Tails need to be inspected, brushed and washed. To access the rectum and anal sacs, gently lift the tail.

Fido has two internal anal sacs—one on each side of his rectum at four and eight o'clock. Each time your dog poops, the sacs secrete a strong earthy-scented fluid meant to alert his pack and enemies of his whereabouts—kind of like primordial e-mail. If you're fortunate, Fido will express adequate fluid with each poop. For many dogs, though, obesity, genetics, parasites or poor diet and the resulting volatile poop consistency tend to clog the anal sacs. When this happens, Fido scoots his rear on the ground or manically licks and nips his bum to relieve the pressure. Clogged anal sacs must be emptied to avoid infections and other nasty, painful problems. To clear the clog, Fido needs a helping hand—preferably not yours. The veterinarian or professional groomer should be your hand of choice.

Spirit: May the Canine Life Force Be with You

We are now well versed on the canine body, but what about the canine spirit? How do we define the essential nature of dogdom? You know what I mean, that canine je ne sais quoi—that slobbery élan? Mark Twain captured the canine spirit when he observed, "If you pick up a starving dog and make him prosperous, he will not bite you; that is the principal difference between a dog and a man." Dogs are givers and pleasers, asking for little in return. For a few bones or scraps, dogs will do just about anything for their humans.

Your dog faithfully greets you when you return home from work every day. The same can't always be said of your spouse, significant other or kids. Without exception, however, your canine pal will be at the door with her tail wagging like a wiper blade in a monsoon, after patiently waiting for the moment the key enters the lock to scurry over and bestow all her love and joy to you. Even better, your pooch never asks if you secured that raise and she's never distracted by the TV or the latest round of fantasy football. In other words, she always gives you 110 percent.

Without a doubt, there is no greater source of unconditional love, inexhaustible companionship, unyielding loyalty and infinite friendship than your dog. Dogs are skilled listeners, the best, in fact. They are nonjudgmental, they don't interrupt, their attention never wavers (unless liverwurst is involved) and they never ever reveal your secrets, no matter how juicy they may be.

Dogs are extraordinarily brave; they have proved their courage time and again ever since humans started walking upright. Prehistoric cave paintings depict dogs attacking huge prey while hunting with their human companions. Dogs have accompanied humans into battle and many canine "soldiers" have earned medals of honor for their exceptional heroism. Napoléon Bonaparte was once saved from drowning by a Newfoundland, which jumped overboard and kept him above water until rescue arrived. The pooch didn't receive a medal, but rather Bonaparte's admiration: "Here, gentlemen, a dog teaches us a lesson in humanity."

Dogs are also instinctively protective of their human pack and are always alert for intruders. Indeed, they've been the chosen protectors of royalty and regular folk alike for ages. Lewis and Clark brought a Newfoundland named Seaman with them on their travels. On several occasions Seaman protected the camp from bears, buffalo and other wild animals. Dogs are intelligent, hard workers. They assist search-and-rescue units, ski patrols and police officers. Many ranchers and farmers depend on dogs to keep their enterprises running efficiently. Even the United States Department of Agriculture has a Beagle Brigade to sniff out contraband at the borders. And to think these patriotic pooches have never unionized!

Dogs teach us empathy and respect for nature. For many of us, helping care for the family dog is our first experience with chores. This training instructs kids, and some adults, how to be responsible for others. A child who nurtures a dog also learns to appreciate, not fear, animals and nature and takes these important lessons into adulthood. Moreover, kids who grow up with pets may have stronger immune systems and may be less likely to develop allergies, asthma and other problems.

As if you needed more evidence of doggy decency, scores of studies confirm that interaction with dogs reduces human stress. Without a doubt, dogs are beneficial to our mental health. Nineteenth-century English author

Samuel Butler said it best: "The great pleasure of a dog is that you may make a fool of yourself with him and not only will he not scold you, but he will make a fool of himself too." Indeed, dogs remind us that it's important to stop and smell the roses (or sniff around the fire hydrant!). Dogs force us to have fun, to exercise and to actually leave our homes to enjoy the fresh air. Who can resist when confronted with a dog bouncing at your feet, gazing up at you with wide eyes, ball firmly clamped in mouth and a tail wagging so hard that his entire body is undulating with enough force to measure 7.6 on the Richter scale?

Dogs live to please us and they take great pains to ensure that we are emotionally and physically sound. They heal our broken hearts and mend our broken spirits. Just think of the therapy dogs that visit nursing homes or the dogs trained to help the disabled live independent lives. Dogs also make us laugh, and we all know that laughter is good medicine. In addition, dogs inspire us to be creative and to participate in our community, whether it's joining a charity Halloween pet parade or chatting with a neighbor who pauses to admire our pooch. Dogs also encourage us to try new hobbies and activities. People and dogs are a natural team for sporty diversions, such as catch, Frisbee, running or agility. I know of one highly urbanized über-Yuppie who actually joined a hunting club so his German Short-haired Pointer could do what he was born to do.

Now, that's a lot of spirit! Unquestionably, we are duty-bound to nurture our dogs' health and wellness, but we owe our faithful, loving canines *so much more*. Grooming enables us to truly and properly care for their bodies, which in turn allows their spirits to soar and minds to thrive.

3·
Why and When to Care
for Your Dog

And Now the Answer to the $64,000 Question, "Why Care for My Dog at Home?"

Every dog owner shoulders a significant responsibility to care for his canine, and I'm not just talking about providing food and shelter. But, OK, let's talk about those two essentials first because they are, after all, essentials. The food must be nutritious (much more on that later) and the shelter had better be safe, be *inside* your home and include a cushy bed, safe toys and healthful treats. Beyond that, your obligations also include keeping your dog safe, both when you're together and when you leave him alone. Therefore, making your home dog-proof is a top priority. Don't worry—all this is easy to do and I'll be showing you how.

Your pooch also relies on you to monitor and maintain his health. Providing appropriate veterinary care, including regular checkups, vaccinations and preventive medicine for heartworm and parasites, is essential. In addition, you must regularly exercise your dog and teach him to be a good canine citizen so he can safely interact with humans and other dogs. Fostering Fido's emotional well-being and mental health is also imperative, but that's simple: all it requires is spending quality time with him and including him in your life.

Grooming is another doggy duty and it is actually related to all your other responsibilities. (Well, maybe not the duty to exercise, except that you'll want to take Fido on extra walks to show off how beautiful he looks and feels now that he's being appropriately pampered.) The entire grooming process is an expression of love, a concept that your dog fully understands and unquestionably appreciates. While cleaning and maintaining his body, skin and coat, you touch, massage, pet and praise him. As you groom, you are also monitoring his health by inspecting him for parasites, pain, injuries, medical conditions and abnormalities. Indeed, many health problems and nutritional deficiencies manifest in the skin and coat. So grooming is essential to maintaining Fido's wellness.

|||||||||||||||||||||||||||||||||||||||||||||||||||||||||||||||||||||||||||||||||||||||||||||||||||||||||||||

Looking Good Is the Best Revenge

All my years of pampering pooches have taught me that dogs are truly sensitive about their appearance. If you watch dogs leaving a good grooming salon, you'll notice that they have a spring in their step and a swagger in their stride. We feel happy and confident after a successful visit to the beauty salon or barbershop, and so do our canine friends.

Just ask Zelda! She was the family mutt of my friend Davida. As was hip back in the 1970s, the family called in a traveling groomer, who arrived, of course, in a conversion van sporting a shag-carpeted ceiling. Zelda entered the van confident, fluffy and furry and exited the van uneven, nearly bald and humiliated. In fact, Zelda was so embarrassed by her appearance that she disappeared every time Davida's father came home. Day after day, Zelda played with the rest of the family, but as soon as she heard the dad return from work, she went into hiding. Her hideous haircut was too much to bear; she could not allow the pack leader to see her like that. Finally, the dad sat Zelda down for a heart-to-heart and explained that she was part of the family and had to stop hiding from him because he loved her no matter how she looked. I don't know if the haircut had begun to grow in, but Zelda stopped hiding and the family found a better groomer.

|||||||||||||||||||||||||||||||||||||||||||||||||||||||||||||||||||||||||||||||||||||||||||||||||||||||||||||

Top Grooming Myths

Throughout my career, I've heard many crazy ideas about the correct and proper way to care for a dog. As you will learn, I am the "Queen of Doing It Right *Every* Time." Therefore, throughout the book I will examine common grooming myths and put them to rest once and for all.

- Frequent bathing is bad for a dog's skin and coat.
- Some dogs don't shed.
- Some dogs are hypoallergenic.
- A dog with a short coat never needs to be groomed.

- A housebound dog never needs washing, because he doesn't play outside or with other dogs.
- Seasonal shedding takes the place of brushing.
- Bathing once every season is sufficient.
- Cutting the fur around the eye causes blindness. (Of course, this may be true if you stab the dog in the eye with the scissors.)
- Baby shampoo is good for a dog's skin and coat, because it is gentle.

Cleanliness Is Next to Godliness

Obviously, grooming makes a dog attractive and sweet smelling; less obviously it makes a dog happier and healthier. Besides, your pooch is living in your home and I believe I can safely assume that you don't want her smelling like a public toilet at a bus station.

There is no way around the fact that dogs are partial to all things dirty. It's in their genes and a powerful instinct. They enjoy digging in the dirt, sniffing one another's rear ends, rolling in the mud and exploring questionable places. It's all part of being a dog. Don't deny your dog her fun! After all, what harm is there in a little dirt—especially when a simple bath will clear up the grime? Likewise, a small investment in a sticky-tape lint roller can go a long way. If *your* fear of dirt prevents your dog from enjoying herself, *you* need to relax and read on so you can learn to clean your dog at home. It's enjoyable—I swear! The brief time you invest in grooming is a small price to pay for all the joy and unconditional love bestowed by your pooch.

Besides, if you are a well-mannered dog owner, there's a considerable chance your pooch sleeps in your bed. (Indeed, every respectable dog owner knows the cardinal rule of dog ownership: *Thou shalt not move the dog from his sleeping position.*) Let's face it, a dog in bed is much easier to bear if she doesn't smell like an old tennis shoe and her paws are free of any foul debris. To be sure, grooming your dog involves more than a quick bath. You'll be attending to the entire dog, snout to tail, with special attention to the head, nose, eyes, ears, skin, coat, paws, nails and—yes, it's true—the privates and rear too. Now, don't slam the book closed and slink away. We are talking about your best friend and loyal companion. The least you can do for her is to keep her clean *everywhere.*

A Pooch's Body Is His Temple

Unquestionably, regular home care is an important factor in maintaining canine health. For instance, brushing removes dead fur, dandruff and excess dander. It distributes natural oil, which promotes hair growth and healthy skin and coat. Routinely cleaning Fido's ears, eyes and other external organs prevents debris, bacteria and parasites from causing problems. Likewise, frequent bathing reduces the opportunity for skin ailments and dirt-related infections.

While grooming, the human examines, touches and smells every part of the dog. This type of up-close and personal contact allows us to spot embedded debris, painful areas, infections, parasites, skin abnormalities, tumors, lesions or other worrisome conditions. Indeed, inspections often reveal early clues to systemic problems. For example, a dull or dry coat may indicate an illness, nutritional deficiency or allergy. By grooming often, you can discover and correct health issues before they become severe or dangerous. A not-so-gentle reminder: if you find anything unusual or suspicious, call your vet immediately!

Love Is Love's Reward (John Dryden)

Home care is an incomparable opportunity for you to express your feelings for your pal and emphasize just how much you adore him. Grooming is much more than cleaning. It's a tactile and emotional bonanza that fosters trust and companionship. While you groom, you are touching, massaging, praising, rewarding and bonding. In other words, you are pampering your pooch, and who doesn't benefit from a little TLC?

Dogs crave attention from their pack leader. Home grooming, therefore, is a daily reminder to your pooch that you love him. Be sure to praise your dog, pet him and tell him how much fun you are having while you care for him. All this affection will make Fido's spirit soar! Without a doubt, these happy vibes boomerang back to you because it feels marvelous to make someone else happy. At the end of the day, you'll both sleep better, and not only due to Fido's newfound hygiene.

A Furry Cuddle a Day Keeps Your
Doctor Away

As they say in infomercials, "But wait, there's more!" Grooming is also a terrific opportunity for *you* to relax. Indeed, researchers have repeatedly demonstrated that touching and petting your furry friend produces a host of positive human-health benefits. Quality time with Fido can improve your mood, reduce stress, decrease your blood pressure, lower your risk of cardiovascular disease and depression and even increase your fitness—that is, if you fail to secure the bathing area and end up chasing a drenched dog all through the house after his escape from the tub!

Spending quality time with your pooch is also pleasurable, entertaining and downright fun. It provides you with a perfect excuse to ignore the telephone and "take five." We all know that laughter is the best medicine and grooming offers loads of opportunities for laughs. For example, you can sculpt your soapy dog into a variety of objets d'art (try a punk rocker with a Mohawk or a stegosaurus) or blow-dry him to four times his normal size. All in all, grooming is truly good clean fun. In a dirty world, this *is* a good thing.

When to Groom:
How Often Is Often Enough?

Many factors determine how often you should groom your pooch. The correct answer hinges on age, health, breed, coat, weather and lifestyle. I'll provide you with general rules of thumb that cover most dogs. Feel free to discuss your dog's particular needs with a professional.

Before we begin in earnest, as a dog lover I'm required to discuss those poor, unfortunate souls that are left by their "people" (and I use the term loosely) to live outside in the elements—pressing their noses against the window, forever wondering why they're inexplicably excluded from their pack.* If you compel your dog to live outside, denying him a proper warm

---

*Of course, if you're a rancher or a farmer and your outside dog is an actual "working dog" *and* as part of his job he happily resides with the animals he guards, you're exempt from my contempt.

and cozy home, you're probably one of *those* people who believes that semi-annual baths are "good enough." If you *are* one of *those* people, you need to be badgered into submission. Immediately go outside, grab a badger and use it to beat yourself about the head and neck. Cease said badgering once you have beaten some sense into yourself, or the badger becomes disoriented, whichever comes first. Now welcome your dog into your home. Sit down with Fido, apologize profusely, beg for forgiveness and explain his change in circumstances.

For all those who welcome their pets into their family and home with full rights and privileges, several factors determine how often to groom. Unlike humans, dogs don't require daily bathing. If, however, you follow my advice and use the appropriate tools, equipment, products and techniques, you may wash your dog as often as you wish. To determine how frequently your dog actually needs a bath, ask yourself a few questions:

- What breed or mix is my dog? As you'll see, your dog will fit into a grooming category, which determines how often you must perform certain grooming tasks.
- How old is my dog? Fido's age often determines how much grooming he can handle.
- What type of coat does my dog have?
- Where does my dog live, walk and play?
- Does my dog spend time with other dogs, such as at the dog park or day care?
- Is my dog healthy?
- What are the weather conditions and seasons like where I live?
- Has anything unusual happened, e.g., skunk attack, encounter with burs or a rough day at the dog park?
- What is my dog's personality?
- Has my dog recently been sick, vomited or suffered from diarrhea, loose stool, incontinence or other untidy issues?
- Is my dog a messy eater? Are treats or food often stuck in his beard or fur?
- How often do I actually brush my dog?
- How much time am I willing to devote to my dog's well-being?

Grooming Calendar

Home grooming entails much more than a monthly or semimonthly bath. You'll also perform certain tasks on a daily, weekly, monthly, semiannual or yearly basis. For example, you must brush your dog's coat and teeth daily or, at a minimum, a few times a week. Likewise, ears, eyes, paws, naughty bits and skin require weekly attention. I've included a handy calendar and planner on pages 205–7 to guide you through the process and keep you on target throughout the year. Feel free to customize it for your dog and lifestyle.

Keep track of your grooming routine and record the results of each session in a grooming notebook. Date each entry and make note of anything unusual that you find or if your dog's behavior changes. This way, you can track changes and discuss them with your veterinarian.

Categorizing Your Dog

Experts categorize dog coats in many different ways. Depending on where you look, coats may be sorted by breed, length, thickness, texture or color and each classification usually has myriad subsets. For example, a dog may be classified as "double coated." This means that the dog has two layers in his coat: the "outer coat," which is the visible and heavier, more weather-resistant layer of fur, and the "undercoat," which is the layer of fluffy, downy fur underneath. For our purposes, however, whether your dog has a single or a double coat is irrelevant, because she still has to be washed, brushed and dried the same as any other dog. Likewise, in the book I often call that stuff growing on a dog "fur" even though a groomer may call it "hair" because it grows out of a follicle. No matter the terminology, basic grooming techniques are the same for all dogs. Therefore, there's no need to confuse ourselves with impractical, unhelpful and overly technical terms. Just remember these four simple categories:

1. Hairless
2. Dogs with hair ("Hair")
3. Dogs with fur of one length ("Uniform Fur")
4. Dogs with fur of multiple lengths ("Multilength Fur")

The only real differences in care between categories are whether your dog requires regular professional haircuts or just trims; whether the dead fur stays in the coat or falls off the dog; whether you'll be dealing with mats; and how often your dog must visit a professional groomer.

Hairless: A Category unto Themselves

Some dogs actually have little or no coat, such as the Chinese Crested, Peruvian Inca Orchid, the Hairless Khala and the Mexican Hairless, which is also called the Xoloitzcuintli—try saying that three times fast. These rare and ancient breeds are tolerated well by people with allergies so severe that they can't handle even the alleged "hypoallergenic" dogs. Because Hairless dogs are basically bald, their grooming needs are quite different from the typical dog's. Hairless dogs are predisposed to poor dental health and have extremely delicate skin that requires special care and extra protection from the elements. Without protective fur, the skin on Hairless dogs burns easily, and keeping warm in cold weather is difficult. Thus, canine-safe sunscreen, UV-protective clothing and warm weather gear are must haves.

A Hairless dog requires bathing, exfoliating and a bit of moisturizer. The skin is sensitive and prone to rashes and pimples, so owners must be vigilant. Some Hairless dogs do have a dash of hair and that hair requires regular brushing with a small, extra-gentle slicker brush. Hairless dogs should visit a professional groomer about every four to eight weeks. If you own or are interested in Hairless breeds, I recommend that you seek out information specifically about these dogs and talk to your vet and professional groomer.

Everyone Else

The following chart separates most breeds into the categories I use in this book. Naturally, there are always rare exceptions to the rule. A while back, I groomed a Lhasa Apso, which is listed as a Hair dog on my chart. This particular Lhasa Apso's coat, however, did *not* behave like that of a Hair dog: his owner found dead fur everywhere because it fell off the dog rather than remaining in the coat until brushed out. Clearly, this "pedigreed" pooch possessed an atypical coat, which meant that at some point another breed had been added to his genetic mix. I would, therefore, categorize this *specific* Lhasa Apso as a Multilength Fur dog. If your dog's coat displays unusual characteristics, go with the category that covers her coat's actual behavior.

If your pooch is a purebred, find his breed on the chart, which will coincide with a coat category. If your dog has a mixed or uncertain heritage, choose the breed that appears most predominant and cross-check the category based on his coat's behavior.

Hair Breeds	Multilength Fur Breeds	Uniform Fur Breeds
Affenpinscher	Akita	American English Coonhound
Afghan Hound	Alaskan Malamute	American Bulldog
Airedale Terrier	American Eskimo Dog	American Foxhound
American Cocker Spaniel	American Water Spaniel	American Staffordshire Terrier/Pit Bull
Australian Terrier	Anatolian Shepherd Dog	Argentine Dogo
Bearded Collie	Australian Shepherd	Australian Cattle Dog
Bedlington Terrier	Belgian Sheepdog	Basenji
Bichon Frise	Belgian Tervuren	Basset Hound
Black Russian Terrier	Bernese Mountain Dog	Beagle
Bolognese	Border Collie	Beauceron
Border Terrier	Borzoi	Belgian Malinois
Bouvier des Flandres	Brittany	Black and Tan Coonhound
Briard	Cardigan Welsh Corgi	Bloodhound
Brussels Griffon	Cavalier King Charles Spaniel	Bluetick Coonhound
Cairn Terrier	Chihuahua (Long Coat)	Boston Terrier
Cesky Terrier	Chinook	Boxer
Coton de Tulear	Chow Chow	Bull Terrier (all sizes)
Dachshund (Wirehaired)	Clumber Spaniel	Bulldog
Dandie Dinmont Terrier	Collie (Rough)	Bullmastiff
Doodle (primarily resembles Poodle)	Dachshund (Longhaired)	Canaan Dog
English Cocker Spaniel	Doodle (primarily resembles Golden or Lab)	Catahoula Leopard Dog
English Setter	English Toy Spaniel	Chesapeake Bay Retriever

continued on next page

Hair Breeds	Multilength Fur Breeds	Uniform Fur Breeds
English Springer Spaniel	Field Spaniel	Chihuahua (Smooth Coat)
German Wirehaired Pointer	Finnish Lapphund	Collie (Smooth Coat)
Glen of Imaal Terrier	Finnish Spitz	Coonhound
Gordon Setter	Flat-Coated Retriever	Curly-Coated Retriever
Grand Basset Griffon Vendéen	German Shepherd (Lush Coat)	Dachshund (Smooth Coat)
Havanese	Golden Retriever	Dalmatian
Irish Red and White Setter	Great Pyrenees	Doberman Pinscher
Irish Setter	Japanese Chin	Dogue de Bordeaux
Irish Terrier	Keeshond	English Foxhound
Irish Water Spaniel	Kuvasz	Fox Terrier (Smooth and Toy)
Irish Wolfhound	Leonberger	French Bulldog
Kerry Blue Terrier	Newfoundland	German Pinscher
Komondor	Norwegian Elkhound	German Shepherd
Lakeland Terrier	Norwegian Lundehund	German Shorthaired Pointer
Lhasa Apso	Nova Scotia Duck Tolling Retriever	Great Dane
Löwchen	Papillon	Greater Swiss Mountain Dog
Maltese	Pekingese	Greyhound
Norfolk Terrier	Pembroke Welsh Corgi	Harrier
Norwich Terrier	Pomeranian	Husky
Old English Sheepdog	Saint Bernard	Ibizan Hound
Otterhound	Saluki	Italian Greyhound
Petit Basset Griffon Vendéen	Samoyed	Jack Russell Terrier
Polish Lowland Sheepdog	Schipperke	Labrador Retriever
Poodle (all sizes)	Shetland Sheepdog (Sheltie)	Manchester Terrier
Portuguese Water Dog	Sussex Spaniel	Mastiff
Puli	Tibetan Mastiff	Miniature Pinscher
Schnauzer (all sizes)	Tibetan Spaniel	Neapolitan Mastiff
Scottish Deerhound	Welsh Springer Spaniel	Pharaoh Hound
Scottish Terrier		Plott

Hair Breeds	Multilength Fur Breeds	Uniform Fur Breeds
Sealyham Terrier		Pointer
Shih Tzu		Pug
Silky Terrier		Rat Terrier
Skye Terrier		Redbone Coonhound
Spanish Water Dog		Rhodesian Ridgeback
Spinone Italiano		Rottweiler
Sussex Spaniel		Shar-Pei
Tibetan Terrier		Shiba Inu
Welsh Terrier		Siberian Husky
West Highland Terrier		Staffordshire Bull Terrier
Wheaten Terrier (Soft and Smooth Coats)		Tosa
Wire Fox Terrier		Treeing Tennessee Brindle
Wirehaired Pointing Griffon		Treeing Walker Coonhound
Wirehaired Vizsla		Vizsla
Yorkshire Terrier		Weimaraner
		Whippet

Coats: Separating Fact from Fiction

MYTH #1: "My dog doesn't shed."

FALSE: On all dogs except the truly Hairless variety, the coat is constantly renewing itself in a three-part cycle: growth, transition and death. At the end of the cycle, the dead strands fall out of the follicle. When we see the dead strands on the floor, we call it "shedding." With some dogs, however, the dead strands never make it to the floor. Instead, they get tangled in the coat. Even though we don't see this dead fur, it's there. Therefore, regardless of where the dead fur ends up, the coat has "shed," or lost its dead strands.

Many factors, including breed, age, health and individual genetics, determine how rapidly a dog's coat moves from growth to death and, thus, how much the dog sheds. Dogs predisposed to long growth periods seem like they're shedding less because the strands die and fall out *less often*. Dogs with coats that move rapidly to the dying stage aren't necessarily shedding more fur; they're just shedding it *more often*. A dog with a thinner coat merely has fewer dead strands than a dog with a thicker coat. Both dogs, however, do shed.

Like the hair on your head, the coat on a Hair dog has no genetically predetermined length and continues to grow until it either dies or is cut. As we've just learned, contrary to popular opinion, *all* Hair dogs shed. It's just that you never see the dead strands because they rarely make their way off a Hair dog. Rather, the dead strands remain trapped in the coat and, if not brushed out, intertwine with the healthy strands still attached to the follicles and form mats. (See chapter 15, "Dirty Deeds Done Dirt Cheap . . . at Home.")

With a Uniform Fur dog you see all that dead fur *everywhere*! On these dogs, the individual strands grow until they reach a genetically predetermined length and then they stop growing. The strands remain attached to the follicle until they reach full maturity, which is approximately three to four weeks. Once the strands on a Uniform Fur dog die, they fall out of the follicle right through the healthy coat, off the dog and onto your floor, clothes and furniture.

If your dog has both short and long fur, by my categorization, she's a Multilength Fur dog. Many mixed breeds fall into this category. These dogs often appear to be wearing pants or feathers around their back ends and legs and often have longer strands on their tails, undercarriage or neck. Multilength Fur dogs offer the "best" of both worlds: the dead shorter strands slip through the healthy short coat and off the dog onto your furniture. The dead longer strands, however, remain trapped in the longer healthy coat and, unless you brush them out, form mats.

MYTH #2: "My dog is hypoallergenic."

FALSE: Many people believe that certain breeds are "hypoallergenic." The Poodle, the Portuguese Water Dog, the Bichon Frise, Hairless breeds and certain terriers are often considered hypoallergenic. In reality, a bona fide hypoallergenic dog is but a figment of our imaginations. All dogs produce allergens that can cause annoying reactions in some people. It's not the dog's fur, however, that causes the reaction. It's the allergens, namely, dander (dead-skin scales), saliva, urine and sebaceous cells.

Fortunately, some breeds (mostly Hair and Hairless dogs) produce significantly fewer allergens and are, thus, well tolerated by most allergy sufferers, except those with asthma or particularly severe allergies. Also, a dog's coat traps allergens both from his body and from the environment, including dust, pollen and mold, so weekly baths may help alleviate human allergy symptoms.

MYTH #3: "My dog sheds in the spring."
FALSE: Finally let's shatter the biggest coat myth of all, seasonal shedding. In reality, a healthy house canine sheds his coat at a fairly uniform rate throughout the year. Ask anyone with a Husky or Labrador Retriever and that owner will tell you that she finds loads of fur *everywhere* regardless of the season.

In ancestral times, dogs experienced seasonal temperature variations and adapted to their environment by developing thicker coats in the winter and thinner coats in the spring. These canines lived outside *all the time,* as the dog settee had yet to be invented. Anyway, these *wild* animals required seasonal coat changes for survival.

Nowadays, virtually all house dogs live in pleasant, temperature-controlled environments and therefore don't require the ancestral coat to endure weather changes. Think of it this way: your dog has evolved. Yes, if you live near the Arctic Circle and your dog spends an inordinate amount of time outside pulling sleds, or if your dog is exposed to a harsh climate on a consistent basis, he may actually experience true seasonal shedding, since he's likely to grow a thicker winter coat out of necessity. Obviously, there will also be the exceptional house dog with a genetic predisposition for a thicker coat that makes it *appear* as though he's shedding more in a particular season—but he merely has more fur to shed.

For 99.9 percent of house dogs, however, the speed and amount of shedding is controlled by factors other than seasonal changes, including genetics, health, age, inside temperature, exposure to sunlight, breed, nutrition, gender and grooming regularity. Therefore, unless Fido is planning on taking frequent extended vacations in Antarctica to live with a pod of wild elephant seals, he will not experience true seasonal shedding. By keeping your dog in a comfortable, temperature-controlled home, you have fooled Mother Nature. If, however, you notice that your dog undergoes a sudden radical coat loss, contact your vet, as extreme coat changes indicate trouble.

The bottom line: habitually and properly brush your pooch and take him for appropriate professional grooming. If your idea of brushing is three quick strokes through the coat, or if you believe that semiannual professional grooming is adequate, your pooch will develop clumps and tufts of dead fur by the end of each season. That's not seasonal shedding, that's just poor grooming.

Doggy Style, or Hairstyles of the Furry and Famous

Even if your dog doesn't resemble a sculpted topiary or require an intricate breed-specific hairdo, she needs an occasional professional haircut, a trim or at least some expert attention. Yes, even (and perhaps especially) if she's a mutt. This professional grooming is, of course, *in addition to* your home dog care duties. The type of coat worn by your dog determines how often she requires an appointment with a skilled professional groomer. Feel free, however, to bring her in more often!

Task	Hair Dog	Multilength Fur Dog	Uniform Fur Dog
Brush regularly	✓!!	✓!	✓
Bathe regularly	✓	✓	✓
Dead coat falls off dog and onto the floor, furniture, clothes, etc.		✓	✓!!
Mats	✓!!	✓	
Brush to remove dead coat	✓	✓	✓
Needs a full home grooming *at least* once a month	✓	✓	✓
Needs a haircut, preferably by a professional groomer	✓		

Task	Hair Dog	Multilength Fur Dog	Unifor Fur Dog
Needs a coat trim, preferably by a professional groomer		✓	
Needs trim around eyes, ears and paw pads	✓!!	✓	Seldom
Professional grooming minimum	Every 4–6 weeks	Every 6–12 weeks	Every 12–16 weeks

Hair Dog

A Hair dog's coat mimics human hair in that it grows continuously until the strands die and fall from the follicles. Just like you, a Hair dog requires a full professional haircut and grooming about every four to six weeks. This professional attention makes Fido look and feel good and renders his coat more manageable for you at home. Moreover, if you want Fido to wear a particular breed-standard hairdo, take him to an experienced professional groomer who specializes in these complex cuts.

I do expect that you'll supplement the professional grooming with the regular home dog care I discuss in this book. But the only time I'm authorizing you to get within five miles of your Hair dog with *any* scissors is to snip out truly stubborn debris, such as gum or water-resistant, crusty poop. If you are *extremely* careful and you cannot get to the groomer, you may trim around her eyes, ears and paw pads.

Uniform Fur Dog

A Uniform Fur dog certainly saves you money on professional grooming. Your pooch never needs professional haircuts (notice I didn't say *grooming*), because her coat stops growing once it reaches the genetically predetermined length. Alas, there is no such thing as a free lunch and everything in life is a trade-off. Rather than requiring frequent dates at the groomer, your Uniform Fur dog decorates your floor, furniture, clothes, food, walls and just about everything else with her dead fur. Luckily, shedding is made more manageable with lots and lots and lots and lots of brushing at home. Bathing helps too. An occasional trip to the groomer for an expert, meticulous coat cleanup with professional stripping tools also helps remove the dead fur more efficiently and pampers your Uniform Fur dog. Of course, feel free to bring your Uniform Fur pooch to a professional more often, but I recommend at least every twelve to sixteen weeks.

Multilength Fur Dog

A Multilength Fur dog is a coat double feature: short fur that needs infrequent professional attention and longer fur that requires an occasional professional trim. Ideally, a Multilength Fur dog should visit a skilled professional groomer about every six to twelve weeks. The groomer should perform a heavy-duty brush and wash to clear out the dead short fur and brush and trim the longer areas. These services will help keep mats at bay and allow Fido to look and feel fabulous. In between professional grooming appointments and in addition to your regular home bathing and brushing, you'll occasionally need to trim around the eyes, ears and paws and cut out stubborn debris stuck in the coat.

Seasonal Hairdos
Are Grooming Don'ts

Before we move on, let's discuss one of the most frequent questions posed to me by my clients: "Do I need to shave my dog for the summer?" First and foremost, your pooch is susceptible to sunburn and skin cancer, so it makes no sense to cut his coat extra short during the strongest-sun months. The coat shields the skin from the sun's dangerous burning rays and assists the skin with temperature regulation by providing insulation from the heat and cold. Moreover, after the fur is shaved it may grow back irregularly or unevenly, and it takes forever. Therefore, the answer is a resounding **no** to summer haircuts that leave the skin exposed. Indeed, unless Fido is a competing show dog, his coat should be at least one inch long. He should never resemble a baby's bottom or a bowling ball. If your dog's coat is exceptionally long or heavy, you may direct your groomer to remove the undercoat but not severely alter the length.

Many of my clients also ask to skip their dog's haircut in the winter, believing that a dog needs a longer, thicker coat to keep warm. *Au contraire!* Except for those poor dogs forced to live outside, or working dogs with legitimate outdoor jobs, most modern canines live in a temperature-controlled home and have no need for a cold-weather haircut, other than aesthetics. If you do opt for a longer winter cut, leave the body only slightly longer than usual, but cut the legs and paws shorter so snow, ice and salt have no place to cling. Be sure that your groomer makes the winter cut balanced so Fido doesn't resemble an ottoman on stilts.

Moreover, if Fido is cold, rather than drastically changing his haircut, just put a sweater on him! It's much easier. But, please, I beseech you, remove any canine clothing the minute he's inside your nice warm home. Fido can overheat if he's dressed in too many layers. I've seen way too many dogs don their sweaters on the first day of winter and wear them straight through until the first day of spring. Not only will the dog and sweater stink, but prolonged exposure to clothing causes mats, very bad mats!

4.
Building Fido's Staff

Like any celebrity, Fido requires a staff to care for his body, mind and spirit. A dedicated and loving owner wears many hats: personal assistant, personal shopper, physical-fitness instructor, part-time groomer, therapist, sensory expert, safety consultant, scheduler, activity director, chief cook *and* bowl washer. Nonetheless, there are a few jobs we just can't do. So Fido needs to outsource. Building a staff of highly qualified and trustworthy experts is part of *your* job description.

At a minimum, Fido requires a veterinarian. In addition, if *you're* lucky, he'll have a trainer to help him learn his manners. If *he's* lucky, he'll also have someone to entertain him while you're off working to pay for his staff. Of course, Fido needs a professional groomer too. We'll discuss this vital staff member later on in chapter 18, "Yes, Virginia, Every Dog Needs to Visit a Professional Groomer," a mesmerizing and exciting must-read that's close to my heart. You'll laugh, you'll cry—it's better than *Cats*.

Always start your search for any staff member by asking for referrals from the dog and animal people you know *and* trust, such as friends, relatives, coworkers and neighbors. Ask Fido's current staff members and check with local animal shelters and rescue organizations. Narrow your list to the names you hear most frequently.

Then, perform some initial research. Find out if any state or local laws require licensing, certifications or special insurance. Call the local Better Business Bureau and check if the businesses or individuals have received complaints. Snoop around on the Internet too. Peruse the potential staff member's Web site and look at reviews written by clients (but take these with a grain of salt, since it's often the hypersensitive, stubborn or disgruntled clients that have the most to say).

Choosing a Veterinarian

Choosing a veterinarian is one of the most important decisions you'll make. Your veterinarian will be your primary point person on all things canine for many years. This isn't a decision to be made lightly or under emergency circumstances. *You* are your dog's best advocate and he's counting on you to be thorough and selective.

Once you have a short list, make appointments to meet the doctors and tour the facilities. Bring the list of questions below and don't be shy about taking notes.

At the hospital, visit the entire facility, especially the back areas where the animals are housed, the procedures are performed and the supplies are stored. Be nosy and peer into cages and corners, under tables and in the bathrooms to determine if the *entire* facility is clean and hygienic. Inspect the equipment. Is everything in good condition and modern or has nothing been replaced or cleaned since the Carter administration? A good hospital is organized, well maintained and not overcrowded.

When you meet the potential veterinarian, ask as many questions as *you* want. Determine whether you like the doctor's answers, are comfortable with his personality and agree with his philosophy. You want a veterinarian with a good kennel-side manner—one who's willing to listen to *you*, since you know your pet better than anyone. If the doctor is aloof, dismissive, unfriendly or unwilling to answer questions at the meet and greet, he'll be the same way or worse during regular appointments. This isn't the type of care you want (or need) for your best pal. Instead, choose a doctor who's passionate about animals, easy to talk to and willing and *able* to share his knowledge and expertise to improve your dog's life.

A veterinarian's team includes technicians, assistants and office staff. Meet these people too and decide if they're also competent, caring and committed to animals. Chat up the clients sitting with their pets in the waiting room. Do they live and die for this doctor or are they there merely because the fees are cheap and the parking lot is convenient?

Unless you're extremely lucky, your community probably has only one emergency veterinary clinic, so you won't have a choice. Nonetheless, visit the clinic. Familiarize yourself with its location, staff, hours of operation and policies while you're calm and relaxed, not in the midst of a crisis.

Questions for the Veterinarian

- Why did you become a veterinarian?
- Tell me about your education, credentials and licenses and explain what they mean. (If the diplomas and certifications that support his claims aren't displayed, ask to see them.)
- Are you a member of any professional societies?
- How long have you been practicing?
- How long have you worked at this animal hospital?
- Where else have you worked?
- Do you have any specialties or special interests?
- What's your medical philosophy?
- Are surgeries and diagnostic tests, such as blood work, X-rays or endoscopy, performed on-site or will I have to go elsewhere?
- Do you work with specialists or specialty clinics?
- What's your opinion on alternative or holistic medicine, such as acupuncture or chiropractic care?
- Do you have pets?
- Do you work with any animal-welfare organizations? (The doctor should be committed to helping all animals—even those that can't pay. Most veterinarians help animals in need and many animal hospitals offer some aid to clients who may require occasional financial assistance.)
- Do you have any references? (Be sure to call.)

Questions About the Hospital

- What other services does the hospital offer, such as boarding, nail clipping, etc.?
- Is the hospital accredited by the American Animal Hospital Association or other professional organizations?
- Is the hospital licensed and insured? Verify that everything is current.
- How many doctors, technicians and other staff work here? How are they screened and trained?
- Do the technicians or staff have special education or qualifications?

- How will technicians and other staff interact with my pet? Can I meet them?
- If my regular veterinarian is unavailable, whom will I see?
- What are the hours of operation?
- Is the hospital staffed overnight? Who monitors my dog throughout the night and how often is he taken for a walk and to the bathroom?
- Who will answer my questions over the phone and is there a charge?
- Will my doctor answer my questions over the phone?
- Do you provide clients with information, such as a newsletter?
- Are you affiliated with an emergency clinic?
- What are the policies for payment, appointments, cancellations and emergencies?
- Do you have any references? (Follow up with these people and ask probing questions.)

After you've visited all the offices, compare notes and decide where you *and* your dog will be most comfortable and happy. Then, make Fido's first appointment.

Choosing a Trainer

Like babies, puppies and even some older dogs have no idea what they're supposed to do other than eat and poop. It's up to you to show your pooch the ropes and teach her manners. But it's not just about etiquette; a trained dog is safer, because she'll come when called, walk cooperatively on a leash, drop undesirable things from her mouth and be able to play nicely with other dogs and people.

With some dogs, training is a snap. For these dogs, a few good dog-training books and a patient, energetic and dedicated owner will do the trick. Most young pups, however, need at least a puppy class to get them started off on the right paw. Some dogs are more difficult and require rehabilitation and specialized instruction. Moreover, many dogs have *owners* who need training and the dog is along merely for moral support.

Whatever the reason, professional instruction will help Fido blossom. It also enhances your relationship with him and makes you a better owner. But before you enroll in a class or sign a long-term contract, analyze your dog, popular training methods and the trainers in your area.

Begin by evaluating your dog's personality and age. A puppy is a blank slate and requires different training than an adult. Often a basic obedience class and housebreaking hints are all a puppy requires. A rescued dog with a sad history of abuse has unique needs that may require a specially trained animal behaviorist. Likewise, a dog learning to adjust to a new baby requires different training than an adult dog requiring a refresher course.

In addition, trainers and training facilities offer a variety of services at various price points: group classes, private lessons or boot camp where the dog stays with the trainer for several weeks. Community centers and animal-welfare organizations often offer low-cost courses. Consider your budget and time commitment.

Bookstores and library shelves are full of books by trainers and animal-behavior experts. Spend a few hours perusing these books and learn a little about current training philosophies and methods. Brush up on information relating to your dog's breed, rehabilitation needs or specific behavior issues. With a bit of background, you'll be able to speak intelligently with potential trainers and make an informed decision.

Gathering Information

Compile a list of the trainers you're most interested in meeting. Because philosophies and personalities differ greatly, interview and observe a variety of trainers. Since you know your dog best, a good trainer will listen to you and tailor his methods to suit *your* dog, even in a group class. I learned this the hard way.

A while back, I enrolled Benny, my first Portuguese Water Dog, in a group obedience class held at a nearby park. I had told the trainer, who was considered "the best" in Chicago, that Benny was having a difficult time adjusting to the sights and sounds of city living and in particular hated bicycles. After a few weeks of Benny trembling, whimpering and generally freaking out *every time* a bicyclist rode anywhere near the class, the trainer said, "I know how to fix this!" He attached Benny's leash to *his* bicycle and was about to ride away.

"Are you sure?" I asked anxiously. "Benny's clearly afraid of bicycles."

"Trust me, I know what I'm doing," he replied, and rode away. Almost immediately, Benny became incredibly upset, but the trainer ignored him and kept pedaling. Then, the trainer *and* the bike fell over right on top of Benny. Benny was now so terrified that he lost control of his bowels, slipped out of his collar and ran off into the park. Everyone in the class was screaming and running after him and we eventually caught him. I never went back to *that* trainer. Not only had the trainer ignored everything *I* had said, but he also ignored what the *dog* communicated. A good trainer is flexible and willing to adjust to accommodate a dog's particular needs.

Warning Signs

Be wary of any trainer who "guarantees" results. Successful training is dependent on much more than philosophy and technique. Dogs *and* owners are willful. The dog's personality and the owner's patience and time commitment are also critical factors and out of the trainer's control. A good trainer will guarantee that he'll try to make you happy and teach you the proper tools. The rest is up to you.

Always choose a trainer who uses *only* humane and safe methods. Any of the following scenarios are serious red flags. If you observe or experience them, feel free to point and glare at the trainer with horror written all over your face before you scream and run out of the facility. In addition, a call to contact animal-welfare authorities may be in order.

- The trainer uses these words or the equivalent to describe her training techniques: "hang," "hit," "deprive," "pinch," "shake," "beat," "kick" or "choke." If the trainer uses shock collars, be aware that numerous experts now frown upon this equipment and, instead, rely exclusively on positive reinforcement methods.
- You observe any dog being physically or mentally mistreated or placed in danger during training or while at the training facility.
- You see any devices that cause pain, suffering or mental anguish at the facility.

Remember, you have every right and, in fact, are obligated to stop a class or training session if your dog (or *any* dog) is being harmed or if you're uncomfortable with the trainer's methods.

Questions for Potential Trainers

- Why did you become a trainer?
- How long have you been a trainer?
- Tell me about your education, certifications and credentials and explain what they mean.
- Do you participate in any continuing education? (If yes, ask him for details. A two-day seminar is not the same thing as completing a full course with a recognized expert.)
- Are you a member of any industry organizations?
- Have you and the facility complied with all local and state requirements, such as licensing, inspections and insurance? Verify that everything is current.
- How long have you worked at this facility?
- Where else have you worked?
- Do you have any specialties or special interests?
- What's your training philosophy?
- Do you use the same methods for all dogs?
- What's your plan for my dog? (The trainer should ask you about your dog and tailor a plan to meet his particular needs.)
- Do you require vaccinations or medical examinations for canine students? (Avoid trainers or facilities that have no such requirements. Diseases pass quickly between dogs.)
- What is the minimum age for puppy class?
- What type of services do you offer and how much do they cost?
- What are the payment, enrollment and cancellation policies?
- Can my other family members attend or observe class too?
- What will I have to do at home to practice?
- What type of follow-up classes do you offer?
- What happens if I can't get my dog to behave at home?
- What type of materials are handed out at class?
- Will I receive a written contract?
- Do you have any pets?

- Do you perform any community service for animals? (A good trainer is devoted to dogs and makes some effort to help.)
- Can I have some references? (Always follow up and ask for detailed opinions.)

Observe a Class

Veto any trainer or facility that refuses your request to observe a class or training session. Watching the trainer in action is the only way to decide if you'd feel comfortable working with her. As you observe, note whether the dogs and the owners are relaxed and happy. The trainer should be friendly, but firm in a nice way. She should motivate the students and dogs, not scare them.

Listen and scrutinize the instructor as she teaches. Are her explanations and demonstrations clear and understandable or does she rely solely on technical jargon? Watch the students and see if they're able to implement the instructions and perform the tasks. Observe how the instructor handles questions. Does she provide patient answers or does she roll her eyes when a student needs an additional explanation? Does the trainer offer constructive feedback or is she condescending?

Students should leave the class with handouts and homework. (In fact, that's how you actually train your dog—practice!) Ask for a copy to see if it's understandable and realistic. Stick around after the class or session and talk to the participants. Ask detailed questions about why they chose the particular trainer or facility.

Once you choose a trainer, sign up for a trial lesson or introductory class. If you're satisfied, then enroll and sign a contract.

Doggy Day Care

Fido misses you while you're at work or away during the day. Dogs get bored, lonely or anxious spending long stretches of time alone. Indeed, these feelings are often the root of other problems, including destructive chewing or self-mutilation. Dogs also require exercise and frequent bathroom breaks, especially when they're young. If your budget allows, day care will keep Fido happy, physically fit and mentally stimulated. Even if you can afford only occasional day care, Fido will be calmer and happier than if he has to spend every day alone.

Day care is available at many price points and in many forms. For example, a walker may come to your home and take Fido on a private walk or with a group of other dogs. An upscale doggy day care center may pick Fido up in the morning and whisk him off to a huge canine club with an indoor pool and artificial grass to enjoy gourmet snacks and massages until he's returned home at the end of the day. The possibilities are endless and daily services are available in big cities and small towns. All the bells and whistles aside, choosing a doggy day care requires research.

Day care options can be divided into two categories: (1) a walker who comes to your home and (2) a facility that cares for many dogs at once. Before you begin your search, determine which day care situation is best for your dog. Fido's age, health, special needs and personality are important considerations. Puppies should not be around other dogs until they've been fully immunized. Older dogs may not enjoy the rough play of younger dogs. Timid, anxious or aggressive dogs should have individual walks. If your dog isn't well socialized, he'll be traumatized if he's thrown into the mix at a busy day care center. Ask your veterinarian, groomer and trainer to help you decide what's best for your dog.

As you'll do before choosing *anyone* on Fido's staff, devote significant time and effort to researching your options and interviewing potential caregivers and visiting facilities. Even if the options in your area are few, you need to do your homework. The only day care in town may be a terrible place and Fido would actually be better off at home alone.

Using the list at the end of the chapter, call the most promising day care facilities or walkers and ask threshold questions designed to weed out any obvious bad fits. Then, visit the potential day care facilities or interview potential dog walkers in person. Listen to your gut as you collect information. If someone rubs you the wrong way or doesn't ask detailed questions about your dog's health, personality, special needs and play preferences, cross that option off your list.

Choosing a Day Care Facility

Your mission is to find a facility that is caring, convenient and within your budget. The staff members must be well-trained dog lovers. The facility itself must be clean, organized and not overcrowded. A good facility has at least two staff members on duty in case of an emergency so the dogs are **never** left unattended and has no more than ten dogs per staff member.

Once you've narrowed your choices to a manageable number, visit each facility. Time your visit during drop-off or pickup and observe for a few minutes before you announce your presence. Then, introduce yourself and walk though the facility with the owner. If you're not allowed in certain areas, find out why. You must see everywhere your dog will be, so you can determine if he'll be comfortable and safe.

During the tour, use all your senses. Does the place smell like urine and feces or merely like "dog"? Are the lighting, ventilation and temperature comfortable? Scrutinize the safety devices used to prevent canine escapes. On the inside, the facility must have double doors or gates that seal off the exits. The outdoor areas must be completely enclosed by a fence that's at least six feet tall and in good repair to prevent even the most acrobatic dog from leaping over or digging under. Verify that the poop and garbage are cleared away.

Observe the dogs playing. Are they happy or anxious? Study the way in which the staff interacts with the dogs. Do they actively play with and monitor the dogs or merely sit on the sidelines fiddling with their iPods? Are accidents cleaned up immediately? Are skirmishes allowed to continue or do staff members separate the unruly dogs? Are enough toys available to prevent fighting? Are the dogs playing in a big empty room or is there interesting equipment? Are there soft rest areas?

Now ask the probing questions at the end of this chapter. Ask as many questions as you need to be satisfied that your pooch will be properly cared for at the facility. The owner should be happy to talk to you and offer straightforward answers. If the owner is evasive or the answers aren't satisfactory, the interview is over.

Choosing a Dog Walker

A dog walker comes to your home and walks your dog either alone or with a group for a specified time period. Some walkers take the dogs to a dog park or beach and some walk the dogs in the immediate area. If your dog is not well socialized, an individual neighborhood walk is best.

Dog walkers may work for an agency or on their own. If you're considering an agency, always meet the specific person who will be working with your dog. Dogs require consistency, so avoid an agency with rotating walkers.

Once you've compiled your short list and determined who meets your minimum requirements, follow up with an in-home interview using the questions at the end of the chapter. While you're chatting, determine if the person *actually* likes dogs or is merely doing a "job" until something better comes along. The walker should be interested in learning about your dog too. If he's not, show him the door. Moreover, observe how the potential walker interacts with your dog. If it's love at first sight, that's a good sign. Sure, many dogs are hesitant around strangers, but if Fido hasn't warmed up to the person at all by the end of the interview, choose someone else.

Ready, Set, Play During the Day

Once you decide where to send Fido, talk to the facility owner or dog walker again and reiterate your dog's personality and special needs. Sign up for a few weeks to begin with and observe your pooch. If he's happy with the arrangement, then extend the contract.

Expect Fido to be pooped when he starts day care or with a walker. Having fun is much harder work than being cooped up alone in a house with nothing to do but sulk and nap! So don't be alarmed if Fido is sleeping more than usual. After a week or two, he'll be accustomed to the increased activity. Now, remember, even though Fido is exercising his body, mind and spirit during the day, your duties remain the same. Continue to walk, play, exercise and spend time with him. The new day care is a bonus, **not** a substitute for your attention.

Questions for Day Care Facilities and Dog Walkers

Tailor the questions to fit the particular day care facility, dog-walking agency or specific walker you are interviewing. Some questions may not apply.

Threshold Questions
- How long have you been in the business?
- Why did you get into the business?

- What makes your business special?
- Have you complied with all local and state requirements, such as licensing and inspections?
- Do you have insurance and are you bonded?
- Are you a member of any industry organizations? (This doesn't guarantee quality, but it shows the business is striving to meet industry standards.)
- Do you require vaccinations or health certificates? (Avoid any facility or walker that doesn't. Illnesses pass quickly when dogs are in close contact.)
- Do you require dogs to be spayed or neutered or have any minimum-age requirements?
- What services do you offer and how much do they cost?
- Do you offer boarding or overnight care?
- Will the same person be walking my dog every day? (Avoid services that send a variety of people to your home. Fido requires a consistent routine.)
- What are your policies for drop-off, pickup, late pickups, payment, reservations and cancellations?
- What's the sick-dog policy?
- If a dog has a contagious illness, what do you require before the dog is allowed to return?
- How am I kept abreast of my dog's activities? How often do I receive reports?
- *For dogs with special needs*: Will you administer my dog's medicine on a timely basis, monitor his health concerns or feed him a special diet?
- Are you involved in any community service to help animals? (Not a strict requirement, but a dog business should be committed to animals.)
- Do you have any references? (Be sure to follow up.)

Follow-up Questions
- How is the staff chosen, screened and trained?
- Do you/staff members receive any special training in first aid, animal behavior or other areas?

- What's the staff turnover rate?
- Who exactly will be caring for my dog? Can I meet them?
- Who else will have access to my home?
- What are your emergency procedures?
- What happens if my dog is injured? Will you take him to a veterinarian? If yes, where? How will I be notified?
- What are the screening procedures for new dogs?
- How do you determine if a dog is appropriately socialized for a particular group?
- How do you introduce new dogs to a play group or walking group?
- How many dogs are in a play group or on a walk together?
- How do you decide which other dogs will play or walk with mine? Do you separate by age or size?
- What strategies do you use for handling aggressive dogs or repeated troublemakers?
- What happens if a fight breaks out? Is there a time-out area? What is the time-out policy?
- Describe in detail what my dog will do at your facility and show me where he'll be.
- How are the dogs supervised during play?
- What's the staff-to-dog ratio?
- Show me the outdoor facilities. How long are the dogs there? What if the weather is inclement?
- Where do the dogs rest and for how long?
- Will you feed or water my dog? How often?
- Where does my dog go to the bathroom and how often is he taken out to relieve himself? What happens if he has an accident inside?
- Do you take the dogs off-site? If yes, where and when do you go and what safety precautions are used?
- What will my dog do on his walk?
- What time will the walk occur and how long will it last?
- Where do you go and what do you do?
- Are the dogs off leash anywhere?
- Are the dogs ever unsupervised?

- Do you offer transportation services?
- How much does transportation cost?
- What type of vehicle is used? Is it heated and air-conditioned?
- How long are the dogs en route?
- How do you screen the drivers and are they licensed and insured?
- How are dogs restrained in the vehicle?

5.
Nutrition: Food for Thought

R ecently, I vacationed with a few friends and we all brought our dogs along. After two days, Zeke refused to eat his high-quality food. Worse, he developed explosive diarrhea and a nasty rash and had scratched himself raw. I told my friends one morning how concerned I was that Zeke was sick and hadn't eaten in a few days. One of them eagerly replied, "Oh, don't worry! He's been eating fine. I've been feeding him in the morning with my dog. I always mix in bacon grease to make sure my dog eats everything." I was horrified, especially when I glimpsed her supersized package of generic supermarket dog food, and realized that the wood shavings lining her daughter's hamster cage probably had more nutrition.

As Zeke can tell you, diet significantly affects every aspect of your dog's physical and mental well-being—from snout to tail, inside and out. Indeed, diet and disease are closely linked. If *you* consumed food made from recycled offal and laced with chemical enhancers and artificial flavors all day, would *you* be ready to jog around the neighborhood? I think not! You'd also be in a bad mood, lethargic and embarrassed every time you looked in the mirror. Think of how you feel after a junk food binge, and then imagine that was *all you ever ate.* When your dog eats low-quality food and treats, she's not just consuming empty calories, which packs on pounds; her body is being robbed of the building blocks necessary to maintain good health, energy and an upbeat attitude.

In addition to a variety of health risks, poor nutrition wreaks havoc on a dog's skin and coat and decreases his tolerance for grooming. Would you be happy standing at attention in the bathtub with twenty extra pounds on your back? When I mention that a client's coat has gone from shiny, full and healthy to dull, brittle and lackluster, I usually hear, "Oh, we're trying a new food from the grocery store." Once the dog returns to his usual high-quality food, the coat problem usually clears up. Please, don't skimp on dog food.

Remember: Fido can't read labels or ask questions. He's relying on you to make intelligent choices for him. Sadly, most people don't give much thought to where food comes from or how it's grown or manufactured—for themselves *or* their dog. We assume that food is safe because we buy it from a reputable store. Have you ever critically reviewed the ingredients in your dog's food? Can you understand the fancy marketing terms or required legal disclosures? I hope the information in this chapter will encourage you to talk to others, ask questions and seek answers.

You Are What You Eat

The sheer variety of dog food and treats on the market boggles the mind. As you might expect, the choices range from the superpremium to the super disgusting. At the top of the heap you'll find raw and certified-organic formulations manufactured with whole animal proteins (not slaughter-house leftovers or grain fillers), real fruit and veggies, natural preservatives and antioxidants. At the bottom are generic brands made from rendered mystery meats and digests, highly refined flours, hulls and other nonnutritive fillers, harsh chemical preservatives and other additives that have been banned for years in Europe. With cheap dog food, you get exactly what you pay for!

Every dog has unique nutritional requirements and tolerances. Consequently, deciding which food is best for your dog can be tricky. You'll find as many diverse opinions as there are dogs in the world, and Fido will add his two cents as well. A dog's dietary requirements depend on his age, stage of life, weight, breed, genetics, environment, lifestyle, activity level and health. To make the best choice, discuss your dog's individual needs with your veterinarian. Then, talk to trusted friends, your groomer and other "dog people" for recommendations. Reputable stores will inquire about your dog's health, breed and lifestyle before making suggestions. Request samples of several products to try at home before purchasing. If your dog's stomach is sensitive, test the new products one at a time. Otherwise, put out little piles of each food all at once as a taste test. Let your pooch sniff and try each one. He'll usually eat the one he likes best first. Before finalizing your choice, carefully read and compare labels and ask manufacturers tough questions.

Who Regulates Pet Food

In the United States, pet-food manufacturing, safety, nutrition, labeling and advertising are governed by various federal and state agencies. The main federal agencies are the Food and Drug Administration's Center for Veterinary Medicine, the United States Department of Agriculture and the Federal Trade Commission. These agencies field calls from consumers and have enlightening Web sites that include important recall information.

Each state also has its own agencies and regulations. Many states have adopted the model standards for the manufacture, distribution and sale of pet food developed by the Association of American Feed Control Officials (AAFCO). The AAFCO has no enforcement power, but it works closely with the pet-food industry and regulatory agencies. The AAFCO guidelines define the ingredients used in dog food and treats. Once you learn these definitions, you'll be able to understand and analyze pet-food labels.

Nutrition 101

Just like for you and me, diet affects every aspect of a dog's body, mind and spirit. (I get soooo cranky when I haven't had my morning coffee and muffin, how about you?) In order to survive and thrive, dogs must consume certain key nutrients: protein, carbohydrates, fats, vitamins, minerals and water. Understanding Fido's nutritional needs requires me to discuss a few scientific concepts. Don't worry—I'll keep things as simple as possible. No PhD is necessary and there will be no quiz (unless I notice that you're not paying attention).

Proteins
As we all learned in middle school, proteins are essential nutritional building blocks responsible for growth, development, immunity and everything in between. Proteins are made up of amino acids—some of which are produced naturally by Fido, some of which must come from what's put in his bowl.

Dogs are primarily carnivores, and thus meat should be the primary protein in their diets. Why is that? In order to explain, I'll have to put on my dietitian outfit (I've always looked good in a lab coat!) and describe how dogs (and, indeed, all of us) use food in our bodies.

Digestion is the process by which a body (canine or otherwise) breaks down food into nutrients that can be absorbed into the bloodstream. "Digestibility" measures how efficiently a body can do this with a particular food. When Fido consumes protein that's low on the digestibility scale, his body absorbs fewer essential amino acids and other nutrients. Indeed, much of that low-digestibility protein goes right through him and ends up in a spiral pile on your lawn. This is why a dog that eats low-quality dog food will have to eat more to absorb the required nutrition—and why he poops much more than a dog eating high-quality food.

Protein comes from a variety of animal and plant sources. Animal proteins, including eggs, beef, chicken, duck, lamb and fish, offer the most nutritional bang for the buck. Therefore, a protein from a specifically identified animal should be the first ingredient listed on the package of food, and animal proteins should predominate overall. Plants are a less-desirable protein source due to their lower digestibility. Fido must consume significantly more plant stuff than meat in order to absorb the same dietary goodness.

While this seems like a simple story—dogs need meat as their primary food source—the simplicity ends there. "Meat" can mean so many different things, and it's more expensive than plants. When companies have a choice between what's good and what's less expensive, I don't have to tell you what wins out! So, when you look at many dog-food labels, you'll see unfamiliar meat products and a lot of corn, wheat, soy, rice and barley—even though they're not the best protein for your dog.

Carbohydrates

Carbohydrates fuel Fido's factory and supply fiber that aids his digestion. As with all other food ingredients, it's a question of good vs. cheap (evil is apparently busy helping cats take over the world). Although whole grains are better because they retain more nutrients after processing, refined grains, such as flours and fragments like hulls and pulp, are less expensive. Manufacturers of low-quality chow use refined grains to fill their food, which also conveniently provides volume and texture. Fillers usually have unappetizing names like "brewer's rice," "mucilage," "middlings," "pulp," "cellulose," "hulls," "gum," "gluten," "pectin" and "cereal by-product."

A modest amount of whole grains in Fido's food isn't the worst thing in the world. That said, low-quality dog food often substitutes highly digestible animal proteins with corn or other grains that also provide a bit of protein along with carbohydrates. If a carbohydrate is the first or predominant ingredient, put the product back on the shelf.

Fats

Fat is a nutritional workhorse. It's an energy source, it fosters healthy cell development, it keeps the heart and brain healthy and it makes for luxurious skin and coat. In case that's not enough for you, fat also helps the body digest and absorb fat-soluble vitamins, such as A, D and E. Animals and plants are good fat sources and both types may be included in dog food. Fat, however, can degrade when exposed to oxygen, so preservatives are necessary to prevent spoiling.

Cholesterol is not a problem for dogs like it is for humans, so a bit of fat in Fido's food is fine. Fats from a specified animal are preferable to generic fats. Alas, low-quality fats are not just less nutritious than high-quality fats but cheaper too, and cost often rules the day.

Vitamins and Minerals

Vitamins and minerals assist the body with a host of vital activities including digestion, growth, reproduction, immunity, skin and coat maintenance and hormone and enzyme production. They also help the body fight disease and boost the immune system. I could go on and on. Suffice it to say that your grandmother was right when she told you to eat your Brussels sprouts.

All dog food must meet the AAFCO's minimum nutritional standards. To satisfy these standards, manufacturers add vitamins and minerals to replace those lost while processing other ingredients, even the high-quality ones. You know what I'm going to say next. . . . Vitamins and minerals vary in quality, which affects a dog's ability to absorb them. Vitamins from natural sources like fruits and veggies and other high-quality ingredients are more expensive and many people think they're better.

Labeling 101

The label offers many clues to judge whether a particular product is one you'd want your dog to eat. Once you learn the lingo, you can discern the quality and source of each ingredient. You'll also have a general idea about the relative amount of each ingredient and whether the packaging claims coincide with what's actually in the food. Your goal is to buy the highest-quality food and treats that you can afford.

||||||||||||||||||||||||||||||||||||||||||||||||||||||||||||||||||||||||||||||||||||||||||||||||||||||||||

Pet-Food Paranoia

When it comes to the pet-food industry, misinformation, myths and downright lies—not to mention extremely scary truths—are everywhere. Evaluate the credibility and bias of the sources of your information. Remember that everyone has their own agenda. Determine if the claims and allegations can be substantiated by more-objective sources. Talk to trusted professionals, perform extensive research and grill the manufacturer and industry organizations. After you gather and weigh the evidence, draw your own conclusions and buy accordingly.

||||||||||||||||||||||||||||||||||||||||||||||||||||||||||||||||||||||||||||||||||||||||||||||||||||||||||

Learning a few of the AAFCO's standard definitions of ingredients will help you on your path to nutritional nirvana. In addition, those nice folks in the government made sure that labels include some basic information that helps you evaluate a product: guaranteed analysis, feeding instructions, statement of nutritional adequacy, ingredients and the manufacturer's name and address.

Guaranteed Analysis

The labels on pet food must include a "guaranteed analysis" statement of certain nutrients contained in the product: the minimum percentages of crude protein and crude fat and the maximum percentages of crude fiber and moisture. (Some manufacturers list additional nutrients.) In this case, "crude" doesn't refer to my sense of humor. Rather, it refers to a specific method of testing the product, but doesn't tell us a lick about the quality or digestibility of the nutrients. Moreover, if you're comparing dry with canned food, forget about it. The percentages don't account for the amount of moisture in the ingredients, which can vary dramatically. For instance, Chicken has more moisture than Chicken Meal. Unless you're willing to try some complicated math, just make sure you see this disclosure on the label and be satisfied that the manufacturer played by the regulatory rules.

Feeding Instructions

The label must show how much of its food to feed a dog each day. These instructions are just general rules of thumb, so adjust to accommodate your dog's individual nutritional requirements. A sled dog needs to eat more than a couch potato.

The recommended portion size helps you calculate the cost per meal. This is easy math. Divide the amount of food in the package by the portion size to get the number of servings in the package. Then, divide the product's price by that number of servings. If a meal is really cheap, you can safely assume that the manufacturer isn't using the highest quality ingredients.

Moreover, when a manufacturer uses cheap ingredients, it has to bulk up the food with fillers to meet the government's minimum nutritional requirements. This means that the portion size for cheaper food is typically larger than for more-expensive food with higher-quality, more-digestible ingredients. In the end, you'll be buying more of the cheaper food, which usually works out to be more expensive than buying the higher-quality food in the first place.

Statement of Nutritional Adequacy

This statement verifies that the product satisfies the average dog's nutritional needs (as determined by the AAFCO) for a specified life stage, either "puppy" (growth) or "adult" (maintenance). In theory, following the package's feeding guidelines ensures that Fido will suffer no nutritional deficiencies. If your pooch is ill, extremely active or pregnant (which she really shouldn't be, since we've *already* discussed the importance of spaying), talk to your veterinarian to determine if the food meets her special nutritional needs.

Manufacturers can prove nutritional adequacy in two ways: by chemically analyzing the food in a lab or by feeding it to dogs and seeing if they suffer nutritional deficiencies. If the manufacturer does the latter, I'd want to know (and so should you) if the live-dog tests would end up in an undercover PETA video. Frankly, the thought of all those laboratory dogs living in who-knows-what conditions makes my skin crawl and my heart ache. If this bothers you too, ask the manufacturer to explain its testing program, policies and procedures in detail. Ideally, you'll learn that the manufacturer uses live animals only to determine whether dogs like to eat the food (palatability), and relies on lab tests *of the food* for its nutritional data. If you wouldn't want your dog to participate in the tests, then don't buy the food.

Ingredients, Listed in Descending Order by Weight

Here's where we hit information pay dirt. The ingredient list is the most effective way to evaluate the quality of the food. But first we have to learn some AAFCO definitions.

Animal protein is made either from flesh or from by-products. You want to see the flesh of a *specified* animal first on the list, because it scores high for digestibility and low on the gross-out scale, for example, Chicken, Turkey or Beef (I realize there's no animal called a "beef," but just go with it—Beef is slaughtered cattle). Sometimes, manufacturers remove moisture from the flesh and grind it into "meal." Meal is fine as long as it came from a *specific* animal, such as Chicken Meal, Chicken Liver Meal, Turkey Meal, Fish Meal or Duck Meal. (The exception is Lamb Meal, which is rendered and thus not as good.)

As we move down the quality scale, vegetarians may want to grab some smelling salts.

The leftovers at the slaughterhouse (stuff like kidneys, lungs, brains, intestines, necks and feet) are used to make various "by-products." By-products from specified animals are higher quality than those identified generically as Meat By-Products or Poultry By-Products.

Although using by-products in dog food is not as horrifying as it may sound (remember, dogs like to eat many things we don't!), by-products are less digestible than flesh (e.g., Chicken or Beef). No good dog food has a by-product as its *primary* ingredient, and the highest quality foods *never* include them.

If a by-product is identified as a "meal," it was *rendered* and then ground. If a by-product is listed as a "digest," it was *hydrolyzed.*

Rendering is a heating process that reduces the animal material into a fat and protein meal. High-quality dog foods usually have no rendered ingredients, or if they do, they're *way* down on the ingredient list, and they come from a specific animal, like Chicken Fat or Lamb Fat. Generic Animal Fat is not acceptable, because we have *no* idea which animal it came from or where—the roadside or the slaughterhouse?

Rendered *generic* meals, such as Meat Meal and Meat and Bone Meal, are totally gross and should be avoided (and this is from someone who expresses anal glands for a living!). When you see these on a label, you have no idea which mammal died, why it died or where it met its maker.

Finding the answers to these questions is difficult. You'll hear *very* different explanations depending on who you ask. As you might imagine, pet-food activists and industry representatives offer opposing evidence and viewpoints. Credible reports claim that renderers sometimes use dead, dying, disabled or diseased animals, roadkill, restaurant grease, expired meat from grocery stores, euthanized pets, horses or dead zoo animals. Even if some of these reports are exaggerated, the thought of it keeps me up at night. To avoid the issue, and the nausea, don't feed your pooch any product that contains generic rendered ingredients.

Digests are even sketchier. They're manufactured by *hydrolysis*, a method that breaks down protein using chemicals or enzymes. (Sounds bad already, doesn't it?) Manufacturers use this cheap, low-quality ingredient as a leavening agent, stabilizer, thickener, flavoring, flavor enhancer or (gasp) protein source.

Digest from a specified animal is the least offensive because at least we can identify the animal and know that it died at a slaughterhouse. Some examples are: Digest of Beef, Digest of Beef By-Products and Digest of Poultry By-Products. The last digest is vague, but Poultry By-Products are from a slaughterhouse and, at least in theory, means a chicken, duck or turkey. It's anyone's guess with Animal Digest and Poultry Digest. These generic digests are made from *any* animal or *any* poultry as long as the tissue is clean and not decomposed. These ingredients suffer from the same problems as the generic rendered meals. I know that dogs' standards may not be *that* high, since they lick their genitals and sniff their friends' butts, but I'd never want them eating anything made with these really horrifying ingredients.

My vegetarian coauthor has now passed out on the floor and needs those smelling salts. So let's move on.

Other Ingredients to
Know and Not Love

Preservatives

Like all processed food, dog food requires preservatives to prevent it from spoiling. Natural preservatives are more expensive than artificial. You guessed it, folks: cheap, low-quality dog food uses the fake stuff, like BHA, BHT and ethoxyquin (sometimes listed as "E"). These and other synthetic preservatives have been linked to serious health problems including cancer and kidney and liver disease.

Tocopherols (vitamin E), ascorbic acid and other forms of vitamin C, citric acid and rosemary are effective *natural* preservatives. They are the only preservatives you want your dog to eat—ever.

Artificial Colors and Artificial Flavors

Some manufacturers use artificial colors to make their products more appealing to *you*, since dogs can't see many colors. These ingredients do absolutely nothing for your pooch except expose him to potential carcinogens, liver disease and allergies.

High-quality ingredients taste good. If the manufacturer resorts to artificial flavorings, it's a good bet it's trying to compensate for flavorless, inferior ingredients. No good dog food uses these additives.

Sweeteners

Sweeteners have no business in anything Fido eats. Sugar (whether natural or artificial) is *not* an essential nutrient and is bad for Fido's teeth and waistline. Artificial sweeteners have the added problem of being possible carcinogens. If you see a sweetener in an ingredient list, put the food or treat back on the shelf.

Sweeteners go by many names other than "sugar." Natural sweeteners may be listed as "dextrose," "glucose syrup," "crystalline fructose," "high-fructose corn syrup," "fruit juice concentrates," "maltodextrin" or "trehalose." The most common artificial sweeteners are saccharin, aspartame, acesulfame-K, sucralose, neotame, sorbitol and Xylitol (which is toxic for dogs). Don't worry about very, very small amounts, but keep sugar out of Fido's food as much as possible.

|||||||||||||||||||||||||||||||||||||||||||||||||||||||||||||||||||||||||||||||||||||||||||||||||||||||||

Rules of Thumb for Interpreting Ingredient Lists

1. The length of the list doesn't always indicate the quality of the food. I'll take a long list of high-quality ingredients and lots of vitamins and minerals over a short list of cheap ingredients and artificial additives.

2. The ingredient list must show the ingredients in descending order by weight. Keep in mind that flesh is heavy because it contains a lot of moisture. Thus, Chicken may be the first ingredient, but if you removed the water, you might find that the product actually contains more of the lighter (often cheap and less-digestible) ingredients that appear lower on the list.

3. In general, the first six to eight ingredients are the most important because they make up the bulk of the product. A protein from a specified animal should be the first ingredient.

4. Watch for ingredient splitting. A manufacturer can list similar ingredients separately to make you think that it's using less of a lower-quality ingredient. For example, corn is a mediocre, but cheap protein source. Rather than put it first, a manufacturer might order its list of ingredients this way: "Beef, Ground Corn, Meat and Bone Meal, Corn Gluten Meal, Cellulose, Corn Germ Meal," etc. Because Beef comes first, you'd think Beef is the main ingredient. However, when you add up the three "corns," they could well outweigh the Beef. (I don't mean to single out corn. If it makes you feel better, substitute soy or wheat in my examples.)

5. Proteins from a specified animal are better than by-products.

6. By-products are better than rendered meals and digests.

7. Ingredients made from a specified animal are better than ones made from generic "meat" or "poultry."

8. Heat can damage or destroy nutrients. Thus, the more refined and processed the ingredient, the less it offers your dog. For example, whole grains are more nutritious than refined grains; Beef is highly digestible, while Meat and Bone Meal, which is rendered (processed), is not.

9. Avoid all artificial preservatives, colors and flavors.

10. Added sweeteners and salt are red flags. Avoid all products that use any artificial sweetener.

|||||||||||||||||||||||||||||||||||||||||||||||||||||||||||||||||||||||||||||||||||||||||||||||||||||||||

The Manufacturer's Name and Address

In addition to the required name and address, many manufacturers voluntarily include their Web site and phone number on labels. Most people never consider talking to the manufacturer before purchasing food or treats. Unequivocally (one of my favorite fancy words), asking questions is *good* for your beloved furry pal. To make it easy for you, I've included a list of the probing questions to ask before you settle on a product. Look for straightforward answers to as many questions as *you* want to pose. Be wary if the answers are vague or the person on the phone tries to change the subject. You'll have to take the answers with a grain of salt, since the manufacturer is trying to convince you to buy its product. Your gut should help you decide if the manufacturer is trustworthy.

Questions for Food and Treat Manufacturers

- Where do your ingredients come from, the United States or a foreign country? If a foreign country, which one? (At least we know that in the United States pet food is regulated and subject to some government oversight. This is not necessarily the case elsewhere.)
- Where are your products and ingredients manufactured? Who owns and runs the facilities? Are they inspected by the USDA or other government agencies? How often? Any violations or fines?
- Define and explain the terms on your label, such as "natural," "organic," "human grade," "healthy," "gourmet," "premium," "super-premium," "holistic," etc.
- What evidence supports the health or wellness claims I see on the package?
- What are the product's protein sources?
- What types of flavorings, fillers and texturizers are used? Are they natural or artificial? Why do you use them?
- Which preservatives are used and are they natural or artificial?
- Do you use any artificial coloring?
- Do you use any rendered products? Exactly what is the rendered product made from: which animals, where do they come from and how did they die?

- Has this product or any of your products or any ingredients ever been recalled? If yes, what happened?
- Has your company ever been fined or cited for legal or regulatory violations, e.g., misleading labels or unsanitary conditions?
- Do you meet the "nutritional adequacy" requirement with a lab test of the food or do you use dogs? (If dogs are involved, ask for details about where the testing is conducted, who owns, runs and monitors the facility, where the dogs come from and where they go after the test, how they live and whether they're nurtured and socialized. Ask if a recognized independent animal-rights organization monitors the dogs, tests and facilities.)
- Explain your policies and procedures to monitor and ensure the safety of your food.
- Does the company support or promote animal welfare and rescue? How?

Other Label Information

Government regulations often require additional information on the package. For instance, the "net weight" tells you the amount of food by weight inside the particular package. This is important for comparing brands because the size and shape of the package can influence how much food you think is inside. The "use by" (expiration) date is also important to notice. As soon as this date has passed, throw the food away. Also, look for food-storage instructions and disclaimers and warnings.

Learning Label Lingo

A healthy dose of skepticism and common sense helps when wading through all the marketing puffery, vague claims and fancy packaging. Look past the beautiful photographs of frolicking dogs, depictions of nutritious ingredients, vague endorsements and self-certifications.

Many of the terms used on the package, such as "premium," "gourmet," "healthy," "holistic," "organic," "natural" and "human grade," are used to grab your attention. These terms have no standard legal definition, so you can't use them to judge a product without asking the manufacturer exactly what it means by them.

When I thumb through dog magazines, almost every ad I see highlights "natural" in big, bold letters. The dictionary defines "natural" as "present in or produced by nature."* But what's important is how manufacturers define it. After all, horse manure is natural! One manufacturer may mean that its food contains no pesticides or artificial, genetically modified or irradiated ingredients and that its product is minimally processed without chemical solvents. Another manufacturer may mean only that the product contains no artificial colors and preservatives, but all the other ingredients are highly refined and wouldn't be recognizable even if they bit you in the nose. To boost a "natural" claim, low-quality products often adorn their labels with pictures of whole grains, fruits and vegetables that are nowhere to be found in the actual ingredient list.

When I see the word "human-grade" associated with pet food, *I* think that the ingredient could legally be used to make my dinner. The manufacturer, however, may think that it means that the meat was once sold in a butcher shop before it passed its expiration date and ended up at a rendering plant. Until the government regulates marketing terms, it's buyer beware.

||||||||||||||||||||||||||||||||||||||||||||||||||||||||||||||||||||||||||||||||||||||||||||||||||||

Is Organic Better?

Organic is nice but usually more expensive and not necessarily better. The USDA's National Organic Standards Board recently implemented standard definitions for the use of "organic" on *human* food labels: seventy to ninety-five percent of the ingredients are grown and processed without synthetic pesticides, hormones and antibiotics and with environmentally friendly methods. Don't get excited when you see "organic" on Fido's food, though; those human food labeling regulations don't currently apply to pet food and treats. For now, the best thing to look for is a statement on the label from a certifying agent that says it's organic.

Note that organic doesn't mean that the meat is cruelty free, that an ingredient could be used in human food or that the product is healthful. For example, organic white rice or organic wheat flour is actually less nutritious than whole grains grown conventionally. Moreover, many chemicals occur "naturally" on earth, including arsenic and uranium, but you wouldn't want them in

*The American Heritage Dictionary of the English Language, 4th ed.

Fido's food. Always read labels carefully and ask the manufacturer to explain its own definition of "organic."

||||||||||||||||||||||||||||||||||||||||||||||||||||||||||||||||||||||||||||||||||||||||||||||||||||||||||||||||||||||

It's Decision Time

Now that you're an informed dog owner, go out and shop yourself silly. Introduce a new food slowly by mixing it with the old food in increasing proportions for a week to ten days. This gradual changeover will help your dog's stomach and digestive system adapt to the new food. If you move too fast, your pooch may suffer diarrhea or other stomach upset.

Nutritious Snacking in Moderation

I encourage the liberal dispensation of healthful, bite-sized treats while you're caring for your pooch. I'm not, however, granting you permission to go hog wild with the doggy junk food or people food. Treats should never be the mainstay of Fido's diet. Too many empty calories are no good for Fido, even if the treats increase his cooperation during grooming. Just as we've seen with food, treats range in quality and nutritional value. To minimize treat excesses, read and analyze labels with a critical eye, using all the information I've just shared.

Snacks and treats, including rawhide, bones and chews made from animal parts, must meet the same federal and state safety requirements as food. Labels must include the manufacturer's name and address and an ingredient list. Look for a short list of simple, high-quality ingredients, such as a specified animal protein or a whole grain. Ideally, treats should have little or no sugar (sometimes listed as honey or molasses) and no added salt. At all costs, avoid treats containing artificial colors, flavors or preservatives. These chemicals have no place in anything your beloved pooch eats.

As often as possible, offer Fido washed, dog-safe fruits and veggies, which are loaded with nutrients. Apples, pears, bananas and carrots are good choices if peels, pits, seeds, leaves and stems are removed. Additionally, steer clear of foods that are toxic or choking hazards. (See chapter 6, "Keeping Fido Safe and Sound at Home," for a list of common food dangers.)

Table Scraps

I know it's fun to share, but many human foods are dangerous or dreadfully unhealthy for your dog. For example, the steak fat you're sneaking to the dog under the table can give him the runs, and the bone presents a serious risk for choking, internal obstruction or stomach perforation. Table scraps should never exceed ten percent of any dog's diet.

Also avoid the temptation to feed Fido spoiled or old food. If you wouldn't eat it, neither should he.

Some dogs eschew begging and prefer to find table scraps by pilfering unsecured garbage. Garbage often contains mold and bacteria and dangerous foods. So securely dispose of food and keep all trash cans covered and out of Fido's reach.

Use common sense when you see health claims on treats, such as "freshens breath" or "reduces joint pain." Few products contain enough of the spotlighted nutrient or supplement to have a legitimate effect. In addition, be wary of statements that imply that the product is recommended by veterinarians. Unless you ask the manufacturer, you'll never know how many doctors approved the product—was it one or one thousand?

If you like to cook, whip up some healthful homemade treats in your kitchen. Prepare homemade chicken soup *without* salt, garlic and onions, which are dangerous for dogs. Remove the bones and skin, finely shred the chicken and freeze the cooled broth in ice-cube trays for delicious, bite-sized *pup*sicles. If you want to get really cute, freeze the cooled soup in popsicle molds and use long, thin rawhide chews for sticks.

Chef Art Smith is both a close friend of mine and a fellow dog lover. He developed this wholesome treat recipe for his three dogs, who love peanut butter.

Chef Art Smith's Puppy Biscuits

One of the greatest loves of being a family is having family pets. My life has been made complete by Link, Tron and Cochon. These furry children are at my side in the kitchen every day. This is a little treat that they love to share.

Ingredients

2 cups whole wheat flour (I prefer King Arthur brand)

1 teaspoon baking powder

1 cup creamy natural peanut butter

1 cup soy milk

Directions

1. Preheat the oven to 350 degrees.

2. In one bowl, mix the flour and baking powder.

3. In a second bowl, mix the peanut butter and soy milk.

4. Combine the contents of both bowls and knead the dough for 1 to 2 minutes.

5. Flour the table and rolling pin. Roll out the dough until it's ¼-inch thick. Cut out with desired cookie cutters. (I love my little pig cutter.)

6. Place cut cookies on double cookie sheets lined with parchment paper to prevent burning.

7. Bake for 20 minutes and cool on a wire rack.

8. Store in an airtight container. Recipe yields about one dozen small treats.

|||||||||||||||||||||||||||||||||||||||||||||||||||||||||||||||||||||||||||||||||||||||||||||||||||||||

The Obesity Epidemic

Shockingly, about five percent of the seventy-five million dogs in the United States are obese and another twenty to thirty percent are overweight. That's a lot of dogs! Canine obesity is a grave medical problem that not only shortens Fido's life but also severely degrades his quality of life. Fat dogs are more prone to heart disease, arthritis, joint problems, cancer and diabetes, and they experience breathing problems, reduced stamina and personality changes. Anesthesia and surgery are riskier for obese and overweight dogs.

Obesity also affects a dog's skin and coat. For example, a fat dog has excess skin folds that are both unattractive and unhealthy. These skin folds trap oil, bacteria and debris and increase the risk of skin ailments. To make matters worse, an obese dog tires easily and is less mobile. Therefore Fat Fido is less likely to cooperate during grooming, which means his folds remain dirty longer.

Portion control is essential to maintaining a healthy weight. Fido, however, has no mechanism to gauge his food intake and will eat as much as he can, unless he's ill, depressed or suffering from a toothache. So chow restraint is *your* job. Follow the product's feeding instructions and adjust for your dog's *actual*, not perceived, lifestyle, health and activity level. Most importantly, don't surrender when Fido pushes around his empty bowl and peers up at you with sad puppy eyes or relentlessly pokes your leg while you dine on a juicy rib eye. Don't allow your pooch to binge on table scraps or lick the dinner dishes clean *every* night.

Many foods claim to be "low calorie," "light" or "low fat." Talk to your veterinarian before you use a "diet" dog food, because these terms are not regulated. You may be able to use Fido's current food and merely adjust the portion size, which will save money.

If Fido inhales his food, purchase a bowl designed to slow down a speed eater. Not only will this help Fast Fido digest his food, but you'll be less likely to refill the bowl too quickly. In addition, combat obesity by regularly exercising your dog. Frolicking with Fido is a dog owner's duty and also keeps *your* waistline in check.

Water, Water Everywhere

Water is essential to all life. It delivers nutrients to the body, regulates temperature, lubricates tissue and flushes out waste. Dogs require a constant supply of clean, fresh water served in clean, fresh containers. When I say "clean," I mean apply the same standards that you use for yourself. Fido should never drink from the toilet unless you do. In addition to providing a full water bowl at home, always bring water along when you're out on the town or exercising together. One of my favorite new dog products is an ingenious portable bowl that attaches to any standard water bottle.

Many factors, including weather and environmental conditions, health, food intake and activity level, affect Fido's daily water requirements. As a rule, a healthy dog can regulate his water intake on his own, which is why it's important for water to always be available. Changes in drinking habits or fluid loss through vomiting or diarrhea are dangerous and require veterinary assistance.

A slew of fancy doggy drinks are now for sale: bottled spring water, vitamin-enriched water, sports drinks, caffeine-free coffee drinks and non-alcoholic beer and wine. As long as Fido has ample clean, fresh water, these drinks are superfluous. If you want to buy them anyway, reading the label is imperative.

Some products claim that their specific vitamin or mineral additives boost nutrition or alleviate skin problems, joint soreness, bad breath or other conditions. Don't rely on extravagant labels, clever packaging, unsubstantiated marketing claims or vague veterinarian endorsements. Some of these drinks are formulated with artificial flavors, artificial colors and various forms of sugar and salt, which may not be good for your particular dog, especially if he's diabetic or overweight. Always talk to your veterinarian before offering Fido anything other than old-fashioned H_2O.

|||||||||||||||||||||||||||||||||||||||||||||||||||||||||||||||||||||||||||||||||||||||||||||||||||||

Real Dogs Don't Sweat

Dogs don't sweat to reduce body temperature like we do; they have sweat glands only on their feet and paw pads. Instead, dogs pant. A healthy dog, therefore, rarely loses enough electrolytes while exercising to warrant a special replacement or "sports" drink. Water does the job just fine. Veterinarians do occasionally prescribe electrolyte replacement products for *sick* dogs, including those suffering from severe fluid loss due to vomiting or diarrhea. Talk to your veterinarian and read the labels before offering Fido a canine sports drink.

|||||||||||||||||||||||||||||||||||||||||||||||||||||||||||||||||||||||||||||||||||||||||||||||||||||

Clean Bowl, Clean Hands, Clean Heart

Practicing good hygiene keeps Fido healthy. Unwashed hands and dirty feeding utensils and bowls easily spread disease and harbor all sorts of germs. Wash your hands with hot water and soap for thirty seconds before and after handling food and treats. No one wants to eat stale food, so always mind expiration dates and dispose of leftovers at the end of each day. Also, change Fido's water several times throughout the day. Follow storage instructions on the label and discard food and treats with damaged packaging. Dry kibble stays fresher in airtight *food-safe* containers. Wet food must be covered and refrigerated. In addition, watch for food recalls, which are often announced on government Web sites, in the media, at veterinary offices and at pet-supply stores.

Thoroughly wash Fido's food and water bowls and feeding utensils every day or *at least* a few times a week. If, however, Fido eats canned or raw food, his bowls *must* be replaced or washed after *each* meal. A dishwasher is an effective sterilizer; swirling a few splashes of water around in the bowl is not. Clean dog-food bins and treat jars every time you refill. Residual fat remaining in bowls and containers can spoil and contaminate the fresh food or treats. Replace bowls and feeding utensils as soon as they're worn, cracked, chipped or badly scratched.

To Supplement or Not to Supplement—That Is the Question

A huge variety of herbs and supplements are sold for canines. Advertisements and labels make enticing claims. Some assert that the product provides "necessary" nutritional support. Others declare that the product relieves a variety of medical disorders; improves wellness, mood or immunity; clears up myriad skin conditions or allergies or improves skin and coat. The FDA considers animal supplements "drugs of low priority" or food additives, which allows manufacturers considerable latitude with their marketing. Worse yet, canine supplements are not yet subject to the same stringent manufacturing and labeling regulations and quality control as those meant for human consumption. So the price, quality and effectiveness of these products vary dramatically.

The best manufacturers self-regulate, use high-quality natural ingredients from reputable suppliers, adhere to strict manufacturing procedures and provide all the information you need to properly and effectively use the product. Then, of course, it's downhill from there.

Look for the following information on a label:

- A rational explanation of the product's purpose
- An ingredient list. Avoid products with artificial colors, preservatives or flavors

- A list separating the active and inactive ingredients
- Clear directions for use, dosing and storage
- Warnings and cautions
- Expiration date
- The manufacturer's name and contact information

A seal from an industry trade group, such as the National Animal Supplement Council (NASC), is encouraging. According to the NASC, manufacturers displaying its seal must adhere to "strict guidelines for product quality assurance, adverse event reporting and labeling standards."

Be wary of marketing or packaging statements that make therapeutic claims, including curing, mitigating, treating or preventing a particular disease or medical condition. View endorsements critically. If a claim seems ridiculous, it probably is. Contact the manufacturer and ask questions before you decide if the product is worth buying.

Questions for Supplement Manufacturers

- Is the product processed at your own plant or at a contract manufacturer? Where is the factory located? Who inspects the facility?
- Where do *all* the ingredients come from? Do any come from foreign sources?
- Which ingredients are natural and which are artificial? How do you define natural?
- What type of quality-control and safety procedures are in place? Do you track and report safety and adverse-event data? If yes, to whom?
- Have any of your products or their ingredients ever been recalled? If yes, what happened?
- What type of testing was conducted to see if the product works? Were the testers independent?
- Were any animals harmed during manufacturing or testing? (If the product was tested on animals, ask for details and decide if you'd be comfortable using your dog as a test subject.)

Supplement Success

Many veterinarians, including my own, prescribe supplements. My coauthor's veterinarian prescribed vitamin E, milk thistle and a supplement containing S-adenosylmethionine to counteract liver damage caused by her dog's epilepsy drugs. She swears the supplements improved her dog's quantity and quality of life. Many of my clients use omega-3 fatty acids to enhance skin and coat, or glucosamine and chondroitin supplements to counteract osteoarthritis.

Whether your dog could benefit from supplements is a function of age, breed, genetics, health, activity level, diet, stage of life and environment. Your veterinarian will help decide whether your pooch should use them, which ones and the proper dosage. Never use any supplement or herb without prior veterinarian approval.

Supplement Safety

- Never give your dog any supplement or herb unless directed by a veterinarian. They can be hazardous if misused or ingested in incorrect amounts. In addition, they can interact with pharmaceuticals and other supplements or cause dangerous side effects.
- Stop using a product if your dog exhibits any negative reaction or side effect and call the veterinarian immediately.
- Never administer a human product to your dog unless instructed by the veterinarian. Just because a supplement is safe for humans doesn't mean that it's safe for dogs.
- Never use a supplement in lieu of appropriate veterinary treatment.
- Never buy a product with damaged packaging.
- Discard the product as soon as it expires.
- Avoid knockoffs and off brands. If you buy your supplement from a street vendor or shady Internet supplier, you may end up with adulterated, improperly stored or counterfeit products.

6.

Keeping Fido Safe and Sound at Home

Despite all the years I've been around dogs, I'm still amazed when I hear about the things that dogs eat: roadkill, batteries, rocks, cigarette butts, mud, glass, plants, cat poop (considered by many canines to be a delicacy), plastic bottles and food bowls. Indeed, dogs will eat, lick or roll in anything and don't care if it's dangerous. Because of this devil-may-care attitude, dogs are injured at home every day. Many of these injuries, including accidental poisonings, are preventable.

Unfortunately, many dog owners are cavalier about dangers in their own homes or mistakenly believe that "my dog knows better." Well, I can tell you from personal experience—*no* dog knows better. The best way to protect Fido is to understand the dangers and take all precautions to prevent disaster. Fido can't do this; he's too busy rolling around in squirrel poop and rotten leaves.

Dog-Proof Detail

Since it's virtually impossible to watch your dog every second of the day, dog-proofing your home is imperative. This is true whether you're bringing home a new family member or caring for your longtime buddy. Dog-proofing takes preparation and planning on your part. So put on your sergeant's uniform; you're about to inspect the barracks. Get down on your hands and knees and examine your home and yard from *Fido's* point of view. Things look quite different when you're down on all fours. You'll discover all sorts of hazards you never knew existed: chemicals stored on low shelves, dryer sheets that never made it into the trash and insect baits near Fido's dog run. To a two-legged fairly reasonable adult, these situations are harmless. To a curious or bored dog, however, they're attractive and potentially deadly. My dog Zeke is a perfect example because he'll eat *anything*. The *final* time Zeke stayed with one particular dog sitter, he ate an entire bottle of another dog's arthritis pills that were left on the counter in a *childproof* container.

Thankfully, an expensive trip to the veterinarian was all he needed to recover. Next time, who knows?

Pretend You Have a Baby

Baby- and child-safety techniques and products work for dogs too. After all, dogs are really just furry children. Child-safety Web sites and catalogs are excellent sources of information and ideas. Here are some basic dog-proofing ideas that will help you fulfill your duty to provide Fido with a safe home.

- Remove anything that Fido shouldn't have from countertops and accessible shelves, especially in closets, in case the door isn't firmly closed. Remember that Fido can jump—high! My friend's diminutive, elderly, arthritic Cockapoo rarely moved other than to relieve herself outside or waddle slowly over to her food bowl. Yet she managed to leap onto the kitchen counter and make off with a raw steak!
- Install safety latches on cabinets to prevent Fido from accessing dangerous items stored inside. Many dogs are able to open cabinets with only their nose. Verify that doors are firmly closed *every time.*
- Replace all open trash containers in your home. Every garbage receptacle must have a secure lid that will stay on even when pushed over. Cans with pedal openers are most convenient. If you store garbage bins in a cabinet or closet, be sure that door closes *every time.*
- Electrical cords and wires must be inaccessible, especially if Fido is a chewer. Purchase guards that hide wires and cords in a hollow tube and attach to a baseboard or wall. Move any cords that dangle from tables and hide them behind furniture. Never place a rug over a cord, as this creates a fire hazard. Unplug any cords in areas that Fido frequents when he's unsupervised.
- Install safety gates to prevent Fido from entering areas that are dangerous or filled with delicate items. Verify that the gate is strong enough and tall enough to withstand a desperate dog. Use

gates that meet *current* child-safety standards. Older gates may have holes and openings large enough to fit a dog's head or neck.

- Secure or remove all wobbly furniture and appliances. Fido can easily knock over a TV stand with his tail or crash into a table when he's running to catch a ball.
- Cover sharp corners on tables and furniture with bumpers. This is especially important if the corners are at Fido's eye level.
- If you enjoy letting in fresh air, use window guards or safety netting to prevent falls from windows and elevated areas. Sometimes, Fido can't resist his squirrel-chase instinct and may jump though an open window.
- Clear the floor in Fido's play area. He (or you) can trip over toys, chews and other stuff in his running path and acquire a serious injury.
- Fido can easily become tangled in the dangling cords attached to window treatments, especially if he likes to sit by the window and bark. Install child-safety products, such as shorteners and wraps, to tuck cords safely out of the way.
- Plastic bags, especially those that held food, are suffocation hazards. Fido can become trapped in the handle or chew it when he's searching for snacks. Keep all bags out of reach.
- Train your two-legged family members to close toilet lids and all cabinet and closet doors.

Home Alone

Dangers lurk in even the most efficiently dog-proofed home. You must therefore formally inspect your home for doggy dangers *at least* once a week and more often if you have lackadaisical roommates. Better yet, always be on the lookout for hazards. Inevitably someone forgets to put away the dish-washing detergent, leaves a dryer sheet on the floor or doesn't close the door to the pantry and trouble ensues. In addition, dogs and especially puppies require a safe place to stay when no one's home or able to supervise. If given the opportunity, Fido *will* make a beeline for anything that's remotely dangerous or off-limits. This is exactly why I recommend crate training to all my friends, family and clients. A crate keeps Fido contained in a secure area, teaches him good habits and provides him with his own personal space. Eventually, when Fido is older and fully trained, you *may* be able to leave him in a dog-proofed, contained area instead of his crate, but there's no guarantee that he won't get into trouble.

My buddy Doug learned this lesson the hard way. Doug had just adopted Cody, a stunning one-and-a-half-year-old Siberian Husky with bright blue eyes. This puppy was exceptionally energetic and playful. All my pleas to use a crate fell on deaf ears, and instead, Doug locked Cody in the bathroom and went on his merry way. I can still hear Doug confidently announcing, "It's a small area. The dog can't get into any trouble!" Famous last words.

Only Cody knows the actual chain of events, but later in the day, Doug received a phone call from his neighbor. It seems that she found Cody standing in *her* bathtub perched atop a pile of *her* panties, which she had left drying in *her* bathroom. What is more, Cody had chewed the crotches out of every single pantie and had devoured every single piece of her French shell soap. Cody had chewed clear through the bathroom wall—green board, insulation and all.

Cody thankfully came to no harm other than a bad stomachache, and the neighbor, although irritated, exhibited a substantial sense of humor. In the end, the neighbor bought new underwear, the dog burped soap bubbles for days and my friend bought a crate.

There's a correct and safe way to crate train, so consult your veterinarian or dog trainer before you begin. No matter the technique, a few basic rules apply:

- Purchase a crate that's large enough for Fido to stand up and turn around inside. Fido may outgrow his puppy crate, so be prepared to purchase a larger one later on. Donate the old crate to an animal shelter. It'll make you feel good and you'll probably receive a tax write-off.
- Remove Fido's collar and leash before you place him in the crate. If he jumps or panics, he can become entangled and choke, twist his neck or hang himself.
- Remove toys or chews if Fido will be alone in the crate. He can shred the toy or break the chew into small pieces, which become instant choking and obstruction hazards.

- Be careful about bedding choices. For many dogs, a towel or blanket provides safe cushioning. If Fido is a heavy chewer, however, he can shred and choke on the bedding. Talk to your veterinarian about alternatives.
- Place the crate in a comfortable spot that's near the family, not in the corner of a dark, drafty basement. Leave the crate door open when you're home. Dogs are denning animals. As such, Fido needs a sanctuary to relax when he *wants* to be alone. His crate should be a refuge, never a punishment.

Common Household Dangers

All homes are teeming with doggy dangers, some obvious and some not. You may not realize the hazards of everyday items commonly left out on tables and countertops, such as coins, toys or beauty products. The ASPCA's Animal Poison Control Center is the preeminent source for up-to-date facts and figures on everything that's hazardous to dogs and other pets. Your veterinarian and animal-welfare organizations are also excellent information sources.

My goal is to start you down the road of awareness and help prevent a tragedy in your home. When a label states that the product is toxic, dangerous or poisonous to humans, assume that the same is true for dogs. Thus, if Fido eats, drinks, inhales or comes in contact with any actual or even suspected hazard, call the veterinarian immediately and begin first aid.

|||||||||||||||||||||||||||||||||||||||||||||||||||||||||||||||||||||||||||||||||||||||||||||||||||||||||||||||

Other People's Homes

Other people's homes are often filled with doggy dangers, especially homes without pets. My friend John was watching Gabriel, my Portuguese Water Dog before Zeke, while I was out of state. While they were in the yard, Gabriel decided to explore the basement of the apartment building. Some careless fool (very possibly John) had left the door open. John called me the next morning and said, "Gabriel was up all night belching—we thought it was funny. He was pacing and burping all night. Then, this morning his poop was shamrock green and I thought I'd better call you. I looked in the basement and saw rat poison.

I didn't know it was there and I think he ate it." I felt so many emotions simultaneously: anger, fear and loathing, just to name a few. I was too far away to do anything myself, so I ordered my "friend" to take Gabriel to the emergency veterinarian right away. Gabriel stayed at the animal hospital for four days and he eventually recovered; my friendship didn't.

There are many lessons to be learned here:

1. Before unleashing your dog, check the home and confirm all doors are closed and all hazards are cleared up. If you lose sight of your dog, go find him. He should never be unsupervised in someone else's home—you have no idea what's there and the home owner probably doesn't either.

2. **Never** wait to see what happens. Call the veterinarian the minute you witness or sense a problem. With many poisons, the symptoms aren't immediately noticeable. If you wait, your dog will needlessly suffer and his recovery is less certain.

3. Perform an IQ test and background check on anyone watching your dog. I'm sorry to say that pet safety is neither obvious nor a priority for many people. Before leaving your dog with a friend or anyone else, review safety procedures and expectations and verify that your friend *truly* understands. A pop quiz may be in order. As a matter of fact, feel free to give your friend a copy of my book and highlight this chapter.

||||||||||||||||||||||||||||||||||||||||||||||||||||||||||||||||||||||||||||||||||||||||||||||||||||||||||

Food and Beverages

Many of the food and beverages we regularly consume are harmful or deadly for our furry friends. Depending on the food, the amount ingested and the size of the dog, Fido can suffer a variety of ill effects. Here's a list of the most common food and beverage dangers.

Food/Beverage	Effects
Alcoholic beverages	Vomiting, diarrhea, lack of coordination, central nervous system depression, tremors, difficulty breathing, metabolic disturbances and coma
Avocado	Vomiting and diarrhea
Bones	Perforated internal organs, such as stomach or intestines
Caffeine: often found in coffee, tea, sodas and coffee grounds	Vomiting, diarrhea, increased thirst, urination and heart rate, hyperactivity, seizures and death
Chocolate (the darker, the more dangerous)	Vomiting, diarrhea, increased thirst, urination and heart rate, hyperactivity, seizures and death
Citrus *peel, fruit and seeds* (lemons, oranges, limes, grapefruit, etc.)	Vomiting and diarrhea and, in extreme cases, nervous system disturbances
Fat trimmings	Vomiting, diarrhea and pancreatitis
Garlic (raw, cooked or powdered)	Damage to red blood cells and anemia. (Be careful: I've seen garlic powder listed as an ingredient in treats and in treat recipes.)
Grapes	Kidney damage, including failure
Macadamia nuts	Vomiting, muscle stiffness and nervous system disorders, such as increased heart rate, depression, tremors and weakness
Moldy or spoiled food	Vomiting, diarrhea and the effects associated with the toxins in the particular food
Mushrooms (store-bought and wild)	Vomiting and diarrhea. Some mushroom species can cause severe gastric distress, liver or kidney damage or neurological disturbances, shock or death.
Onions (raw, cooked or powdered)	Damage to red blood cells and anemia. (Be careful: onion powder is sometimes used in treats and in treat recipes.)

continued on next page

Food/Beverage	Effects
Potato eyes and trimmings	Vomiting, diarrhea, loss of appetite, drowsiness, confusion, behavioral changes, weakness and slowed heart rate
Raisins	Kidney damage, including failure
Rhubarb	Vomiting, diarrhea, loss of appetite, drowsiness, confusion, behavioral changes, weakness and slowed heart rate
Tree-fruit *stems, leaves, pits and seeds*. The fruit is fine. (e.g., apples, apricots, cherries, peaches, etc.)	Vomiting and loss of appetite. In severe cases, weakness, loss of coordination, breathing difficulties, shock, coma and death. Pits and seeds are also choking and obstruction hazards.
Salt	Electrolyte imbalances
Tomato *leaves and stems. The ripe* tomato itself is fine.	Drooling, loss of appetite, vomiting, diarrhea, drowsiness, behavioral changes, slowed heart rate and central nervous system disturbances, such as weakness, depression or confusion
Yeast dough (raw)	Obstruction and rupture danger as it expands in the stomach or intestines
Xylitol (found in many diet foods, gum and candy)	Sharp drop in blood sugar, depression, loss of coordination and seizures or liver damage

Although technically not a food, tobacco is extremely dangerous too. Fido may eat a cigarette butt left in an ashtray or on the sidewalk. The nicotine in tobacco can cause severe vomiting, depression, elevated heart rate, a drop in blood pressure, seizures, respiratory failure and even death. If that's not reason enough to stop smoking and forbid anyone in your home from smoking, I don't know what is. Oh yes, there's the problem of secondhand smoke too. Fido's lungs are smaller and more delicate than yours.

Decorative and Household Items
Dogs will eat *anything*: home decor, craft and sewing supplies, clothing, office supplies, small appliances, books, small toys and Super Balls—just

about any everyday item. Anything smaller than Fido's mouth is a potential hazard for choking, internal obstruction and perforation. Some items, like batteries, contain chemicals that are poisonous and can wreak serious havoc if chewed or ingested. The easiest way to avoid trouble is to put things away or store them in *closed* containers out of Fido's sight. Tidying up not only protects Fido; it forces you and your roommates to adopt good cleaning habits.

Flowers and Plants

The list of flowers and plants dangerous to dogs and pets is long—toxicologists have identified more than seven hundred. I've listed some of the most common below. Visit the ASPCA's Animal Poison Control Center for a complete list. In addition, consult with your veterinarian and a reputable nursery or landscaper before purchasing or installing plants in your home or yard.

Aloe vera	Elephant's ear	Narcissus
Amaryllis	English ivy	Oleander
Autumn crocus	Gladiolus	Peace lily
Azalea	Holly	Philodendron
Bird-of-paradise	Hyacinth	Poinsettia
Castor bean	Hydrangea	Pothos
Chrysanthemum	Iris	Rhododendron
Clematis	Kalanchoe	Sago palm
Cyclamen	Lilies	Schefflera
Daffodil	Mistletoe	Tulip
Dieffenbachia	Mother-in-law	Yucca

Whether toxic or not, keep all flowers and plants out of Fido's reach. Hang them or display them on shelves or tables high enough that Fido can't knock them over. In the yard, set up a barrier around the garden. Poisonous flowers and plants can cause a range of reactions from mild stomach upset to seizures to organ failure. If Fido ingests leaves, stems, flowers, bulbs or seeds, call the veterinarian promptly and begin first aid. These plants are dangerous:

First Aid for Poisoning

Sometimes you'll observe Fido coming into contact with a toxin. Many times, however, you'll merely smell it, see it on his body or notice his strange behavior. If you have even the slightest suspicion that Fido has been poisoned, call the veterinarian and begin first aid. Time is of the essence; safe recovery often depends on obtaining medical care within a small time window.

The signs of poisoning include the following:

- Vomiting
- Diarrhea
- Fever
- Abdominal pain
- Trouble breathing
- Muscle tremors or twitching
- Lack of coordination
- Nervousness
- Listlessness
- Seizures
- Coma

First take a deep breath so you can remain calm, clearheaded and organized. Collect everything involved in the incident, including packaging and containers. Save anything that Fido has chewed or vomited in a sealed plastic bag for later analysis. Then **IMMEDIATELY** call your veterinarian or emergency veterinarian or the ASPCA's Animal Poison Control Center at **1-888-426-4435**. The Animal Poison Control Center charges a small, but worthwhile, fee, so have your credit card handy.

If Fido is exhibiting serious symptoms, such as seizures, difficulty breathing or loss of consciousness, call your veterinarian and prepare Fido for **immediate** transport to the animal hospital. The veterinarian will call the Animal Poison Control Center if necessary. You must concentrate your efforts on getting Fido to the doctor right away.

If possible, have the following information handy for your call:

- Information about the poisonous or toxic substance or product, including the container or packaging
- The details of the incident, such as how long ago the exposure occurred, when you discovered the problem and the quantity of the poison at issue
- The pet's age, breed, sex, weight and health concerns
- The symptoms you've observed

Never induce vomiting, allow Fido to drink, wash him or do anything to treat the poison *until directed by a veterinary expert*. Even water or shampoo may activate or react with the harmful substance. Always have your pet first-aid kit handy and be sure that it's stocked with a turkey baster or dropper to administer three percent hydrogen peroxide, which is often used to induce vomiting. If you're directed to go to the animal hospital, bring everything you've collected.

||||||||||||||||||||||||||||||||||||||||||||||||||||||||||||||||||||||||||||||||||||||||||||||||||||||||||||||||||

Toiletries, Chemicals and Cleaners

Many household cleaners and chemicals, and even cosmetics and grooming products, have enticing smells that seem to call out to Fido for a lick. Once consumed, the chemicals can cause severe medical problems, including diarrhea, vomiting, nervous system and respiratory disturbances, organ damage and failure, seizures, coma or death. Many of these items also have poisonous fumes or cause skin and eye irritation if Fido touches them.

Always read and strictly adhere to a product's use and storage directions. And I mean follow the directions with painstaking exactitude—there's no wiggle room. For example, if a cleaning agent says to avoid contact until dry, don't let Fido into the room until you are 110 percent sure that it is. Fido is smaller than you and closer to the ground, and spends a significant amount of time sitting and sleeping on the floor. As a result, he's more likely than you to become sick from prolonged exposure to the chemicals and cleaners used in your home. If possible, switch to natural cleaners that don't rely on toxic chemicals. Baking soda, vinegar, lemon juice and water can do many wonderful things! However, natural cleaners can be harmful too, so don't be lulled into a false sense of security. For example, citrus-based cleaners may cause vomiting, diarrhea and central nervous system disturbances if ingested.

To be safe, keep Fido away while you're using any chemical or cleaner. Open windows and clear the air before you bring him back into the room. Store *all* products on high shelves, preferably behind closed doors. Likewise, the containers themselves should be tightly closed in case Fido knocks one over.

Medication

Before we get into specifics, let's be sure we all understand basic medication safety: unless you're directed by a veterinarian, **never** give any prescription, over-the-counter or herbal medication to your dog. Even though human drugs are sometimes prescribed for pets, the dosing is usually different. If human medications are misused, your pooch can suffer serious, life-threatening effects.

Always store medications safely out of Fido's reach. Curious dogs can chew right through childproof pill bottles, tubes and other packaging in no time flat.

Although *all* over-the-counter and prescription medications are potentially harmful to pets, these drugs are especially dangerous; even one pill can be disastrous:

- Acetaminophen
- Anticancer drugs
- Antidepressants
- Aspirin
- Cold medicines
- Diet pills
- Ibuprofen
- Vitamins and supplements

Indoor Pesticides, Baits and Traps

Insects and rodents can invade even the cleanest homes. Combating an infestation usually involves strong chemical pesticides and rodenticides that can harm your pooch *and* you. In addition, baits and traps contain poisonous chemicals that smell enticing to your pet. These items should be used only in areas that are *completely* inaccessible to your dog, such as inside closed cabinets.

Pest-control chemicals can have serious and life-threatening effects on your pet, including gastrointestinal problems, bleeding, seizures, organ damage, respiratory distress, coma and death. I'm not messing around here; even one mothball can seriously harm your dog. If you employ a professional exterminator, discuss pet safety and request and read product labels and warnings *before* your home is treated.

Dog-Proofing Your Yard

Your yard is probably one of Fido's favorite places to hang out. (Notice that I did *not* say "live in" or "spend an inordinate amount of time alone in.") The first rule of thumb is an oldie but goodie: **never** leave your dog unattended in your yard or in anyone else's either. He can be stolen, be attacked by a wild animal (nowadays a problem even in cities), escape or dig it to pieces. In addition, verify that Fido has a shady spot with a fresh water supply while he's outside. Put him inside while you mow the lawn. Many dogs are agitated by loud noises and a mower can make a projectile out of anything it rolls over. Choose plants, shrubs, trees and flowers that are safe for pets.

Pesticides, weed killers and fertilizers are potentially poisonous to your dog. Even the "natural" products may be toxic when ingested, inhaled or contacted. If you're using pest-control products and baits in your yard, carefully read and follow the directions for use and storage. Request and read the pesticide product information if you're hiring a professional exterminator. Some products remain on plants or grass for an extended time, which means Fido will be exposed to the toxins longer.

Always remove Fido's food and water bowls before applying any yard chemical. Never let Fido eat the treated plants or grass and keep him away until the pesticide is thoroughly dry.

Devote some time to studying green, nontoxic alternatives to chemical pesticides. Talk to a reputable landscaper or nursery. In addition, many books, magazines and Web sites are devoted to organic gardening and are excellent sources of current information on prevention and control of pests using less-toxic means.

Yard dangers aren't limited to those that grow. My coauthor's friend had a beautiful Rough Collie that died while tethered in his yard. The dog chased a squirrel in the backyard and sadly his neck snapped when the chain ran out and forcefully pulled him back. If you have a pool, be sure that the gate is closed and the fence sturdy and high enough to prevent Fido from jumping over and swimming without supervision. Remove all standing water so Fido won't drink it and mosquitoes won't breed in it. Inspect the fence, gates and other enclosures frequently to ensure that no escape is possible. Crafty dogs may jump over or dig under fences, pull down chicken wire and slip between fence posts.

Going Green for Fido's Sake

Everyone is talking about "going green" and eating, living, working and playing in ways that are less harmful to our fragile planet. Adopting a green lifestyle not only helps the earth but allows our furry friends to live in a healthier environment. Going green, however, takes patience and research. Here are a few tips to get you started.

• Recycle

The most obvious and most compassionate way to recycle is to adopt a "used" dog. Shelters and rescue organizations are full of wonderful dogs waiting for a home, and many reputable breeders have dogs that need to be re-homed. In addition, purchase dog toys, accessories and bedding made with recycled and eco-friendly materials.

• Reduce Exposure to Environmental Toxins

Your home and yard are filled with toxic chemicals that harm you and your pet. Reduce everyone's exposure by using environmentally sound cleaners, pest-control products and home goods that emit low fumes. Purchase grooming and food products that are formulated without synthetic chemicals. Read labels and choose products that have pronounceable and recognizable ingredients. In addition, choose products that contain ingredients grown and manufactured using eco-friendly techniques and are not tested on animals.

Natural and eco-friendly gardening techniques have been around since people first domesticated wheat and rye approximately thirteen thousand years ago. Now is a good time to get back to our roots and learn how to grow without harming the earth. Doing so will help Fido, since he ingests yard and gardening chemicals every time he licks them off his paws or eats grass.

• Reduce Fido's Environmental Impact

Landfills are clogged with poop-filled plastic grocery bags. Reusing plastic bags is admirable, but those bags take centuries to decompose. Instead, use biodegradable bags, which can drastically reduce the decomposition time, especially if the bags are composted. At the very least, these bags are manufactured from corn or other sustainable ingredients instead of polyethylene, a plastic.

- **Reuse**

Fido doesn't mind if you line his crate with an old towel or blanket as long as it's clean and has no frays or tears, which can make the item a choking hazard. In addition, repurpose your old towels, sheets, blankets, newspapers and gently used crates, collars and leashes by donating them to local animal shelters and rescues.

||||||||||||||||||||||||||||||||||||||||||||||||||||||||||||||||||||||||||||||||||||||||||||||||||||

Safe Toys, Chews and Bedding

Just because the package says a toy or chew is "dog safe" or "indestructible" doesn't guarantee that an accident won't occur. You are on the front lines of toy, chew and bedding safety, so choose wisely and be vigilant.

Toys

In 2005, I lost my beloved Gabriel at two and a half years old. Gabriel loved to chew those allegedly indestructible nylon bones. One day, he started having severe diarrhea and I rushed him to the vet. After various veterinary delays, one of the doctors *finally* noticed that Gabriel had swallowed a small piece of one of those "indestructible" bones. He had surgery to remove the resulting internal blockage, but died four days later. Gabriel's death was one of the most difficult moments in my life and I still miss him *every day*. I've been on a mission ever since to ensure no one else suffers a similar heartbreaking loss.

Make intelligent toy choices. Don't buy a toy merely because it's cheap or cute. Rather, inspect the toy and determine if it will withstand your dog's chewing strength and activity level. Many cheap toys (and poorly made expensive toys) can rip easily and expose dangerous fillings or break into small pieces, which become instant choking or obstruction hazards. Fido should not be able to close his mouth with the toy or ball inside. If you have multiple dogs, size *really* does matter. A small ball appropriate for a little dog is a choking hazard for her larger sibling.

You'll confuse Fido if you give him toys shaped like items that you don't want him to chew. Fido can't tell the difference between his toy purse or cell phone and the real thing. For the same reason, don't allow him to play with *your* old clothing and footwear. Besides, these items aren't made for this purpose and small pieces can easily break off.

Whichever toys you bring home, be sure that each one is made with nontoxic materials. Avoid toys with removable or small parts, such as eyes, decals or ribbons, including children's stuffed animals, which aren't made to withstand canine jaws. Likewise, don't let Fido play with or chew on wooden toys, because they can splinter and injure his mouth or digestive tract.

Once you determine the type of toy that's safe for your dog, go hog wild and make some fun purchases. Fido should have a variety of playthings: toys and balls to fetch and chase, puzzle toys that stimulate his mind and, if he's not a heavy chewer, soft fluffy toys to carry around and cuddle. If Fido has a softer mouth, he might enjoy the flexible latex or rubber toys that squish. If Fido is a heavy chewer, stick with hard rubber toys or heavy-duty rope toys and forgo stiff vinyl or plush toys that can break apart easily. Dogs also love toys that make noise and can entertain themselves trying to figure out where the sound is coming from.

Dogs are notoriously messy, so you must inspect and wash Fido's toys *at least* once a month. Do this more often if he's a heavy chewer. Read the label; many plush toys can be machine washed and dried. Clean rubber, latex and vinyl toys by hand in hot water and mild dish-washing soap and then thoroughly rinse and air dry. Bleach is a no-no since it leaves harmful residue on the toy. If a toy is ripped or broken, the squeaker is hanging by a thread or the stuffing is visible, throw it away immediately.

Chews

Dogs love to chew. Chewing releases energy, entertains and helps clean teeth. (Please note, however, that chewing is *not* a substitute for regular dental care.)

Pet-supply stores are a vegetarian's nightmare, but bliss for Fido. Just about every animal body part is available as a chew: tendons, tracheae, bully sticks, bones, ears, hooves, snouts and the ever-popular rawhide. Before bringing one of these tasty morsels home, talk to your veterinarian about appropriate chew choices for your dog. Experts disagree about the safety of rawhides and other chews. If your furry pal is a power chewer, rawhide and other animal body parts are **not** a good idea. Hard rubber toys specifically designed for heavy chewers are safer.

Like with all products these days, the country of origin is an important consideration. I buy rawhide and chews sourced and manufactured in only the United States, Canada and countries that monitor and regulate production, sanitation and labeling.

That said, just because a chew (or any product) is made in the U.S.A. doesn't guarantee that it's safe or well made. If the chew looks cheap, has an artificial scent or flavor or is dyed or bleached to a strange or unnatural color, *don't* buy it. Chews should be the same color you'd find in nature: rawhide and body parts are usually cream, tan or light brown—not glow-in-the-dark white. Every year, I cringe when I see bright red candy-cane-shaped rawhide around the holidays. There's absolutely no reason to expose Fido to chemicals used for the sole purpose of making the product attractive *to the human.* Fido couldn't care less about the color or shape—he just wants to chew.

Don't toss Fido a rawhide or chew and then leave for work. All chews are potential choking and obstruction hazards. Fido can quickly break off or shred a chew into small pieces that he can swallow whole. In addition, chews can upset a sensitive stomach and cause vomiting or diarrhea. Thus, Fido must be supervised at all times while chewing. Take a chew away if your dog is devouring it too fast or breaking it up. I don't give rawhides to Zeke because he inhales them in about two minutes and throws them up shortly thereafter.

Bully sticks and other chews made from animal parts smell ghastly when they are squishy and wet. Take a wet chew away and allow it to dry and harden before returning it. Immediately throw away chews that are breaking up, splintering or gnawed down to a stub. Wash your hands with soap and water after handling a chew, since they've been known to carry salmonella.

Bedding

Every dog needs a bed to call his own—even if he spends most of his time in yours. Beds are available in every size, color, fabric and shape and at every possible price point. Moreover, beds are filled with all types of stuffing and some have fancy features like electric warmers. Choose a bed that's large enough to accommodate your dog comfortably when he stretches out and built to withstand his activity and chewing level. If Fido is arthritic or extremely athletic, consider a bed that's heated or filled with therapeutic memory foam. Many dogs prefer beds that are higher on one side so they feel protected. Dogs also enjoy sleeping on soft blankets or towels. Lucky dogs have a bed or blanket in several areas of their home.

Inspect and wash Fido's bedding at least every month. If the bed has a foam core, toss when it begins to crumble. Likewise, replace the cover of the bed if it's ripped or torn.

Seasonal Safety

Summer and Spring

Before bringing Fido along to a picnic, cookout or party, ask yourself whether he'd rather be home in the air-conditioning. Fido may have neither the personality nor the desire to attend a party. Definitely leave him at home if he's young, old or ill, because he'll have a difficult time remaining comfortable in the heat. Always watch your dog for signs of heatstroke or heat exhaustion and bring him to a cool location, preferably in air-conditioning, if he is overheating. (See chapter 9, "Fun with Fido," for details.)

Also determine whether the festivities will allow you to supervise Fido at all times. Remember that some dogs aren't proficient swimmers and most dogs cannot control themselves around food, especially meat sizzling on a barbie. Moreover, alcohol and dogs don't mix. A small sip of your gin and tonic can be toxic. Always keep Fido on leash unless your party is located in a safe, fully enclosed area. Finally, verify that Fido is welcome where you're going. He can never be left alone in a car, especially in warm weather.

In addition, keep your dog away from other people's gardening pesticides, fertilizers and lawn chemicals. Insects and parasites, such as mosquitoes, spiders, fleas and ticks flourish in warm weather. Visit your veterinarian for a yearly heartworm check and parasite medication. Remember to administer these crucial medicines in a timely fashion. (See chapter 10, "Annoying Allergies and Pernicious Parasites.")

||||||||||||||||||||||||||||||||||||||||||||||||||||||||||||||||||||||||||||||||||||||||||||||||||||||

NEVER LEAVE A DOG (OR ANY ANIMAL) ALONE IN A CAR!!

Not only am I yelling—I'm stomping my feet, holding my chin at an indignant angle and crossing my arms firmly across my (well-toned) chest. Even in mild weather or in the shade, the inside of a car can reach a deadly temperature in a matter of minutes, and Fido can die from heatstroke. Rolling down the windows does nothing but provide an escape opportunity or easy pickings for a pet thief.

In the winter, the temperature inside a vehicle plummets quickly and Fido can literally freeze to death. If you leave your motor running, carbon monoxide can rapidly build up inside the car.

Anytime you see an animal alone in a car, call the police or search out the owner. Feel free to chastise the owner for endangering her pet.

|||||||||||||||||||||||||||||||||||||||||||||||||||||||||||||||||||||||||||||||||||||||||||||||||||||||||||||||||||

Winter and Fall

All responsible, caring owners must undertake certain precautions to protect their pooches from cold-weather hazards. Despite their fur coats, dogs can suffer from hypothermia or frostbite, especially on the tips of their ears and tails. Use your common sense; if you can't hear over your chattering teeth, your dog is probably cold too. Young, elderly or sick dogs may need additional weather protection and shouldn't be exposed to harsh weather. (See chapter 9, "Fun with Fido.")

When the thermometer begins dropping and frostbite and hypothermia are scary and real possibilities, Fido should be living *inside* your home. If you nonetheless continue to believe that it's acceptable to force Fido to live alone outside in the elements, at least help him survive. His shelter must be raised off the ground, insulated, filled with safe, warm bedding and appropriately sized. He must have a constant supply of fresh, *unfrozen* water and additional wholesome food because he burns extra calories shivering— I mean, keeping warm.

Once it turns cold, winter-proof inside your home. Move Fido's crate and beds to warm, dry and draft-free areas. Erect a barrier around fireplaces that can't be easily knocked over. If you use space heaters, keep Fido far away and never leave him unattended in a room where one is in use. He can burn himself if he's too close or knock it over and start a fire. Since you'll be limiting outdoor playtime, devise indoor activities for your dog. Play catch, chase or hide-and-seek or practice tricks; just limit Fido's couch time. (See chapter 9, "Fun with Fido," for additional ideas.)

Holiday Safety

When planning your holiday celebrations, don't forget about Fido. Dogs enjoy celebrating with the rest of the family, but some holidays are more dog friendly than others. Dogs are extremely curious, especially puppies. Never leave Fido unsupervised in a room with holiday decorations, plants or treats. If Fido is anxious during celebrations, talk to your veterinarian about strategies for helping him remain calm and happy.

If you're using candles, place them well out of Fido's reach and never leave the room while they're burning. Dogs don't understand fire and have no idea that their fur is flammable. One of my clients left her Cocker Spaniel alone in the dining room with lit candelabras on the table. The dog jumped onto the table to feast on the goodies, tipped over a candelabra and set his long belly fur on fire. Thankfully, someone noticed right away, threw a towel around him and wet him down in the kitchen sink before he was seriously injured.

Fourth of July

Even though it seems logical to bring Fido along to outside celebrations, sometimes it is better to leave him home. Fourth of July is *not* a dog-friendly holiday. Many dogs are easily spooked by fireworks. Indeed, dogs often become noise sensitive as they age.

When fireworks are booming, Fido should *always* be inside, sequestered in a safe, quiet room. Never leave Fido unattended in your yard on July 4 (or any other time). Stray fireworks can land there or the noise of neighboring fireworks can scare him and he'll desperately try to escape. Whether or not he succeeds, he can seriously injure himself.

If you do bring Fido with you, keep him on leash at all times. Your normally calm dog may dart off unexpectedly and terrible accidents happen to dogs off leash, especially when you throw pyrotechnics into the mix. Fido should be nowhere near cherry bombs, Roman candles, sparklers or anything else that involves fire and gunpowder. If he gets too close, he can be burned, lose an eye or suffer hearing loss from the explosions.

Immediately dispose of all unused fireworks and remnants, as they are toxic if ingested. After the holiday, look for firework pieces when you're out walking or playing. Protect everyone's pet by throwing away anything you find.

Valentine's Day and Easter

Although otherwise unrelated, both Easter and Valentine's Day are chocolate- and plant-intensive holidays. As you know, chocolate is extremely toxic to dogs. So exercise extreme caution with your chocolate bunnies and heart-shaped boxes of bonbons. Flowers and plants are popular on these holidays too. Thorns can injure your dog if he steps on or swallows them. Easter lilies, tulips and other spring flowers are extremely toxic if eaten and must be kept far away from Fido.

Halloween

Halloween is a controversial holiday for dog owners. Ever since the first cave dog donned a saber-toothed tiger costume, people have been debating the merits of dressing up dogs. If Fido doesn't mind dressing up—and you've verified this with an objective third party—go right ahead and have a ball. Whether he's Bark Vader, Dogzilla or Hairy Potter, his costume must be comfortable and not obstruct his vision, hearing, breathing or movement. **Never** force Fido to wear his costume if it makes him stressed, scared or nervous.

While trick-or-treating, keep Fido on a short leash and under control at all times. Take him home the moment he becomes uncomfortable or anxious. Watch him closely so he doesn't eat any candy or wrappers. Pumpkin seeds are a problem too. They can get lodged in Fido's throat or intestines. Eating a pumpkin may upset Fido's stomach, and larger pieces of flesh and tough skin can cause dangerous internal blockages.

Halloween decorations should be placed out of Fido's reach. If Fido knocks over a jack-o'-lantern, he can suffer serious burns or start a fire. Likewise, chewing or swallowing fake cobwebs, plastic skeletons or glow sticks can be harmful.

In addition to joy and laughter, trick-or-treaters bring many extra escape opportunities. Even the most confident dog can dart out the door if spooked by a costume or an enthusiastic guest. It may be best to keep Fido away from the commotion in a comfortable and safe closed room.

The Holiday Season: Thanksgiving, Christmas and Hanukkah

The holidays are joyous and exciting, but offer many opportunities for canine injuries. If you can't resist feeding Fido from your holiday table, keep the portions small and skip turkey bones, fat trimmings and greasy potato latkes. Don't leave Fido alone in the kitchen with leftovers or overflowing garbage cans. Dogs can perform extraordinary feats of agility and strength when food is involved.

One Thanksgiving my family and I were all standing around the kitchen chatting as the turkey cooled on the stove top. Ivan, my Giant Schnauzer, tore into the room, hopped onto the stove, snagged the turkey, sat in the middle of the room and began devouring our dinner. His paws dug so deeply into the flesh that he looked like a lion on a wildebeest. Not knowing what else to do, I bypassed the customary "triple dare" and "triple-*dog* dared" my sister to retrieve the bird. She declined, however, when Ivan bared his fangs and growled menacingly. With no Chop Suey Palace in the vicinity, we ate our festive meal at a Greek diner. Ivan, of course, had diarrhea for days.

Holiday decorations can be a problem too. Erect a barrier around your Christmas tree so Fido can't knock it over or drink from the water in the tree stand. The electrical cords attached to Christmas lights, and anything on the lower branches of the tree, attract curious canines. Moreover, tinsel, ornaments, ornament hangers and room decorations are dangerous if ingested. Fido can easily swallow small items, like dreidels, which can cause obstructions—they aren't too comfortable coming out the other end either. Holiday plants, such as holly and mistletoe are particularly poisonous. Poinsettias are less dangerous, but will still make Fido ill if eaten. Gifts also generate hazards. Ribbon, yarn, tape, balloons, gift-wrap accessories, batteries and small parts of toys are choking hazards.

Holidays and celebrations can be overly exciting, isolating or stressful for your dog. Dogs are creatures of habit and any change in routine may be upsetting. In many homes, routines go out the window as families host overnight guests or celebrations. Be sure that all your guests know and understand your pet-safety rules.

Observe your pooch throughout the celebrations. Watch for behavior changes that could indicate stress or sickness. Be ready to remove him from the activity if he becomes anxious or aggressive. Fido may be much happier in his crate or bed. Humans are also often overwhelmed or anxious during holidays. Your dog will respond to your emotional state and body language. Be sure to spend some extra quality time with him. This will improve your mood and help Fido's too.

|||||||||||||||||||||||||||||||||||||||||||||||||||||||||||||||||||||||||||||||||||||||||||||||||||||||||||||||||||||||

Live Animals Make Lousy Gifts

Not everyone shares your love of animals, and even animal lovers may be reluctant or incapable of assuming the responsibilities, time commitment and expense of a pet.

Animals are not returnable or disposable and, therefore, should **never** be given as a gift. Instead, wrap up a creative stand-in for the living, breathing animal, such as a picture, toy, food or cute collar and leash. Better yet, purchase a gift certificate from a local shelter or rescue. This allows the recipient to decide for herself whether she's ready, willing and able to welcome a pet into her family.

Besides, the holidays are a dreadful time to introduce a new pet into a household. Your routine is altered, celebrations take you away from home and you're probably too busy to provide your new family member with the required care, stability, love and attention. Wait until after the holidays. Local shelters and rescues will be overflowing with rejected holiday gifts that are anxiously awaiting their new home.

|||||||||||||||||||||||||||||||||||||||||||||||||||||||||||||||||||||||||||||||||||||||||||||||||||||||||||||||||||||||

7.
Always Be Prepared for Emergencies

Nowadays, we're bombarded with public service announcements and products related to disaster and emergency preparedness. I *still* have fifteen rolls of duct tape and plastic sheeting in a back closet! Yet, no emergency or disaster plan is complete unless it includes our pets. A bit of practice and preparation will allow you and Fido to survive life's worst-case scenarios, whether a natural disaster, a medical emergency or an everyday mishap. So grab your neckerchief; we're going to make like a Boy Scout and always be prepared.

Doggy ID

Don't let Fido ever leave home without his American Express card or, more critically, his collar and tags. On the identification tag, consider listing your cell phone number *and* a number for someone out of the area in case phone lines are inoperable during an emergency. Check Fido's tags often and re-place them when the information changes or becomes illegible.

Since Fido has no back pockets in which to carry his wallet, implant a microchip identifier inside him. Have no fear—the government won't monitor his bank account, and black helicopters won't follow him down the street. The chip merely allows shelters and veterinarians to locate the owner of a lost dog easily and quickly. The chip, which is about the size of a grain of rice, is injected into the skin between the shoulder blades. The procedure is easy and inexpensive and many organizations offer microchips on a reduced-fee or no-fee basis. As soon as your contact information changes, update your file with the microchip company. If your dog is lost or his collar is removed, you want him to possess all the tools to ensure his safe and speedy return.

Locations of Animal Hospitals and
Transportation Options

Review the phone numbers, operating hours and locations of your veterinarian's *and* emergency veterinarian's offices. If you are not great with directions, take a dry run when you are calm to learn the fastest routes. If you don't drive, prepare a plan for alternative transportation. Ask a neighbor or friend to be your emergency transport. Some cities have emergency pet taxis, but if your dog is seriously injured, waiting for its arrival may not be an option.

Pet First-Aid Kit, First-Aid Manual and
Emergency Stickers

Although I hope you never have to open the box, a canine first-aid kit is an essential safety item. I recommend that you purchase a travel kit for your car or backpack too. First-aid kits must always be fully stocked with unexpired products, so check the contents several times a year. Replace items as you use them or they expire.

A pet first-aid manual is another vital safety item (one for humans is a good idea too). First-aid books include comprehensive instructions on caring for your injured or sick pet until veterinary help is available. The American Red Cross publishes easy-to-understand and useful books. Read and review your manual several times a year so you'll be relatively prepared should an emergency arise. If you have questions or need clarification, talk to your veterinarian.

Finally, on all outside doors place stickers alerting emergency personnel that you have pets. These stickers are available at veterinary offices and stores. Replace the stickers at least once a year or when they fade.

Poison Control and Emergency
Information Card

Always keep the ASPCA's Animal Poison Control Center's twenty-four-hour hotline number handy and don't be shy about using it. The number is

1-888-426-4435. Stop reading right now and copy and complete the Emergency Information Card at the end of this chapter. Then, laminate it and hang it in a conspicuous location in your home and place copies in your car, your purse or backpack and your own disaster kit. I have mine taped inside the cabinet door above my kitchen telephone. Prepare a card for each pet and attach pictures and vaccination and veterinary records. Verify the information yearly and update as needed.

Disaster Planning

The number one rule of disaster planning is simple: **NEVER leave your pets behind**. IF YOU LEAVE, THEY LEAVE. No exceptions. If the situation isn't safe for *you*, it's definitely not safe for *your pets*. Left alone, they'll have no food or water and no one to keep them safe. The Federal Emergency Management Agency (FEMA), the Red Cross and local and national animal-welfare organizations are excellent resources—so use them!

Plan and prepare before disaster strikes. No matter where you live, a natural or man-made disaster is always possible. At a minimum, your disaster plan must include the following:

1. A list of safe places to go *with* your pets within a one-hundred-mile radius of your home. Except for service animals, Red Cross shelters don't accept animals. Call ahead to hotels, motels, friends and relatives to verify that they'll accept Fido. If you can't find a place to stay *with* your pets, research veterinary hospitals and boarding facilities in the safe zone. Don't leave Fido in an animal shelter unless you have absolutely no other choice. Shelters will be overwhelmed and inundated with animals in peril.

2. Along with your disaster kit, prepare one for your pets. Assemble a separate kit for each pet. Use an extra crate or pet carrier to hold the supplies. Clearly label the container with your pet's name, your name and contact information and your veterinarian's phone number. The kit should include: Fido's picture, his medical records and vaccination history and a copy of the Emergency Information Card. Place all paperwork in a zip-top plastic bag. An extra collar with tags, a harness, leash and first-aid supplies and

a manual are also necessary. Include a can opener, bowls and a seven-day supply of food, water and medicine. Replace perishables every six months. Plastic poop bags, a toy and a blanket are essential too.

3. Arrange for a neighbor or friend to fetch your pets if you're not home and then meet you at a designated location. Give the person your house keys and a copy of the Emergency Information Card and show her where the pet disaster kits are stored.

The moment you learn that a disaster is even remotely possible, begin evacuation preparation. Even if everything turns out fine, you'll have practiced for the next time. Call ahead to your safe haven and make reservations or alert your friend or family of your potential evacuation. Bring all pets inside your home. **NEVER** leave a pet penned or chained outside, especially if disaster is looming. Move to a safe area in your home *with your pets* and await further information. Don't let your pets run free inside. If they're scared, they may hide and you don't want to waste valuable escape time hunting them down. If you're not home, call your designated pet wrangler and arrange to retrieve your pets.

As you're leaving your home *with* your pets, write "pets evacuated" on the emergency stickers or with permanent marker on all outside doors. This will prevent emergency personnel from wasting valuable time searching your home. Grab your pet and human disaster kits and get the heck out of Dodge. When you return home, be mindful of new hazards caused by the disaster and keep your pet home and closely supervised until things return to normal.

Finding Your Lost Dog

Regardless of how conscientious and careful you are, Fido can end up lost. Dogs have been known to slip out the front door or dash off if a leash breaks. Your chances of recovering your pet are a million times better if he's wearing an identification tag *and* he has a microchip. Collars can slip off; chips are permanent. Most veterinary offices and shelters have equipment to read a microchip. If the information is current, Fido will be back in your arms that much sooner.

The moment you realize that Fido is missing, do the following:

1. Grab a recent picture of your pet and roam the area where he was last seen. Call your pet's name as loudly as you can. He may be scared and hearing your voice is likely to draw him to you. In addition, talk to everyone you meet on your search. They may have information that will lead you to your dog.

2. Contact all local shelters and animal-welfare organizations, animal-control agencies and veterinary offices, as well as the police. Provide a detailed description of your dog and any information about the incident.

3. Visit the local shelters every day. You know exactly what your pet looks like. A shelter worker may have a different idea of what light brown, spotted or short hair means. Moreover, many dogs may fit your description.

4. Advertise! Prepare a flyer with your dog's picture, your contact phone numbers and e-mail address and information about his last known whereabouts. The announcement should include a detailed description of your pet, such as breed, gender, age, weight, color and any special markings or characteristics. Always leave out one identifying detail to protect yourself from a scam artist trying to prey on your desperation. Likewise, never include your home address. Hang the flyers on signposts and telephone poles and in stores, animal hospitals, libraries, coffee shops and other locations in the area. Place ads in newspapers, online and on the radio.

5. Alert your neighbors. Go door-to-door; ask people who live and work in the area if they've seen your dog. Place an article of your clothing on the front porch so your dog can smell home. Dogs have been known to return after many months and many miles of travel.

|||||||||||||||||||||||||||||||||||||||||||||||||||||||||||||||||||||||||||||||||||||||||||||||||||||||||||||||||||||||||

Beware of Lost-Pet Recovery Scams

It's despicable and unforgivable, but evil people may try to play on your heartstrings while you are searching for your lost pet. Always leave one detail off the advertisement. If someone calls or e-mails claiming to have your pet, ask her to describe your dog. If the person doesn't mention this characteristic, she's *not* trustworthy. Moreover, if the story seems far-fetched, it probably is. Be wary of any person who asks for money *before* returning your pet. Most Good Samaritans are not motivated by financial benefit. Always arrange to meet a stranger in a public place, such as an animal shelter, a pet-supply store or a veterinary office. Don't pay a reward until you have your dog *firmly* in hand. If you believe that someone has stolen your pet or is trying to scam you, contact the police.

IIIIIIIIIIIIIIIIIIIIIIIIIIIIIIIIIIIIIIIIIIIIIIIIIIIIIIIIIIIIIIIIIIIIIIIIIIIIIIIIIIIIIIIIIIIIIIIIIIIII

How to Help a Lost or Stray Dog

If you see a dog alone, she needs help. A lone animal is in immediate danger from cars, evil people, other animals, starvation and disease. Don't walk or drive away. Aside from your moral duty to help a defenseless animal, karma is involved. If you help a dog in a time of need, someone will help yours.

Be cautious when approaching the animal. Even friendly, well-trained dogs can bite or run if scared or hurt. If you feel comfortable, catch the dog and attach a leash or other restraint. In a pinch, use your jacket, belt or tie as a leash. Both my coauthor and I always keep a few leashes in the car for this purpose. Ask a passerby for help if needed. If you can't catch the dog or you're uncomfortable, call animal-control officials or a local shelter. Wait with the dog until help arrives.

If the dog has a tag, contact the owner and keep the dog safe until you can reunite him. If he has no identification, take him to the nearest veterinary office or animal shelter to scan for a microchip. If the dog has no chip, hang "Found Dog" announcements in the area. Before relinquishing control, call the police, the city pound, local shelters, animal-welfare organizations and veterinary offices. Many people file lost-dog reports. If you can't keep the dog or find him a new home, you'll have no choice but to leave him at a shelter that accepts strays. At least he'll be safe, and hopefully, he'll find a new home.

EMERGENCY INFORMATION CARD

Pet Name:
Age:
Breed:
Circle one: Male   Female   *Circle one*:   Spayed/Neutered   Intact

Physical description (include color and distinguishing marks)

Microchip Company Name: Identification Number:
Address:
Phone: Web site:

Health Issues or Allergies:

Owner Name:
Address:
Home Phone: Work Phone: Cell phone:
E-mail:

Secondary Emergency Contact:
Relationship:
Address:
Home Phone: Work Phone: Cell phone:
E-mail:

Primary Veterinarian:
Address:
Phone:
Directions:

Specialty Veterinarian:
Address:
Phone:
Directions:

Emergency Veterinarian:
Address:
Phone:
Directions:

ASPCA's Animal Poison Control Center: 1-888-426-4435   www.aspca.org

Important Web sites:

Location of first aid kit and manual:

Location of pet disaster kit:

Designated Guardian:
Relationship:
Address:
Home Phone: Work Phone: Cell phone:
E-mail:

Alternate Guardian:
Relationship:
Address:
Home Phone: Work Phone: Cell phone:
E-mail:

Additional Information:

In attached envelope:

Recent photograph
Important veterinary records
Vaccination history

Caring for Fido If You Can't

No one likes to think about death and dying. Nonetheless, if you pass away or become ill or incapacitated, Fido still requires love and care. Pets can be forgotten during times of emotional upheaval. Without a contingency plan, Fido could end up in an animal shelter with a dismal future. If you're not around, Fido needs to be placed in a caring, loving and responsible home so he can continue to thrive. If you have everything in place before disaster strikes, Fido's life will be minimally interrupted and he'll be loved, happy and safe. And, in the end, that's what really matters.

Think carefully as you select Fido's guardian and alternates. Talk to the candidates and choose people that you believe in your gut to be completely reliable and trustworthy; you'll be in no position to oversee the situation. The guardians must be willing and able to assume *all* the emotional, financial and time commitments of pet care. Once a year, talk to Fido's guardian and alternates and verify that they're still willing and able to perform their duties.

Many people include pets in their wills and *officially* designate guardians and money for a pet's care. Relatives or heirs can always challenge your will, especially if they aren't dog people or are particularly bitter because you didn't leave *them* your fortune. To minimize problems, hire a reputable lawyer who specializes in wills and trusts to prepare legal documents that comply with relevant state laws.

Most state laws don't recognize bequests made *directly* to an animal. Pets, however, can be cared for through a "trust." A trust allows you to allocate money solely for the *care* of your pet in the event of your death, illness or incapacitation. You assign a trustee to dole out the funds to a specified guardian. The guardian is legally bound to use the funds to care for your pet. Depending on the state law, you may be able to include detailed care instructions.

It will probably come as no surprise that my lawyers require me to state "in no uncertain terms" that I'm neither a lawyer nor a law firm and that this book is no substitute for the advice of a licensed attorney who is familiar with applicable state law.

8.

Go, Fido, Go! Traveling With and Without Your Furry Pal

Ask someone what comes to mind when the words "travel" and "dogs" are mentioned together. For most people, it will be one of two images: (1) Lassie, desperately crossing the Scottish Highlands, fighting with every last breath to return to her boy while she ignores the fact that Elizabeth Taylor and Roddy McDowall are stealing her precious screen time, or (2) Snoopy on the road, his empty bowl perched jauntily on his head, a hobo-style stick-and-handkerchief pack slung over his shoulder. Thankfully, your dog can travel much more comfortably if you're educated and prepared.

Overnight Travel: Should Fido Stay or Should He Go?

Traveling with Fido is well worth the extra effort as long as he's *genuinely* thrilled to be on the road. Some dogs are born to see the world, and some are happier at home. While planning my recent hiking trip to the Smoky Mountains, I had to decide whether to bring Zeke and Arthur along. We were driving to Tennessee and staying in a dog-friendly cabin. Both dogs enjoy the car; both are healthy and easygoing. So far, so good. Then, I thought about what we were planning to do on the trip. Zeke has a short coat and he's agile, energetic and large enough to foil a bald eagle hunting for dinner. So I knew he was coming. Arthur, however, was a different story. His long coat would be a nightmare on trails and a magnet for dirt, burs and parasites. He's small and I was genuinely worried that a bird of prey would swoop down and carry him away. (I'm not kidding—this can really happen.) Moreover, he's slow and I knew that after about five hundred feet I'd be carrying him up the mountain. So Arthur stayed home with a responsible and trustworthy friend while Zeke and I packed our dirks and (faux) buckskin shirts and explored the mountain wilderness.

Analyze the details of your trip in light of Fido's age, health, physical fitness and personality. If in doubt, leave him home with a competent and reliable caretaker. We'll discuss these options later on. The rigors of travel can be especially difficult for young, elderly, ill or physically impaired dogs. For example, if Fido is arthritic, he can't safely hike to a campsite or stay cooped up in a crate in a cold, drafty cargo hold. Puppies shouldn't be around other dogs until fully vaccinated (around four months old). Older dogs are often too frail or cranky to withstand the mental and physical demands of travel.

Next, realistically assess your dog's personality. Is he easygoing and adaptable or does even a slight change in routine make him anxious? Does he enjoy being away from home? Is he a nervous Nellie in a new environment? Does he live and die for outdoor activity? Is he keen to be around strangers, crowds and other dogs? Will he mind being left alone in an unfamiliar place? Does he get carsick? Will the stress of a flight take years off his life? Abandon wishful thinking and be objective.

A pretrip veterinary examination is always a good idea. Discuss your vacation plans in detail and solicit an unbiased opinion. The doctor may recommend specific vaccinations, medication or parasite preventatives based on your destination.

Even if Fido is waiting by the door with his bags packed, there are a few more factors to consider. Verify that your *particular* dog is welcome *everywhere* you plan on visiting and on *every* mode of transportation. Hotels, homes, attractions, campgrounds and airlines often have restrictions based on age, size or breed. Call well ahead of your trip and ask detailed questions about the current applicable rules and regulations, fees and paperwork requirements. Once you are fully informed, adjust your itinerary accordingly.

Now think about what you'll be doing on your trip. Where will Fido stay while you're off eating and sightseeing? He can't be left alone in the car—**ever.** Many theme parks and attractions offer on-site "pet checks." Call each facility and determine if your pooch would be comfortable and welcome there. Some facilities offer overnight accommodations, but may not be staffed through the night. If Fido will be spending large amounts of time in a kennel or in his crate back at the hotel, there's no reason to bring him along.

Ascertain whether you'll need to take any additional precautions to protect Fido from local environmental hazards, such as native plants, insects and parasites. (See chapter 10, "Annoying Allergies and Pernicious Parasites.") Consult parasite and vegetation maps and talk to officials at each destination for current and accurate information. Discuss your findings with your veterinarian and determine if the risks are worth the hassle.

Unless you're staying exclusively in private homes and not visiting any attractions with Fido, you'll need paperwork from your veterinarian certifying Fido's health, his vaccination history and other information. The specific requirements vary depending on where you are visiting and lodging. Call ahead and ask; then decide if you are willing and able to comply.

In the United States, pets can travel freely across most state lines with only a health certificate or proof of rabies vaccination. Hawaii, however, has strict controls on animal visitors, including a quarantine. If you're traveling to another country, contact the appropriate consulate or embassy. Most countries require detailed paperwork, quarantine, proof of microchip, blood tests and proof of vaccinations for a variety of diseases.

||||||||||||||||||||||||||||||||||||||||||||||||||||||||||||||||||||||||||||||||||||||||||||||||||||||||||||||||

Crate Expectations

No matter where his travels take him, Fido needs a crate. Whether you're driving, flying or traveling on the *Queen Mary 2*, Fido's crate must be in good condition, sturdy and well ventilated. The door must latch securely without being locked, in case Fido must be removed in an emergency. In addition, the crate or carrier must be large enough for Fido to stand up and turn around inside. If the crate is too big, he can be injured if it bounces around. If Fido is flying, his particular crate must be approved by the airline.

Clearly label the crate using indelible ink and include your name, permanent address and cell phone number and your travel information and temporary-contact details at your destination. If flying, add the flight number, the destination city and the name of the person accompanying or picking up the dog. Also, print the words "LIVE ANIMAL" in LARGE letters and place arrows indicating UP on all sides of the crate. Tape a current photo of your dog on the top of the crate in case he's lost.

Regardless of the mode of transportation, acclimate Fido to his crate *well before* vacation—I mean four or more weeks before. Allow Fido to explore it, snack, drink and nap in it and take some practice trips around town in it. Confine him for a few hours at a time so he won't be surprised on vacation. If he already uses a crate and it's sturdy enough for travel, great—but get Fido used to moving while inside it. Don't forget to clip his nails so they won't get caught on the crate.

||||||||||||||||||||||||||||||||||||||||||||||||||||||||||||||||||||||||||||||||||||||||||||||||||||||||||||||

Overnight Safety

Whether you're staying at a hotel, campsite or private home, a bit of dog-proofing is required at every destination. As soon as you arrive, determine Fido's bathroom arrangements; he'll probably have to go NOW! Then, inspect for indoor dangers, such as electrical cords, hazardous chemicals and open garbage bins. Whenever Fido is outside, he must be on leash and in your control. He's unfamiliar with the sights, smells and sounds in the new location and may get spooked and bolt. If Fido will be using a yard, check for hazards and verify that it's fully enclosed and that the fence is in good repair. If you'll be staying or playing outside, look for natural hazards like poisonous plants, wild animals and open bodies of water or nearby cliffs. (See chapter 6, "Keeping Fido Safe and Sound at Home," and chapter 9, "Fun With Fido," to learn more.)

Motor Vehicles: Cars, Trucks and Motorcycles

Some dogs go bonkers when they hear the words "Wanna go in the car?" To them the car offers an endless opportunity to see the world and travel comfortably with their pack. Other dogs, however, are scared sick (sometimes literally). These dogs are anxious because they have no idea what's going on or dislike the noise or the motion. These dogs often shake, drool, foam at the mouth or vomit.

If your dog is afraid or becomes carsick, introduce him to the car slowly over a period of weeks well before your trip. During the training period, reward Fido with bite-sized treats so his stomach will be less likely to turn queasy once you start moving.

Begin by bringing Fido into the car and sit with the engine off while you praise him and bestow treats. Once he's comfortable, turn the engine on. Of course, be sure the garage door is open so no one is asphyxiated. Keep the praise and treats coming until Fido overcomes this hurdle. Then, go for a short ride, maybe only a minute long or just up and down the driveway. Repeat the short rides every day until Fido seems calm, or at least his drooling has decreased. Now gradually increase the duration and distance of your trips. Quite frankly, this is not a bad way to introduce any dog, especially a puppy, to the car.

If Fido's car sickness isn't diminishing, visit the vet to rule out a health problem, such as an inner-ear disorder. If Fido is healthy, the vet may prescribe medication to decrease his vehicular anxiety. Don't use any over-the-counter or herbal remedies unless directed by the vet.

Dogs Don't Come Equipped With Automatic Restraints

You wear a seat belt and so should Fido. A loose dog in a moving vehicle is a danger to himself and to people inside and outside the car. The dog can distract the driver, block her vision or impede her ability to steer or use the pedals. An unrestrained dog may randomly decide to jump out an open window, which is exactly what happened to a client of mine. She was driving with her windows half-open and her Golden Doodle, Sammy, loose in the car. Sammy spied a squirrel and jumped right out the window and into the road. Sammy's owner slammed on the brakes and opened the minivan door. Sammy was standing in the middle of the road, stunned, and then slowly limped back into the van. Thankfully, the street wasn't busy and no serious damage was done. Sammy's legs and her ego were bruised—the squirrel got away.

In an accident, an unrestrained dog will be thrown around the car or through the windshield at life-threatening velocity. According to Bark Buckle UP, a national pet-safety program, an unrestrained 60-pound dog in a car traveling at 30 to 35 miles per hour will cause an impact of 2,700 pounds. The dog probably won't survive and the driver and passenger may be harmed if they collide with the dog. If the dog survives, he'll be injured and scared and, thus, more likely to bite rescue workers or interfere with their work. Moreover, the dog could escape from the wreck and be hit by another vehicle or cause another crash.

Now that you understand why a restraint is necessary, which one should you choose? Purchase a restraint specifically designed and tested for dogs rather than making your own. Restraints attach to your vehicle using a variety of gizmos. The size of your dog determines the best style of restraint. Doggy car seats raise small dogs up so they can see outside while safely attached to the car's seat belt. Harnesses that attach directly to the seat belt are more comfortable for medium and large dogs.

Crates and pet carriers are fine as long as they're well ventilated and *firmly* attached to the vehicle. Otherwise, the crate will become a dangerous projectile in a crash. Built-in vehicle barriers are available from the factory on many cars. These gadgets form a cagelike structure in the back of the vehicle.

Whichever restraint you choose, practice installing it in the vehicle *and* on your dog *before* you rev the engine. Never restrain Fido in the front seat. If the air bag deploys, the impact can kill him. Remember, restraints are only effective when they are used. So even if you're running late, buckle up the dog—every time!

And Another Thing . . . More Vehicle-Safety Rules

Although Fido loves to feel the breeze through his fur, it's way too dangerous for him to ride with his head out the window. Unless he's wearing goggles and earmuffs, debris, bugs and air pollution can damage his eyes or cause internal ear injuries. The cold air being forced inside his nose and lungs can harm Fido's respiratory system. Worse yet, his head could hit a tree branch, a mailbox, a side-view mirror, a road sign or even a bus.

Fido must **never** ride in the back of a pickup truck. He could jump out, fall out or be thrown from the vehicle. Tethering Fido to the truck bed doesn't make him any safer. If he's thrown from the truck bed, he'll be strangled or dragged by his neck behind the moving vehicle.

Whether you're human or canine, motorcycles have inherent risks since they're open and offer little protection in a crash. Nonetheless, Fido can ride along on a motorcycle as long as he's properly restrained. New canine protective gear is available: sidecars, carriers, trailers, helmets and goggles. The more enclosed he is, the safer Fido will be in an accident. If he's not restrained, he can jump or be thrown off the moving cycle.

And remember . . . **NEVER LEAVE A DOG (OR ANY ANIMAL) ALONE IN A VEHICLE!**

Long Rides

On long car trips, make frequent stops—at least every few hours—to let Fido relieve himself, stretch and drink plenty of water. Many people forgo feeding Fido in the car because his stomach may be upset by the motion. Thus, feed your dog a light nosh a few hours before departure and then at your destination. Additionally, anytime Fido leaves the car, he must be on leash and, as always, wearing his collar and ID tags. To avoid escapes, I always attach the leash before I unbuckle my dogs.

Air Travel

If you thought air travel was difficult for humans, imagine how a dog feels. He's separated from his best friend, stuffed in a box and placed on a conveyor belt that meanders though the bowels of a noisy and stuffy airport. Along the way he's bombarded with earsplitting and unfamiliar sounds and nothing looks or smells familiar. Then, he's tossed around by indifferent strangers, lobbed onto another conveyor belt and fed into a big, uninviting cave. Inside he's surrounded by huge stacks of weird-looking bags and supplies. His crate is vibrating and his ears are ringing. The cave door slams and then all of a sudden his crate begins swaying, his ears feel like they'll explode and it's cold. He has no idea what's going on, where he is or if he'll ever see his best friend again. And that's just takeoff!

Air travel is neither pleasant nor easy for our four-legged friends. Forget the wonders of flight and the physics that allow a megaton piece of machinery to soar through the air; as far as Fido's concerned, flying is for the birds—it's too mentally and physically taxing. Moreover, pets are lost or killed on commercial flights every year. Many more are injured while trying to break out of their crates or running around in the cargo hold after escaping. If Fido is small enough to fit under your seat in the cabin, he may fare better, but he will still have no idea what's going on and is likely to become extremely anxious. Fido should fly only when absolutely necessary.

Every airline has its own take on dogs in flight, so call ahead. Many major carriers allow only service dogs in the cabin or limit the number of dogs on board and in cargo. Here are a few additional facts to check before booking the flight:

- Minimum and maximum age for flying
- Health and breed restrictions. Never fly dogs suffering from respiratory disorders or short-snouted dogs as cargo. The temperature and oxygen fluctuations in the cargo hold can be deadly.
- Size requirements for a dog flying in the cabin
- Cargo-hold temperature-control and pressurization procedures
- Crate requirements
- Procedures for feeding and watering en route. Specifically ask if you can include frozen water in his bowl so Fido can drink during the flight as it thaws.
- Procedures for delays. If Fido will be off-loaded during a delay, determine where he'll be waiting. He may be sitting on the tarmac in the cold or rain, and if he escapes, the results can be deadly.
- Fees
- Required paperwork and medical certifications

Mandatory Flight-Safety Rules

Once you've decided that Fido can fly, you must exercise extreme caution to ensure his trip is safe.

1. Book direct flights to minimize the chance Fido will get lost or miss a connection. Avoiding holidays, weekends and other busy times should (hopefully) minimize the opportunity for delays.
2. Travel on the *same* flight as your pooch. Unaccompanied animals have no one to watch out for them other than airline personnel. Remember, not everyone is a dog lover. Enough said.
3. Be mindful of the weather. In the summer, don't fly in the middle of the day; in winter, avoid frigid mornings and nights.
4. Ask your veterinarian about the appropriate collar. Fido needs his ID tags, but certain collars, such as choke or metal-pronged

collars, can easily catch on the crate and harm your dog. If you're uneasy with Fido wearing his collar in the crate, clip it on the front door or tape it on top and be sure he has a microchip.

5. Verify your flight the night before in case of changes or cancellations and reconfirm Fido's drop-off and pickup times and locations.

6. Reschedule the flight if Fido is sick on travel day.

7. Feed Fido several hours before the flight so he's less likely to have an upset stomach once he starts moving.

8. Run Fido around and have him relieve himself as close to departure as possible so he'll be tired during the flight.

9. *Personally* place Fido in his crate, and check and recheck that the door is securely closed.

10. If Fido is riding with you, do not send him through the X-ray machine. Take him out and *then* place the *empty* carrier on the conveyor belt. Don't laugh; one of my clients actually sent his new puppy through the machine. The dog, now a few years old, *seems* fine. He does, however, have a *radiant* smile.

11. Tranquilizers are a no-no unless your *veterinarian* prescribes them and the airline approves. Altitude can alter a drug's effect and interfere with a dog's ability to regulate his body temperature. Ask your veterinarian about natural remedies to decrease anxiety *before* you administer any.

12. Watch as Fido's crate is being loaded on the plane. If you don't see him, ask the gate agent to check for you.

13. Once you disembark, run—don't walk—to the baggage claim and immediately retrieve your dog. Examine him and take him to a local veterinarian if something isn't right.

Trains, Buses and Ships

Pet dogs are rarely welcomed on trains, buses or ships even as cargo. Service dogs, however, travel with the passenger. Before making any travel plans, call ahead for each company's rules, regulations and fees. Most of the "Mandatory Flight-Safety Rules" apply here too.

Traveling Without Fido

Don't feel guilty. It's OK to leave Fido behind as long as you've arranged safe and enjoyable care. Begin your search well ahead of your trip. Competent friends and relatives and the best pet sitters and boarding facilities book up way in advance, especially during the holidays. If you wait until the last minute, you never know what you'll get.

Choosing the best people or facility to care for Fido while you're away is a time-consuming but critical job. You'll need time to research and visit the kennels, meet the sitters and analyze your options. Even if the choices in your area are limited, you'll need to check them out thoroughly. If the only boarding facility or pet sitter in town is dreadful, Fido would actually be better off with your elderly uncle Louie.

Fido will be most comfortable with familiar people and places. If you use a dog walker or if Fido attends doggy day care, start your search there. If Fido's caretaker handles overnight stays, lucky you and lucky Fido! If you need to find another option, do your homework.

Although hybrids exist, caretakers are divided into three main categories: (1) family or friend, (2) a pet sitter and (3) a boarding facility. Each option has distinct advantages and disadvantages. Fido's age, health and personality and your budget are also important factors to consider. If Fido is older, ill, nervous away from home, timid, aggressive, not well socialized or requires a great deal of attention, he should stay at home with a sitter or with a familiar friend or relative. Puppies without full immunity and sick dogs should avoid places where lots of dogs congregate, since their weak immune systems are less able to fight off contagious diseases and parasites. If, however, Fido is well socialized, easygoing and healthy, a boarding facility that offers *many* play opportunities may be a good choice.

Choose wisely; you don't want Fido to view your departure as a punishment. Remember, dogs are gregarious; they need to be with people and feel the love. If you disappear and Fido is alone except for the two times a day a sitter comes or he's cooped up in his crate for twelve hours at a time or he's languishing in a concrete run at a low-end kennel, he'll be quite upset. Indeed, this is when many dogs become anxious, bored and destructive. Don't open yourself up to a call from Fido's attorney and all that negative publicity. It's much easier to make a good choice.

Friend or Relative

Pros

- Fido won't be alone at night.
- Fido stays in a home environment.
- He receives personalized attention.
- Playmates are available if the caretaker has other pets or children.
- Cost is free or inexpensive.

Cons

- You're at the mercy of an unpaid volunteer, who may ignore your instructions or have no common sense *whatsoever*.
- Home may not be properly dog-proofed.
- Caretaker may be away at work during the day.

Before you ask a friend or relative to watch your precious pal, consider whether Fido is comfortable with that person, her home and her roommates. Has Fido spent much time there and if he has, did he enjoy himself? Did Fido play nicely with other pets or family members, especially children? If your friend doesn't have a dog, is her home full of hidden dangers or can it be dog-proofed? Is it full of expensive furniture and delicate antiques?

Does your friend work long hours or carouse all night? If Fido will be left alone for long time periods, find a different caretaker. In addition, carefully consider how responsible and trustworthy this friend or relative *actually* is. Would your sister know not to leave her chocolate bar on the counter, to put away her bottle of ibuprofen or to keep the yard gate closed at all times? Does your nephew share your philosophy about dog care and is he as committed to canine health and happiness? Is your neighbor willing to treat your pooch like his own, let him sleep in his bed and pamper him like you do? Moreover, will your friend or relative abide by *your* wishes and instructions or will she feed Fido bacon for breakfast, lunch and dinner?

Most importantly, decide if the person has ample common sense. A client left her beautiful Wheaten Terrier, Sandy, with her brother. The brother had business that required him to be away all day, and rather than leave the dog alone, he took Sandy to their mother's house. Seems like a responsible thing to do, right? The mother had dogs and a large yard—even an electric fence, so Sandy couldn't run away.

The mother placed an electric collar on Sandy and left her in the yard with her dogs. A few hours later, she checked on the dogs and noticed that Sandy was missing, but the mother didn't look for the dog or call for help. Later on, Sandy reappeared in the yard. The mother *assumed* everything was fine; she didn't inspect the dog, take her to the veterinarian or call the owner.

The owner retrieved Sandy a few days later and immediately noticed several *huge gaping holes* matted over with dried blood on her back. Frantically she asked her mother what the heck had happened. The mother shrugged her shoulders and replied, "Oh, Sandy *was* gone for a couple hours, but she came back. She seemed OK, so I didn't call you." After further interrogation, the owner learned that coyotes frequently snatch dogs from the area, and deduced what happened. Coyotes had stolen into the yard and attacked poor Sandy. Not only was she viciously bitten, but she was shocked by the electric fence as the coyotes dragged her away. It's a miracle that Sandy broke free, made her way home and didn't bleed to death. Unfortunately, there are loads of clueless dog owners, and the mother was one of them. Sandy eventually recovered, but she has large scars across her back.

Anytime you leave your dog with someone else, triple-check that the person understands how to care for a dog properly, how to keep him safe and what to do in case of an emergency. Better yet, purchase a copy of my book and have the person read it before your pooch moves in. Don't forget to bring back a generous thank-you gift so your friend or relative will be pleased to watch Fido again.

Paid Caretakers

When choosing a pet sitter or boarding facility, begin with referrals from the reliable and rational dog people in your life, including Fido's veterinarian, trainer and day care staff. Don't just request names; have the referrers describe their experiences in detail. Pet-sitting services often have multiple employees, so request the names of specific sitters.

Professional organizations, such as the National Association of Professional Pet Sitters, Pet Sitters International and the Pet Care Services Association (boarding facilities) have locators on their Web sites. These organizations certify that a member business meets specific standards of safety and care. Membership is no guarantee of quality, but it is an indication the company is at least making an effort.

Once you've compiled a list, perform some preliminary research. Determine the applicable state or local requirements for licensing, insurance and bonding. In addition, make inquiries with the local Better Business Bureau. Peruse the Internet and visit rating sites, but analyze the information with a skeptical eye, since the most difficult-to-please people are often the most vocal reviewers.

Now start making calls. Talk with the business owners to screen out obvious duds or ones that fail to meet your minimum requirements. The business owner should be straightforward and willing to provide detailed answers.

Review your results and then arrange for the people who would actually be watching your dog to come to your home for a chat, or in the case of boarding facilities, schedule on-site visits. Reject any business that refuses a personal interview or tour of the facility. The business obviously has something to hide. Try to choose businesses that help animals in need. It's always nice to support people who care deeply about animals. Remember, every potential caretaker must pass your gut-reaction test and ask you extensive questions about your dog.

Pet Sitters

Pros
- Fido remains at home, where he's most comfortable.
- Sitter will water your plants and take in your mail and newspapers.
- If you pay for it, sitter will stay overnight.
- At home, Fido won't be exposed to other dogs that may be sick.

Cons
- Fido may be home alone for long stretches of time.
- Fido may be home alone overnight.

- Multiple sitters may care for your dog.
- A stranger will be in your home unsupervised.

Pet sitters offer a variety of in-home services. A sitter can visit your home and feed and walk your pooch several times a day, water your plants and collect your mail, stay overnight or remain with your dog 24-7. It's a matter of your budget and the services available in your area.

If you can afford a sitter visit only two or three times a day, Fido may be safer and happier in a boarding facility, where he'll receive more attention (if you pick a good one). For me, leaving my dogs alone through the night is simply not an option. Barring a life-threatening emergency, I never let my dogs stay alone for more than five or six hours and certainly never overnight. But, hey, that's me. You do whatever allows you to sleep at night.

A good pet sitter, especially one that stays overnight, acts as a foster parent, so that Fido is comfortable and happy with little disruption in his routine. The sitter should play with, walk, entertain, groom, inspect, feed and cuddle your dog and take her to the veterinarian if needed—everything you do.

Screening Questions for Pet Sitters

- How long have you been in the pet-sitting business?
- Are you a member of any professional organizations?
- What makes your business special?
- Are you licensed, insured and bonded? Is everything current?
- What services do you offer and what do they cost?
- Will your sitters stay overnight or perform any home services, such as water plants or collect mail?
- What are your policies for payment, reservations and cancellations?
- Will I receive a written contract?
- How do you choose, screen and train your staff?
- What type of background checks do you perform and what is the turnover rate?
- Who will be visiting my home and have access to my keys and alarm information?

- Will the same person be caring for my pet the entire time? (Avoid services that send a variety of people to your home. Fido requires a consistent routine.)
- Is the sitter able to handle my dog's special needs, including administering medication or monitoring an illness?
- How do I verify whether the sitter shows up for all visits?
- How often do I receive progress reports?
- How long are the visits, what exactly does the sitter do on a visit and where will she take my dog?
- How do you verify that I've returned from my trip in case I can't reach you?
- Do you have any references for your business and for the particular sitter? (Always follow up with the references and ask pointed questions.)

In-Person Interview for Pet Sitters

During the interview, analyze the sitter's demeanor and body language. Is he professional and serious, caring and responsible? It's also important to watch him interact with your dog. Fido's ESP may be able to sense something you can't. By the end of the interview you'll be able to tell if the sitter has *any* rapport with your pooch. The sitter should ask you detailed questions about Fido's health, schedule, routine, personality, preferences and special needs. If he doesn't, escort him to the door and politely say "good riddance."

- How long have you been a sitter and why did you choose this job?
- What experience or special training do you have?
- Do you have pets? Will they accompany you?
- Will anyone accompany you on your visits or during your stay?
- What will you do with my dog?
- Can you handle my dog's special needs?
- What emergency or disaster plans do you follow?
- What will you do if my dog has a medical emergency?
- Do you drive and have a car?

- How will my pet get to an animal hospital in an emergency?
- How will you contact me for updates and questions? How often?
- Ask some hypothetical questions to determine if the sitter can think on his feet and cope with emergencies:
    - -What if you arrive and can't find Fido?
    - -Will you let Fido off leash?
    - -What if Fido isn't eating?
    - -What if you have a personal emergency and can't make the visit?
    - -Will you leave Fido in the car or tied up in front of a store?
- Do you have any references? (Be sure to call if you like the sitter.)

Boarding Facilities

Pros
- Fido stays in a secure environment with trained staff.
- Fido will not be alone overnight.
- Fido has many opportunities for play with other dogs and interaction with people.
- The facility may offer additional services, such as grooming or training.

Cons
- Your dog may spend too much time in his crate or kennel.
- Fido is exposed to numerous dogs that may carry illnesses or parasites.
- An unfamiliar environment may stress out your dog.
- Fido may not receive much personalized attention.

Today, most boarding facilities have come a long way from the cramped, lonely kennels of old where dogs languished in uncomfortable cages or dog runs with little or no opportunity for play. Depending on where you live, you may have limited choices or a huge variety of facilities ranging from a private home to a traditional kennel to the full-blown canine resort with private rooms boasting flat-screen TVs, twenty-four-hour webcam, organized activities and spa treatments. Your choice is merely a function of your budget.

Screening Questions
for Boarding Facilities

- How long have you been in business?
- How did you get into the business?
- Are you a member of any industry organizations?
- How is the staff chosen and screened?
- Do staff members receive any special training in first aid, animal behavior or other areas?
- What is the staff turnover rate?
- Have you complied with all local and state requirements, such as licensing, inspections and insurance? Is everything current?
- Do you require vaccinations or health certificates from boarders? (Avoid any facility that doesn't. Illnesses pass quickly from dog to dog in close quarters.)
- Do you require dogs to be spayed or neutered or have any minimum-age requirements?
- What services do you offer and how much do they cost? What is included and what is extra?
- What are your policies for payment, reservations and cancellations, drop-off and pickup? What if my plans change and I need to extend Fido's stay?
- Will I receive a written contract?
- Could you describe a typical twenty-four hours in your facility?
- Where will my dog stay? Avoid any facility that houses more than one dog per space unless *you* request sharing.
- Where will my dog go to the bathroom and how often will he be taken out to relieve himself? What happens if he has an accident inside his sleeping area?
- Can my dog's special needs be accommodated? For instance, if Fido is nervous, can he stay in a quieter section of the kennel? Will the staff be able to maintain his special diet or monitor his health issues?

- How many staff members are on duty? (During group play sessions, the ratio should be no more than ten to one.)
- Are the dogs unsupervised at any time, while alone or in groups?
- How many people are on-site overnight? (If the answer is none, the interview is over.) Ascertain the details about the overnight staff and their duties.
- Can I have references? (Take the time to call and ask detailed questions.)

On-Site Visit

Before announcing your arrival, hang back and observe. Look for required licenses and inspection certificates, which should be prominently displayed. Watch how the staff interacts with the customers and dogs. Chat with customers and ask probing questions.

During the tour, everywhere you go must be clean, organized and not overcrowded. Literally sniff around as you visit the facility—it should smell like dogs, not feces or urine. The lighting, ventilation and temperature should be comfortable too. Peer into the crates or dog runs and verify that they are clean and appropriately sized. Confirm that each dog has individual food and water bowls. The dogs should sleep on a raised platform, not on a concrete floor. Ask to see the exact space where your dog will stay. Observe and listen to the dogs. Kennels should be loud and full of happy, relaxed dogs. Do you hear joyful barking or crying and whimpering? Watch the staff; are they excited to be around the dogs or are they merely doing a job? Watch a play session to see if you approve of the way the dogs are supervised and managed. Are the staff members gentle, attentive and kind or rough and aloof with the dogs? Study the security devices. Are they sturdy enough to prevent escapes? Be sure that your dog wouldn't be able to break free or hop a fence or squeeze underneath.

Examine the entire facility, including any outdoor spaces. Outdoor runs and play spaces must be protected from the elements or not used during inclement weather, except for quick bathroom breaks. If you're not allowed to visit particular areas (other than administrative offices), cross the facility off the list.

As you're touring, ask these questions:

- What makes your facility special?
- Who will be caring for my dog? Can I meet them?
- How do you screen new dogs and introduce them to others at the facility?
- Can I bring bedding or toys from home?
- How much time per day will my dog be confined and where?
- What does my dog do when he's out of his crate or run? (Be sure that you understand exactly what you're getting. Some facilities offer activities on an à la carte basis, meaning that you must pay for additional play sessions, walks and pampering.)
- Which dogs will my dog play with and how do you decide?
- What type of individual attention will my dog receive?
- How often is my dog's crate or sleeping area cleaned?
- How often will my dog be fed and watered? Can you administer a special diet or medication?
- Do you offer any special services?
- How can I check on my dog and how often?
- What types of safety devices and precautions do you use to prevent escapes and injuries?
- What are your procedures for emergencies and disasters?
- What happens if my dog is sick or injured?
- Which veterinary hospital do you use?
- Will you take my dog off-site? If yes, determine the particulars and whether the supervision and transportation are safe.

Trial Run

Wherever Fido will eventually stay, arrange a trial run before your vacation. Fido should spend the night at your friend's or relative's home or stay at the boarding facility over a weekend. If you are using a pet sitter, arrange to be away so the sitter can visit or stay with Fido as if you were already out of town. This trial allows you to work out the kinks in the arrangements way before you actually leave town.

Fido's Packing List

Whether Fido is traveling or staying behind, you'll need to pack his suitcase. Pack these items regardless of Fido's travel plans:

- **Food and treats in airtight containers.** Pack extra portions in case you extend your trip or are delayed. Fido's stomach won't be happy if you switch brands on the road.
- **Food and water bowls.** If space is at a premium, purchase collapsible bowls.
- **Medication.** If Fido takes multiple pills, arrange them in a clearly labeled travel pillbox. Bring parasite and heartworm medication if you'll be away when they're due. Pack dosing instructions and extra prescriptions for emergency refills.
- **Leash, harness and collar with current licenses and ID tags.** Verify that Fido's license, vaccination and permanent ID tags are current and legible. Attach an extra tag listing the contact information at his destination, whether it's with you or a caretaker. Carry a recent photo of your dog with you at all times or provide one for his caretaker.
- **Crate, bedding and maybe a portable gate.** Most boarding facilities have crates, but ask to bring Fido's if he is particularly attached. Fido should have his favorite blanket or toy too. If you're leaving him, throw in an unwashed article of your clothing to remind Fido that you will be coming back. If Fido will be staying in someone's home, consider packing a portable gate or fence to keep him out of restricted areas, like your great-aunt Bertha's all-white living room packed with delicate figurines of big-eyed children participating in a variety of charming activities.
- **Poop bags and enzymatic cleaner for accidents.** These supplies are unnecessary at a boarding facility. Otherwise, you can never overpack these items. If Fido uses wee-wee pads, bring an adequate supply.
- **Toys and chews.** Fido will be more comfortable with a few of his favorite items.
- **Grooming supplies.** Whether he's with you or a caretaker, Fido requires some basic grooming. Plus, dirt happens, so it's better to be prepared. Pack a travel grooming kit with the basics: Fido's brush, shampoo, conditioner, a sponge, cotton balls, ear wash, eye cleaner and canine sunscreen. Rather

than wasting your breath explaining how to use the supplies, give the caretaker my book and highlight the how-to chapters.

- **Canine first-aid kit and manual.** Purchase a travel-sized kit and manual. Check the kit before each trip to be sure that it's fully stocked with unexpired items.
- **Safety restraints.** If Fido will be in a car, pack his safety restraint. If his caretaker will be driving him, explain and demonstrate how to use it. If appropriate, install the device in the caretaker's vehicle.

If Fido Is Traveling With You, Add These Items to His Suitcase

- **Bottled water.** Fido must be well hydrated during the journey and water may not be readily available along the way. Bring water everywhere you go. If you don't want to share with Fido, carry a portable bowl.
- **Emergency information.** Pack a copy of Fido's Emergency Information Card and his current veterinary records. Compile a list of veterinary and emergency clinics along your route and at all destinations. Ask your veterinarian for recommendations or visit the American Animal Hospital Association's Web site to find local hospitals. Call ahead and obtain the directions to each facility. Navigating unfamiliar roads is difficult in an emergency.
- **Current vaccination history, required health certificates and other documentation.** Bring extra copies and store them in a second location in case you lose the originals.
- **Special equipment for activities.** Canine safety equipment is not always available on the road. Bring everything you need from home, such as a life jacket for boating, a dog pack for hiking, canine sunscreen and protective clothing and footwear.

If Fido Is Staying Behind, Pack These Additional Items

- **A fun surprise for the caretaker.** There's nothing wrong with bribery.
- **Information packet.** This packet should contain everything anyone wanted

to know about Fido but was afraid to ask. If the caretaker has information about Fido's routine, his special needs and emergency assistance at her fingertips, Fido will be comfortable, happy and safe while you're away. Once you compile the packet, you'll be able to use the basic information every time you travel—just update as necessary.

1. *Fido's Emergency Information Card.* If Fido is sleeping out, provide written directions from the caretaker's location to your veterinarian and emergency clinic.

2. *Authorization for veterinary care and petty cash.* Prepare a notarized letter permitting the caretaker to seek veterinary care and guarantee payment in the event of an emergency. Leave payment information for emergency veterinary care and cash for incidentals.

3. *Your itinerary and contact information.* The itinerary must include a day-by-day, blow-by-blow list of your movements: flight information, travel routes and the names, addresses and phone numbers of every place you're staying or visiting. Provide cell phone numbers and e-mail addresses for you and anyone else traveling with you. If an emergency arises, the caretaker needs to know where to find you.

4. *Local emergency contact.* List the names, addresses and phone numbers of nearby reliable friends, neighbors or relatives who are willing to help.

5. *Detailed care instructions.* Describe Fido's daily and nightly routine, his feeding and medication schedule and your rules for treats and table scraps. In addition, discuss your rules for walking and exercising and where and when Fido is allowed off leash. Describe Fido's sleeping habits and where he stays when he's alone. If Fido has any illnesses or behavioral problems, explain the issue in detail so the caretaker isn't surprised or overwhelmed. In addition, list his quirky behavior, his fears and his play preferences. If Fido is scared in thunderstorms, hates children or chases squirrels, the caretaker needs to know so she can avoid problems.

6. *Detailed bathroom instructions.* Describe Fido's bathroom habits, including how often he goes, where he prefers to go and any signal you use to encourage him to go.

7. *Safety rules.* Even if the caretaker is an expert, it never hurts to offer a refresher course on dangerous foods, poisonous plants and common household hazards. Many people aren't aware of the doggy dangers in

their own home. Have the caretaker read chapter 6, "Keeping Fido Safe and Sound at Home."

8. *House rules and instructions.* If Fido's caretaker is visiting or staying in your home, list your rules for guests, overnight visitors, and computer use, and note areas that are off-limits to people and dogs. Prepare a list of emergency repair services and instructions for household appliances and systems.

Departure

Feed Fido a few hours before departure to minimize the risk of motion sickness. Run him around and tire him out right before you leave so he'll be calm when he begins his travels or his stay with a caretaker.

If Fido is staying at home, gather your instructions and supplies in one place for the sitter's convenience. If Fido is sleeping out, bring these when you drop him off.

Before you leave, painstakingly review everything with the caretaker. Ask probing questions to verify that the person is listening to you drone on. Paint a picture of Fido's normal behavior so the caretaker will know if something changes and will seek veterinary assistance. Leave no stone unturned. Fido can't speak up for himself.

If someone is staying in your home, reiterate the house rules. Demonstrate how to use appliances, the alarm and other household systems. If the sitter is staying overnight, show her where she'll be sleeping, how to work your shower and where you keep extra supplies.

When you leave, don't make a big fuss. Pat Fido on the head and pretend you're just running out to pick up a quart of milk. Most dogs can't tell time, so if you've left him in good hands, Fido might not realize how long you're gone.

9.
Fun With Fido

Welcome aboard the *Love Your Dog Boat*! We're expecting you. I'm your cruise director, Billy McCoy, and I'm responsible for all the activities and entertainment on this ship. I promise, we have something for everyone! Fido has already set his course for adventure and his mind on a new romance. He's chatting up that foxy apricot Poodle in the sparkly caftan standing on the curving grand staircase next to Doc. Isaac is waiting to fix you a Shirley Temple. Captain Stubing just blasted the horn and we're leaving port.

Having fun with your dog seems like an obvious part of the human-canine relationship. Indeed, for some, this comes naturally and easily. Many people, however, would rather slip Fido extra treats instead of engaging in a quality play session. Treats, however, are no substitute for your time and attention, and your busy schedule is no excuse for failing to entertain and exercise your pooch. Heck, it's good for *you* too!

Fido isn't capable of planning his day and depends on you to foster his physical and mental fitness. Pull out your Canine Guardianship Contract and turn to page 325, Section 101.2.4.5 (A)(2)(g)(iii), which states: "As an owner, you assume without exception the duty to exercise Fido's body, mind and spirit a *minimum* of sixty minutes per day for the duration of his life." Playing only on the weekends is a deal breaker. Truly, why risk becoming entangled in a messy lawsuit filed by your aggrieved, ignored, fat, out-of-shape and depressed dog? Don't worry, though, you can break up the required playtime into smaller increments over the course of the day and still satisfy the spirit of the contract.

The Many Benefits of Physical and Mental Exercise

Primitive dogs were always on the move hunting and surviving. These tasks required almost-constant mental and physical exertion. In more recent history, humans employed dogs as herders, swimmers, guards and hunters—dogs had real jobs. Now most pet dogs spend their days unemployed and stuck at home with nothing to do but sleep. It's no wonder that many dogs get into trouble with destructive chewing or suffer from separation anxiety or depression. Busy, stimulated dogs are less likely to have behavioral problems. Fido needs a new job description that includes daily mind and body work.

Fortunately, stimulating Fido's body, mind and spirit is as easy as playing and exercising together. Whether you're a canine or a human, exercise in combination with a healthful diet maintains a trim waistline, tones muscles, builds cardiovascular health, strengthens bones, improves joint mobility and increases the quality and quantity of life. Exercise also increases mental alertness and provides a positive outlet for canine energy. Aside from eating, Fido's main goal in life is to spend time with you and bask in your attention. The togetherness wrought by exercise and playtime demonstrates to Fido the depths of your affection, which makes him very happy indeed.

How to Choose Appropriate Activities

You and your dog have countless choices for fun both outside and indoors. Ponder the factors below to help guide your selections. Be honest and realistic when you assess everyone's capabilities. If you choose wisely, establishing and sticking to an exercise or play routine is easy. *Before* beginning any exercise or rigorous activity, consult with Fido's veterinarian and *your* medical doctor. The doctors can help you develop a safe routine based on everyone's health and physical status.

Canine Factors

Age
Puppies should not engage in rigorous physical activity that involves intensive or repetitive jumping or running until their bones and joints are fully formed and mature, which is at approximately eighteen months old. Your

veterinarian can help you decide when *your* pup is ready. Older dogs often have joint problems and require less-strenuous and shorter exercise sessions.

Breed and Physical Characteristics

Research the history of your dog's breed or breeds and tailor the activities to her heritage, historical job description and physical characteristics. Herding and working dogs like Bearded Collies, shepherds, sheepdogs and cattle dogs and Siberian Huskies and Alaskan Malamutes need extensive physical exercise to channel their natural high-energy levels. Smaller dogs with shorter legs, like toy and miniature breeds, can't exercise as far or as long as the big guys. Pugs, Boxers, Shih Tzus, Lhasa Apsos, Bulldogs and other short-snouted dogs have trouble regulating their body temperature and can overheat quickly if they exercise too briskly. Similarly, giant dogs like the Saint Bernard and Mastiff often have congenital medical conditions that limit their ability to participate in more vigorous activities. Always consult with your veterinarian to determine what's appropriate for your dog.

Health and Stamina

Physical limitations, including obesity, muscle and joint health, fitness level, genetics, illnesses and disabilities must shape your activity choices. A dog with a heart or breathing condition should not be jogging four miles a day. Similarly, if either you or Fido is under the weather or in a bad mood, don't engage in rigorous activity until everyone recovers.

Fido cannot play with others unless his vaccinations are current. Puppies and dogs with immature or weak immune systems are especially susceptible to contagious diseases. Remember, puppies must wait to fraternize with others until they have completed the full series of initial vaccinations and boosters. Every dog owner has a duty to minimize canine illness, even if it means that you and Fido are stuck at home for days while his conjunctivitis or stomach virus clears up.

Nice weather encourages even the laziest human and canine couch potatoes to engage in some outdoor activity. Rein in your excitement and consider everyone's *actual*, not perceived, fitness level when choosing an activity. If you and your pooch spent the winter curled up on the couch watching *Sex and the City* reruns, with a super-sized bowl of buttered popcorn in one hand and the latest scandal rag in the other, don't attempt to run a 5K the first time out. Both of you must start slowly and gradually build endurance over time, based on your doctors' recommendations.

Preferences

Assess your dog's personality, his temperament and the types of activities he enjoys. Then, do the same for yourself. It's your responsibility to choose activities that Fido will enjoy and not fear. Think about how Fido feels and reacts to these factors:

- Wrestling or rough play with other dogs
- Timid or aggressive dogs
- Groups of dogs
- Crowds of people
- Strangers
- Children
- Loud noises
- Water
- Heights
- Motorized vehicles
- Fast-moving people and objects, such as strollers, bicycles, joggers, skateboarders or in-line skaters
- Balls
- Squirrels, birds and other common wildlife

Never force Fido to participate in an activity that scares him or makes him uncomfortable. Anxious dogs are more likely to become aggressive, bite or run away. So if Fido is afraid of children, don't jog through a crowded playground or stop to let a kid pet him. The idea is to make exercise and playtime enjoyable and successful so you'll both want to do it again and again.

Obedience Skills

You and your dog are canine ambassadors. Good behavior in public can reinforce or change people's attitudes about dogs. Accordingly, you must control Fido at all times. Outdoor activities include a myriad of distractions, including squirrels, joggers, bicyclists, balls and other dogs. Fido's ability and *desire* to follow directions like "Come" and "Stay" are, therefore, important considerations. In addition, many outdoor activities, such as jogging, require Fido to behave on leash, remain by your side without pulling and safely navigate streets, intersections and crowded public areas.

If Fido needs to brush up on his listening, leash or heeling skills, your first activity together should be an obedience class. Obedience training will enhance your bond and exercise Fido's mind.

Human Factors

Your health, personality, physical abilities and preferences are all important factors to consider when choosing activities. In addition, think about the following issues.

Budget
Many of the most fun and rewarding activities are free or low cost, such as walking, jogging, visiting the dog park or playing with neighborhood dogs. Equipment-intensive activities, like bicycling or agility, can be enjoyed at a wide range of price points. Fido doesn't care if you have the fanciest sports equipment; all he wants is your time and unfettered attention.

Convenience
Dogs require daily physical and mental stimulation. I know you have a busy schedule, so choose activities that are conveniently located and require little advance preparation. Save the more elaborate activities for the weekend. If the best dog beach is thirty-five minutes away, go there on special occasions.

Goals
Do you want to have fun, improve fitness, lose weight, compete, socialize or help the community? These goals are not mutually exclusive and many dog activities allow you to satisfy them all.

Environmental Factors

Parasites

Mosquitoes, fleas and ticks love to prey on dogs and humans enjoying the outdoors. Avoid parasite-infested areas and keep current with Fido's parasite preventatives too. For additional information, review chapter 10, "Annoying Allergies and Pernicious Parasites."

The Weather

Consider the current weather conditions and the forecast for the duration of your outdoor activities. Weather changes can occur rapidly. Some dogs become anxious in thunderstorms or overheat quickly. If Fido is upset or uncomfortable, neither of you will be having any fun.

Don't force Fido to play, exercise or remain outside if the weather is inclement, too hot, humid, wet or frigid. Weather extremes are dangerous for you and your dog. Moreover, puppies and older and ill dogs are sensitive to extreme weather conditions. Inside playtime is a safe, pleasant alternative.

Cold Weather Safety

Dogs love to chase leaves in fall's crisp wind and romp in winter's snow. To determine how long Fido should stay outside, temperature is not the only factor to consider. Just as you would do for yourself, evaluate the windchill, sun strength, humidity and dampness in light of Fido's age, health, size, weight, physical fitness and coat texture. Skinny or thin-coated dogs have less insulation from the cold. Smaller dogs get cold more rapidly than larger dogs because they have less body mass to produce heat. Moreover, young puppies, elderly or ill dogs and those with breathing problems are extremely sensitive to cold or snowy and wet weather. Without a doubt, no one other than Arctic sled dogs should be exerting himself outdoors or remain exposed to harsh and/or wet conditions for extended time periods.

As silly as he may look, Fido requires a winter wardrobe to protect him from the elements, even when he's just walking around the block. If Fido has a thin or short coat, he definitely needs additional insulation from the cold. Purchase functional coats or sweaters or splurge on designer duds. Don't forget to protect Fido's paws from the cold, rock salt and other winter chemicals, which dry out the pads and cause them to crack. Chemicals also collect on unprotected paws and Fido can get sick when he licks them. The options for canine footwear are surprisingly vast. Whether you choose waterproof hiking boots or disposable booties, have Fido wear them around the house so he'll be accustomed to them before the weather turns nasty. Fido's clothing and footwear should be snug, but not impede his movement. Dry the gear after each use and wash it regularly.

If Fido won't wear footwear even for all the dog biscuits in the world, apply a dog-safe protective paw balm before venturing outside and wipe off his paws when you return. Remove any snowballs or ice attached to his fur or stuck between his toes or paw pads. Be sure to dry him off all over too.

Be especially mindful of antifreeze and windshield-wiper fluid while you and Fido are outside. These chemicals can be downright lethal, even in small amounts. A twenty-pound dog can die after ingesting only one tablespoon of antifreeze containing ethylene glycol. The "safer" antifreeze contains propylene glycol, but it's still poisonous if ingested in larger amounts. Unfortunately, some people are careless about these fluids and they collect in puddles, driveways, garages, streets, parking lots and other places our dogs frequent. To make matters worse, dogs are attracted to the sweet smell and taste. If you suspect your dog has ingested antifreeze or any other poison, begin first aid and call the veterinarian IMMEDIATELY!

Keep Fido away from frozen lakes, rivers or pools, which often have thin ice. Moreover, ice-covered paths, stairs and sidewalks are slippery. Believe it or not, I think you'll be hard-pressed to find a lawyer, even the most desperate sort, to represent Fido in his slip-and-fall case. Without a windfall settlement, you'll be faced with large medical and physical-therapy bills associated with Fido's broken leg, not to mention the extensive mental anguish from missed playtime.

|||||||||||||||||||||||||||||||||||||||||||||||||||||||||||||||||||||||||||||||||||||||||||||||||||||||||||||

Winter First Aid

Despite their fur coats or fancy wardrobes, dogs can suffer from frostbite or hypothermia. Use your common sense: once Fido is wet or begins to whine, shiver or slow down, outdoor play is over.

Frostbite

Frostbite occurs when tissue is exposed to severe cold, which causes the skin to freeze and impairs circulation. The tips of the tail, ears and nose are particularly vulnerable, along with paw pads, since snow, ice and frozen mud can accumulate there. If you still haven't neutered your dog, his scrotum can suffer frostbite too. (The thought of that alone should persuade you to neuter Fido ASAP!) Severe frostbite is dangerous because the affected area often requires amputation.

Watch for the signs of frostbite:

- In the early stage, pain or swelling and pale or gray skin. The skin may be hard and cold to the touch.
- In the advanced stage, the skin is red or black. The skin will fall off if untreated, and life-threatening infections can quickly develop.

If you suspect frostbite, immediately bring the dog to a warm location and call the veterinarian. Begin slowly warming the affected area. Cover the area with warm—not hot—moist towels. **Never** apply direct heat with a heating pad or blow-dryer. **Never** rub or massage the area. As soon as the dog begins to warm up, wrap her in fresh, dry towels or blankets and transport her to the animal hospital for veterinary assessment and treatment. Even after recovery, the frostbitten area may suffer permanent circulation problems, which means that the dog will be more sensitive to cold.

Hypothermia

Hypothermia is a serious emergency that requires urgent medical attention. Exposure to cold and damp conditions can cause a dog's body temperature to drop precipitously. When this happens, the body can't produce adequate body heat and bodily functions become rapidly impaired. In severe cases, hypothermia can be fatal. Therefore, as soon as Fido exhibits *any* discomfort in the cold, bring him inside.

The signs of hypothermia include the following:

- Shivering
- Decreased mental alertness
- Lethargy or weakness
- Slow and shallow breathing

- Muscle stiffness
- Slowed heart rate or weak pulse
- Dilated pupils
- Impaired consciousness: dog is not responding to stimuli or commands

Immediately bring a hypothermic dog to a warm area, call the veterinarian and begin to slowly raise the dog's body temperature. If the dog is suffering from mild hypothermia, wrap him in warm—*not* hot—blankets. If possible, warm up the blankets in the clothes dryer. Alternatively, fill plastic bottles with hot water and wrap them in blankets or towels to avoid burning the dog's skin. Place the insulated bottles on the dog's less-furry areas, including the undercarriage and armpits. Keep the dog dry, since you'll be transporting her to the veterinarian as soon as she begins to warm up.

||||||||||||||||||||||||||||||||||||||||||||||||||||||||||||||||||||||||||||||||||||||||||||||||||||||||||||||||||||||||||||||

Warm Weather Safety

Wherever your warm-weather adventures take you and your pooch, be sure that she has continuous access to abundant fresh, cold water and shade. Too much sun can burn Fido's skin. Indeed, Hairless breeds and dogs with short fur or white or light-colored coats actually sunburn rather quickly and all dogs are susceptible to skin cancer. Fido's fur coat offers only modest protection, especially if it's cut short or shaved.

If possible, limit Fido's exposure during peak sun time, which is from about ten a.m. to four p.m. depending on your location and the season. In addition, slather on the canine-safe sunscreen or dress your pooch in UV-protective clothing. Dogs tend to sunburn on the ears, eyelids, lips, nose and tail tips, undercarriage and other exposed or sparsely furred areas. Remember that sidewalks, sand, blacktops and other surfaces reflect the sun's rays directly onto your pooch's undercarriage. If your dog develops signs of sunburn, such as red, peeling or blistering skin or hair loss, contact your veterinarian promptly.

Be aware of warm-weather disease transmission as you walk around town and visit parks and celebrations where dogs congregate. Unfortunately, some owners refuse to clean up after their dogs. The abandoned piles of festering poop sometimes transmit disease or worms and other horrible parasites, so steer clear. Moreover, these fecal scofflaws give all us responsible pet owners a bad rap. I always carry a few extra bags to clean up deserted doodie. "Here's an extra bag" is an effective conversation starter.

Common sense must rule the day. Warm weather quickly heats the ground and Fido's feet aren't protected by cushy gym shoes. Hot sand or pavement can burn Fido's paw pads, and exercising on hard asphalt is taxing to his joints. Try to run and play on dirt, gravel or grass. If Fido's paws are sensitive, buy him lightweight booties for protection.

Heatstroke and heat exhaustion, the milder form of the condition, are serious concerns for dogs playing or exercising in hot and/or humid weather. Heat and humidity can interfere with a dog's ability to regulate his body temperature, especially if he is young, elderly, obese, ill or diabetic or has breathing problems. Dogs left outside without adequate shade and fresh water or in a car are at risk too.

||||||||||||||||||||||||||||||||||||||||||||||||||||||||||||||||||||||||||||||||||||||||||||||||||||||||||||||

First Aid for Heatstroke and Heat Exhaustion

Heatstroke and heat exhaustion are grave medical emergencies that require a quick and calm response to prevent collapse, organ failure or even death. Stop exercising immediately if Fido exhibits any of these symptoms:

- Rapid breathing or panting
- Excessive drooling or thick and sticky saliva
- Lack of coordination or staggering
- Bright red tongue or bright red or pale gums
- Refusal to obey commands
- Weakness
- Lethargy or depression
- High fever
- Vomiting or diarrhea
- Collapse or shock

The moment you suspect heatstroke or heat exhaustion, bring the dog to a cool location. If an air-conditioned area is unavailable, move into the shade.

Immediately call the veterinarian and begin to cool the dog *slowly*. Place the dog in a cool—*not* cold—bath, or loosely wrap her in cool—*not* cold—moist towels. **Never** use ice or icy water. Once you've begun the cooling process, promptly transport the dog to the veterinarian.

|||||||||||||||||||||||||||||||||||||||||||||||||||||||||||||||||||||||||||||||||||||||||||||||||||||||

Grooming Tips for Outdoor Activity

Fur is a debris magnet. Keeping Fido neat and trimmed, especially on his paws, between the pads and toes, and on his undercarriage, will minimize the dirt and detritus that attach to his coat. Fido should visit the groomer for a regular pedicure because long nails can break, tear or rip off during play.

Whether Fido is returning from a walk around the block, a day at the beach or a hike in the mountains, he requires a few minutes of grooming TLC to keep him healthy and safe. Inspect him thoroughly and remove any dirt, debris or parasites. Spot wash or bathe him as needed. If your feet are sore, imagine how Fido feels after playing without shoes. Run a footbath and share the relief.

Safety Rules for Outdoor Activity

Playing and exercising in the great outdoors offer many fringe benefits. Fresh air is invigorating, sunshine supplies vitamins for the body and nature's sites and sounds are mentally stimulating. Enjoying outdoor activities, though, requires attention to safety rules.

Whatever outdoor activity you choose, you'll need a few pieces of basic equipment:

• Sturdy leash. Choose the length and style that allow you to control Fido comfortably. Many joggers prefer hands-free leashes. When you're moving through streets and congested areas, keep the leash short and walk next to your dog. If he is walking ahead of you, a driver may not see him since he's lower to the ground.

- Harness. A harness won't strain Fido's neck as he exercises. They're a good choice for small dogs, those with tender necks or dogs that pull.
- Collar with current identification tags and licenses. Fido should also have a microchip in case his collar is lost.
- Clothing or boots to protect Fido from the weather and ground debris. Also, be prepared for sudden weather changes. I always keep a few towels and blankets in my car in case we get caught in foul weather.
- Nutritious snacks, water and a travel bowl
- Plastic bags. If you've run out, use a leaf, a piece of paper, garbage or anything else you can find; just don't leave any poop behind.
- Travel-sized canine first-aid kit to keep in your car or backpack and a copy of Fido's Emergency Information Card
- Charged cell phone in case of human or canine emergencies
- Small notebook and pen. Dogs are date magnets. You may want to record phone numbers and arrange canine and human playdates.

The single most important thing you can do to keep Fido safe outdoors is to keep him on leash and in your control unless you're *inside* a fully enclosed area. I've seen and heard of way too many accidents and tragedies because an owner removed the leash too early and allowed the dog to run free or failed to keep a tight grip on the leash when the dog ran after a squirrel. Dogs don't always go where you expect, especially if they're spooked or excited or they spy a distraction.

Moreover, don't let Fido eat *anything* off the ground. Many dogs are connoisseurs of garbage and animal feces. Nothing is too gross: used Kleenex, old pizza crusts, candy wrappers, used bandages or anything else that people or animals discard. Garbage and debris can be sickening, dangerous or spread contagious disease and parasites.

Don't exercise once a week and expect Fido to engage in rigorous activity. Work him out daily to build stamina. Warm up at the beginning of play or exercise sessions. When you're through, cool down with a leisurely walk.

||||||||||||||||||||||||||||||||||||||||||||||||||||||||||||||||||||||||||||||||||||||||||||||||||||||||||||||

An Easy Stretch

I perform this stretch with Zeke before and after we run, to stretch and warm up his hardworking hind-leg and rear-end muscles.

Gently place Fido on his back so his legs are in the air. Start at his hip and slowly and lightly rub your hand down the side of one back leg to straighten it. Move the leg in a natural motion so it doesn't strain or hyperextend. Hold the leg straight for five to ten seconds and release. Stop right away if Fido resists

or yelps. Now repeat with the other back leg. When Fido stands up, he may shake. This releases stress as he literally "shakes it off."

As you play or exercise, observe Fido continually for signs of fatigue or injury. Never push him to his physical limits. Pause for bathroom and rest breaks. If Fido slows down, stops, begins panting heavily, limps, whimpers or displays any signs of discomfort, immediately stop and rest or call it a day. Dogs often continue to play even if they're injured or near collapse. *You* are the only thing between Fido and overexertion.

Continually survey the terrain and traffic. Fido isn't wearing shoes, so look out for broken pavement, rocks, glass or other debris. If you are playing in an area frequented by hunters, dress Fido in a brightly colored shirt and watch for animal traps. Wear reflective clothing at night and use reflective collars and leashes too.

In addition, **never** leave Fido unattended. Whether he's tied up to a post in front of a store or to a tree, he's in danger while alone. Dog theft and torment by strangers is not limited to cities. Besides, Fido can hurt or strangle himself on the leash if he becomes upset while you're gone. Similarly, verify that Fido is welcome at your destination. Some parks and public areas prohibit dogs (the nerve!). If you forget to check and you learn that Fido isn't welcome, find somewhere else to play. Never leave Fido unattended in a car no matter the weather.

Primer for Outdoor Activities

The opportunities for having fun with Fido outdoors are endless. Here are some of my favorite activities.

Old-Fashioned Frolic

People and their dogs have been playing catch and fetch together for millennia. These old favorites can be enjoyed anywhere. Always play in a fully enclosed area so Fido has no opportunity to run off and get hurt or worse. Use dog-safe toys or tennis balls. Wood, branches or rocks can break Fido's teeth or injure his mouth and tongue.

Dog Park

Few activities offer the fun and socialization opportunities of a good dog park. Where else can you and Fido find an enclosed area filled with dogs in the mood for fun and fellow dog lovers interested in networking, dating, schmoozing and information sharing? Taking a few precautions will make your visit safe and enjoyable.

- **Health Concerns:** Don't go anywhere near a dog park if Fido isn't fixed. Actually, go directly to the veterinarian and spay or neuter your dog; DO NOT PASS GO; DO NOT COLLECT $200. In addition, before you step foot into the park, be sure that Fido's vaccinations are current and that he's healthy. Absolutely *no* puppy is allowed at the park until all his vaccinations and boosters are complete *and* your veterinarian gives you the all clear.

  If Fido is under the weather, skip the dog park; he's more susceptible to contagious diseases and he's likely to be cranky with other dogs. If he's recently been sick, even if it's minor diarrhea or vomiting, keep him home until your veterinarian says he's ready to be around other dogs. I couldn't sleep at night knowing that one of *my* readers endangered other dogs with a contagious illness.
- **Licenses:** Check with the city or state about licensing requirements and park rules. Most dog parks require a rabies tag and a local license in addition to a dog-park tag.
- **Preliminaries:** Before letting Fido off leash, walk *inside* the park and close

the gate so he can't escape, and verify that the park is securely and fully enclosed. Scan the area for poop, broken bottles and dangerous debris; be a good citizen and clean up. Bring your own fresh water and bowl so Fido doesn't have to share with unknown dogs or drink from stagnant, dirty or salty water.

- **Personality:** *You* are legally and morally responsible for your dog. Be mindful of his personality. Fido shouldn't be at a dog park if he's scared or aggressive around other dogs, kids or people. Socialize him slowly before setting him loose in a park.

    Unfortunately, not every dog owner is responsible, so *you* must watch your dog at all times. It's easy to become engrossed in conversation with an attractive dog *owner* while Fido runs amok. Little dogs can accidentally get trampled in a group of rampaging big guys or a fight can break out over a tennis ball. Keep Fido away from noticeably aggressive or sick dogs and dogs with lax owners.

- **Dog Gone Fun:** Let Fido be a *dog* in the dog park. He's going to wrestle, run like a crazed lunatic, roll in stinky grass, dig and drool. He may even be the hump-ee or hump-er. It's all part of normal dog play as long as no one has her hair on end, is baring her teeth or is biting. Don't ever be shy about reprimanding an owner who is not controlling an aggressive dog or not cleaning up.

||||||||||||||||||||||||||||||||||||||||||||||||||||||||||||||||||||||||||||||||||||||||||||||||||||

Volunteer at the Dog Park

Organize a cleanup and fix-up day at the parks where you and Fido hang out. Gather a group to mend fences, erect poop-bag holders and clean out dangerous and ugly debris. This is a nice way to support your community and meet new people.

||||||||||||||||||||||||||||||||||||||||||||||||||||||||||||||||||||||||||||||||||||||||||||||||||||

Delightful Dog Paddle

Swimming is wonderful exercise and it's gentle on aching joints. Most dogs enjoy swimming (and some are truly born to swim, such as Portuguese Water Dogs, Golden Retrievers, Labrador Retrievers, Poodles and

Newfoundlands), but not every dog takes to it. Don't toss Fido in the water to see what happens. If he turns tail and runs, don't push him. Try a different activity.

Introduce Fido to the water slowly to determine if he's interested and capable of staying afloat on his own. Teach him how to exit the water too. He may not instinctively understand how to use the steps in a pool or a ramp on a dock. If he feels trapped in the water, he may panic.

Fido can enjoy a dip in a pool, pond, lake or ocean as long as it is clean. Stagnant and dirty water harbor algae, bacteria and other evils. Many beaches post information about water quality. If humans shouldn't be in the water that day, neither should your dog. If you're swimming in the ocean or wetlands, watch for signs indicating jellyfish, sharks, alligators, crocodiles or other dangerous water creatures.

Closely supervise Fido at all times while he's in the water. Continually monitor currents, tides and undertow and keep him out of deep water. Even strong swimmers can tire unexpectedly or get spooked, so be ready to jump in. Moreover, even though Fido is cool in the water, the sun can burn his delicate skin. Use dog sunscreen on his nose and ears and reapply often.

Don't let Fido drink the water while he swims. Salt, pond scum, amoebas, pollution and other water toxins may upset his stomach. Be mindful of hot sand on delicate paws and don't let Fido eat any dead fish or garbage that washes up onshore.

After swimming, use ear wash to remove excess water from Fido's ears. Always bathe Fido after swimming too. Chlorine from a pool and salt from the ocean can dry out his skin and coat. Likewise, algae and other flotsam from lakes and ponds leave stinky and irritating residue. Carefully wash the sand and dirt from Fido's paws and between the pads.

A Topknot-ch Idea for Unobstructed Vision

Fido needs unfettered vision while playing. If he has long hair hanging in his face, put it up in a "topknot," a canine ponytail. All you need is a small hair elastic, which is available wherever kids' hair or grooming accessories are sold. I prefer elastics treated with powder, since they're less likely to stick to or break off fur.

Face your dog. Place your fingers in an L shape, and using your thumbs and index fingers, gather the hair as you move. Start at the outside corners of the eyes, move up to the tops of the ears and then across the head to the center. Your thumbs are the comb forming a part as you go. Pretend that you're putting your own hair into a ponytail.

Arrange the topknot so it's not pulling skin or fur before you wrap the elastic band around it. If it's too tight, your dog will look like she attended a Botox party with Joan Rivers. I'm serious. I've seen dogs with topknots so tight that they couldn't close their eyes. There should be a small pouf at the base of the topknot and it should be flexible, but not flop around as the dog moves, and the eyelids should remain in their natural position.

Most elastic bands dry out and weaken after a week or so. First, try to break the rubber band apart by pulling on it. If that doesn't work, grasp the base of the topknot and gently work the rubber band up to the top.

||||||||||||||||||||||||||||||||||||||||||||||||||||||||||||||||||||||||||||||||||||||||||||||||||||

Walkies and Runnies

After a four-year and fifty-pound hiatus, my dog Gabriel inspired me to get off the couch. He had so much excess energy that I knew I had to do something—and quick, before he trashed my house. Running was easy and inexpensive. My veterinarian gave us the green light when Gabriel was about eighteen months old. We gradually worked up to four-mile runs about four days a week until he died. Now Zeke is my faithful running partner. Like Gabriel, Zeke would eat everything in sight and rampage nonstop through my house. As soon as he was old enough, my veterinarian said to start running. Running channeled Zeke's energy and calmed him down.

Dogs are the best running partners. Zeke is rarin' to go no matter the time of day. In the morning, I never have to wait for him to peel the cucumbers off his eyes and take out his curlers. At night, he's not worn-out from work. As soon as he spies my running shoes, he's waiting by the door with wide eyes and a wagging tail.

Most dogs love to run, but not all. Recently, I brought Arthur along for a trial "run" and he quit after a quarter of a mile. He looked up at me, sat down indignantly and refused to move a muscle. I had to wear him around my shoulders like a Cocker Spaniel stole all the way home.

Don't start with jogging right away; begin with walks and increase the distance and intensity over time. If possible, run and walk on gravel, grass or dirt. Asphalt and concrete heat up and are hard on joints and paw pads. Carry water for Fido and let him rest often. When you're finished, clean his paws and pads and inspect them for injuries and excess wear and tear.

Hiking

Sharing nature with your pooch is rewarding and extremely enjoyable as long as you practice safe hiking. Dogs are affected by altitude and rough terrain just like humans. Start slowly and work up to longer and more-rigorous hikes over time. Fido may do just fine on the way up the trail. If he's worn-out on the way back, however, he's more liable to slip, hurt himself or refuse to go any farther. Stop often and allow Fido to rest, drink and eat a wholesome snack. During the breaks, check his paws for injuries and remove any debris stuck in his fur.

Keep Fido on a leash and under your control at all times. Dogs have no concept of trail markers. On a recent hike with Zeke things got a bit hairy (or furry, I should say). When we reached the top of a cliff, Zeke became overwhelmed with excitement and he started running around and jumping in circles. At one point, he landed right on the edge of the trail—and it was sixty feet straight down from there. Had he not been on leash, he would have gone over the edge.

Never leave Fido unattended; he can run off or be attacked. Some of the wildlife, even the cute ones, may carry rabies and are often downright mean. Watch for birds of prey that might consider Fido a tasty meal and swoop down and try to grab him. If Fido is bitten by anything, end your hike and call the veterinarian immediately.

Don't let Fido eat anything on the trail. Bring nutritious snacks and sufficient water. Poisonous berries and plants and stagnant, dirty or contaminated water are dangerous. Keep him away from any animal droppings, as they sometimes contain parasites and disease.

Consider dressing Fido in protective clothing to shield him from the elements, dangers underfoot, irritating plants and ticks. If Fido is wearing a backpack, keep the load light. A dog should carry no more than twenty-five percent of his body weight. Have Fido practice with the backpack at home and gradually fill it so he's used to wearing it well *before* you hit the trail. Fido shouldn't wear a pack if he's a puppy, prone to joint and muscle problems or new to hiking.

Be mindful of weather conditions. Don't hike on humid and hot or frigid days. Both you and your dog must use sunblock. Certainly, head back if you see a storm on the horizon.

Although a posthike grooming session can be a bit time-consuming, it's well worth the effort. Be sure to remove all ticks, parasites, burs, thorns or other plant materials that are embedded in his skin and coat.

Go for the Gold: Sports

If you can imagine an activity to do with your dog, chances are there's a competition for it. One San Diego hotel holds an annual canine surfing competition. Sports channels frequently broadcast extreme dog sports like dock diving, where a dog races down a long wooden dock and leaps across the water to retrieve a toy, or flying-disk competitions where dogs flip and jump to catch disks thrown from far away. A quick Internet search will locate national organizations and local groups that can provide information on training and competitions.

Canine training and obedience facilities often offer agility classes. Dogs run through and over tunnels, ramps and jumps and weave like slalom skiers through rows of flexible poles. Many dogs absolutely love the mental and physical challenges of agility. During a competition, dogs are timed as they run though an obstacle course. Because this is a rigorous activity, ask your veterinarian if your dog is up for the challenge.

Obedience classes are enjoyable and useful. Fido will be so happy to spend time together, he won't even notice that he's in school. Once you and

Fido are adept, compete in an obedience competition or join a musical free-style group, an activity that combines obedience and choreographed movements set to music.

Breed-Based Activities

Take a moment to think about Fido's heritage. Historically, breeds had specific jobs. For example, Basset Hounds, with their long ears and highly developed sense of smell, assisted hunters in locating prey. Border Collies and Old English Sheepdogs herded farm animals. Find an activity that emphasizes the job your dog was meant to perform. Hide snacks in your yard and set your Beagle loose to uncover the treasure. Join a hunting club for your pointer, spaniel, terrier or hound, but dress her in orange to keep her safe from other hunters. Or buy a stuffed squirrel and play fetch. A farmer may require help herding his sheep or a golf course may need a dog to keep birds off the grass. Here in Chicago, the Park District occasionally uses Border Collies to chase seagulls and geese away from beaches and parks. The possibilities are limitless.

Tour de Fido

It's difficult and dangerous to control your dog if he is running alongside your bicycle, especially in high-traffic areas. Instead, have him ride in a dog trailer attached to your bike. The sights and sounds along the way offer myriad opportunities for mental stimulation and Fido will be pleased as punch to be out of the house and feel the wind in his fur. Once you arrive at your destination, it's playtime!

Dog trailers are sold at many price points. Be sure that the model you choose has a strong restraint system so Fido will remain inside even if you ride right through a squirrel convention. Purchase a trailer with a cushy seat, adequate shock absorbers and ventilation, as well as reflectors and a safety flag for visibility. In addition, verify that the trailer attaches securely to your bike.

Don't bring Fido along until you're adept at stopping, starting and maneuvering the bike and trailer. Practice with the trailer empty and gradually add weight. Likewise, allow Fido an opportunity to investigate, sniff and sit in the trailer before you take him for his first ride. If necessary, use treats to entice him inside. Begin with short rides and gradually work up to longer journeys. Always check on Fido as you ride. Avoid busy streets, especially at high-traffic times. Even with the safety flag, drivers may have a hard time seeing the trailer. Well-maintained bicycle paths are best. If Fido will be riding with his head out of the trailer, use dog goggles to protect his eyes from airborne debris and bugs. Stop smirking—it's for safety, not a fashion statement.

Set Sail

Boating is another activity that many dogs enjoy. Boat surfaces are wet and slippery and Fido isn't wearing deck shoes, so all canine sailors must wear a properly sized life vest specially made for dogs—no exceptions! If possible, place a nonslip mat in the area Fido likes to stand. While on board, supervise him at all times. The water can get rough and he can fall overboard. Even strong swimmers can panic and drown.

Primer for Indoor Activities

Staying inside when the weather is too hot, too cold or too rainy is no problem. The indoors offers many opportunities for fun and frolic with Fido. Indeed, every activity need not have a physical benefit. Mental stimulation and emotional bonding are important too.

Old-Fashioned Activities

Time-honored activities like catch or fetch are enjoyable inside too. Be careful how hard you throw a toy if you're playing near fragile knickknacks. Clear Fido's path so he doesn't trip or slip and fall. For variety, hide treats around the house for an afternoon treasure hunt. If Fido enjoys company, invite his friend over for a (well-supervised) playdate.

Share the Sofa

It's OK to participate in an occasional quiet activity. My favorite day of the week is Sunday afternoon. Zeke, Arthur and I sit on the sofa and watch TV together. Bonding is a two-way street; Zeke and Arthur help me relax and make me feel like I'm never alone, and they feel loved and appreciated.

Mental-Agility Games

Puzzles offer entertaining task-oriented play that exercises Fido's mind and increases his paw-eye coordination. These toys require Fido to figure out how to release treats. Fido may have to push a lever, force the treat out a small hole or slide a door to obtain his reward.

Beauty Shop

Treat Fido to an afternoon of pampering using all the dog-care skills you've learned in my book. Not only will Fido look and feel good; he'll appreciate the quality time spent together. If you're not in the mood for grooming, play some New Age music and bestow a relaxing massage or an extended belly rub.

Canine Community Service

Whether we walk on two or four legs, we should all help our community. Many volunteer opportunities allow Fido to come along and help out. Even if he can't participate, Fido will be proud of you for helping dogs in need.

Charity Walks and Runs

Many animal-welfare organizations and other worthwhile charities hold walkathons, fun runs or races to raise money and awareness. These events offer you the opportunity to exercise your dog, meet people and help the community. Be sure that Fido enjoys being around other dogs and crowds and is physically fit enough to handle the exercise. If not, borrow a shelter dog or a friend's dog or sponsor a participant.

Therapy

Therapy dogs are pets trained to interact in specific and meaningful ways with strangers who need a little extra TLC and encouragement. For example, dogs participate in reading programs at libraries and schools. Humane-education programs use therapy dogs to illustrate lessons. Many nursing homes, hospitals, residential group homes and prisons welcome therapy dogs too. The dogs offer impartial, enthusiastic encouragement, stimulation, love, affection and entertainment. For many patients, animal-assisted therapy provides lifesaving emotional support and helps them overcome physical and emotional challenges.

You can't, however, just show up at your neighborhood hospital and let Fido loose. First, he must be evaluated to determine if he possesses a suitable personality as well as training and certification. Not all dogs fit the bill. Therapy dogs must love people of all ages, relish tactile contact even from strangers and be comfortable around all people regardless of their age, size, shape, gender or ethnicity. In addition, dogs must be well behaved and understand basic obedience rules.

If you think your dog is a good candidate, contact local and national therapy-dog groups. These organizations evaluate, train and certify dogs, offer insurance and provide information and assistance.

Search and Rescue

National and local organizations train and certify volunteer search-and-rescue teams. Volunteers and their dogs work alongside professional rescuers and law enforcement in times of crisis. This activity requires a significant commitment of *your* time and resources. The rewards, however, are tremendous and you and your dog can save lives.

Animal Welfare

Animal-welfare organizations and animal rescues and shelters always need monetary support, which I wholeheartedly encourage. There are also many other ways to help. Here are a few suggestions:

- Use your new dog-care skills to groom shelter dogs and improve their body, mind and spirit. Whether you're bathing or completely making over a dog, your efforts will help her find a permanent home. A dog is much more adoptable if she looks like a pet rather than a grubby street dog. Every time I groom a shelter dog, I can see and feel the relief the dog experiences when all the old fur and dirt come off. Moreover, the interaction and attention from a caring human lift the spirit of a shelter dog, which makes her more attractive to potential adopters.
- Donate your expertise. Organizations always need assistance with financial and business planning, management, publicity and fund-raising.
- Donate your time. Shelters and rescues need volunteers to do just about everything: enter data and maintain donor files and Web sites, walk dogs, clean cages, transport dogs, staff adoption events and organize fundraisers.
- Take a working vacation at an animal sanctuary. Animal sanctuaries care for animals that often have nowhere else to go. Some of these animals are

old, infirm or not adoptable. Many sanctuaries encourage visitors to volunteer on-site, which allows you to interact directly and meaningfully with the animals.

- Adopt a new pet at the shelter and encourage every person you meet to do the same, whether an old friend or a stranger in the checkout line. Many people don't know about breed rescues and specialty shelters, so spread the word.
- Report animal abuse or neglect immediately even if the perpetrator is your friend, neighbor or family member. If you're worried about repercussions, file an anonymous report.
- Speak out about animal-welfare issues, such as the horrors of puppy mills, animal abuse and neglect and the importance of spaying and neutering pets. Monitor legislation and write to lawmakers about animal issues. Join local and national animal-welfare organizations.

Celebrate with Fido

Our pets are blessings from above and they deserve to be rewarded for all the unselfish love, emotional support, friendship and joy they give. Celebrating the human-canine relationship is a fun (and clever) context to bring two-legged and four-legged family and friends together. Plan a party for Fido's birthday or adoption day or to celebrate his graduation from obedience school. Throw a shower to welcome a friend's new canine bundle of joy. Canine celebrations also provide a natural opportunity to help the community. Ask guests to bring a donation for a shelter in lieu of a gift. Shelters often publish wish lists of items they need.

Unleash your creativity and get wacky with themes, decorations and activities. My coauthor had a *Bark* Mitzvah to commemorate her dog's second birthday (about thirteen in human years). Filbert wore a doggy yarmulke and the cake was decorated to resemble a book. How about serving human guests champagne for Fido's third birthday, which is when he turns about twenty-one in human years? Play musical chairs with dog and owner teams or buy washable finger paint to make colorful paw-print party favors. Hold a talent or costume contest and award prizes. Rent agility equipment to keep the dogs entertained. The possibilities are endless.

Offer your canine guests wholesome but tasty dog treats, such as Chef

Art Smith's Puppy Biscuits (see pages 82–83). Serve your human guests cupcakes or cookies decorated to resemble the guest of honor (be careful to place the human treats out of the dogs' reach!). Provide multiple bowls of water and enough toys for everyone. Clean up any accidents immediately. When it's time to serve the canine cake, separate the dogs and feed them simultaneously to avoid food fights. Closely supervise the mayhem and promptly remove agitated, tired or aggressive dogs.

If the party is outside, verify that the area is fully enclosed and secure, then let the dogs chase one another until they fall over. Provide a shady spot to rest and extra water.

Saying Good-bye

Unfortunately, fun with Fido must end one day. Learning to cope with the loss and opening your heart to a new furry pal is a challenging and heart-wrenching journey. Sometimes, you'll have advance notice and you must make that most difficult but humane decision to euthanize a sick dog. Other times, the loss is a total shock. In both situations, the grief is real. A mourning pet owner feels many emotions: anger, sadness, confusion, denial, guilt, sorrow, lethargy and sometimes relief. To many, the loss of a pet is just as serious and devastating as the loss of a friend or family member. Grief is personal and everyone mourns in different ways and for varying lengths of time.

Grieving is a process and emotional support is crucial. Of course, there are coldhearted, thick people who will say, "Why are you so upset? It's just a dog." If you find that you have no one to talk to or need a little extra TLC, many veterinary schools have wonderful hotlines that offer free assistance zto bereaved pet lovers. In addition, the Internet is full of informative Web sites and supportive online communities. Your veterinarian and local animal-welfare organizations and shelters are also excellent resources.

Both my coauthor and I lost a beloved dog unexpectedly. We found solace in our friends and family as well as the written word. I still cry like a baby every time I read "The Rainbow Bridge," a touching poem shared by grieving pet lovers everywhere. It's available all over the Internet. Many beneficial books on pet loss are available and some are written specifically for kids experiencing death for the first time. My personal favorite is *For*

Every Dog an Angel by Christine Davis, a book given to me by my coauthor after Gabriel's death.

Don't ignore your grief. Rather, find a meaningful book or poem, make a scrapbook, write a song, compile a DVD of pictures and music or hold a memorial service. It's important to participate in a ritual that allows you to acknowledge your emotions.

The most powerful healing, however, comes when you open your heart to a new furry friend. More than eight million dogs are waiting in animal shelters and rescues right now for their forever home. Whether you want a purebred or a mutt, there's bound to be a perfect dog waiting for you.

10.

Annoying Allergies and
Pernicious Parasites

llergies and parasites are the most common skin problems suffered by dogs. Arming yourself with knowledge will allow you to relieve your itchy dog and protect him from deadly illnesses carried by creepy-crawlies.

Annoying Allergies

Like humans, dogs can suffer from allergies. An allergic reaction occurs when a dog is exposed to an "allergen," which can be any foreign substance either inside or outside the body. Allergens cause the immune system to overreact and produce a response, such as itchiness or a rash. Dogs typically begin to show initial allergy symptoms as young adults, although puppies and older dogs occasionally develop allergies too. Many breeds are genetically predisposed to allergies, such as the Dalmatian, Golden Retriever, Poodle, Lhasa Apso, Pug and English Bulldog and many setters, terriers and schnauzers.

The severity of the reaction varies by dog and often increases with each exposure to the allergen. Similarly, the more allergens he's exposed to simultaneously, the more severe the reaction can be.

Today, allergy diagnosis and treatment are sophisticated and often effective. Veterinary allergists and dermatologists are also available to treat severe cases. Canine allergies are sorted into four general categories.

Inhaled Allergies

Just like humans, many dogs are allergic to particles in the air. Seasonal allergies are usually caused by inhaling allergens in the environment, such as the pollen of blooming plants, trees, grass and weeds. Once the season passes, the allergy symptoms clear up until the next year. Year-round inhalant allergies are usually caused by particles the dog breathes in the home like dust and mold. The first clue that your pooch is suffering from inhalant allergies is usually the maniacal scratching caused by her incredibly itchy skin.

Food Allergies
Dogs may have food allergies to beef, chicken, dairy products, wheat, soy, corn, eggs, food additives or food colorings. In addition to the usual itchiness and skin irritations, food allergies may cause vomiting, diarrhea and excessive gas. I'm not talking about a few extra toots; I mean room-clearing, hair-curling flatulence, so don't feed your allergic dog near an open flame.

Contact Allergies
When Fido's skin touches an allergen, it triggers a reaction, such as a rash or hair loss. The reaction is usually localized to the area of contact, which helps diagnose this type of allergy. Snoozing on a wool blanket, bathing with scented grooming products or touching residue from household cleaners are all common sources of contact allergies. Dogs are frequently allergic to chemicals in flea and tick collars and will experience severe skin irritation and hair loss in the neck area.

Insect-Bite Allergy
Insect bites sometimes trigger allergic reactions. Fleabite dermatitis is one of the most common canine allergies. When an allergic dog is bitten by a flea, the flea's saliva causes a local and systemic reaction. The dog begins to itch all over and she scratches, chews and licks, which often leads to a secondary infection. All this discomfort, however, is easily prevented by eliminating fleas from the dog and her environment.

Symptoms

Dogs and humans are allergic to many of the same allergens, but often exhibit different symptoms. (Psst: don't tell them, but dogs are a different species.) For example, allergens in the air cause people to sneeze, but dogs to itch. A dog's face, ears, paws and undercarriage are usually itchiest. As a result, dogs often rub their face on the floor, paw at their ears, chew their feet or lick their belly and unmentionables.

Common canine allergy symptoms include the following:

- Inflammation
- Excessive scratching, licking or chewing, especially if your dog is focusing on a particular area
- Rashes, bumps or blisters
- Thickened, discolored or stinky skin
- Hair loss
- Inflamed ears or chronic ear infections
- Difficulty breathing

It's important to visit the veterinarian for diagnosis and treatment as soon as you see the first symptoms to reduce the risk of secondary infections. For example, if you ignore a rash, the itchiness will drive Fido batty and he'll lick, chew and scratch himself excessively. If he keeps at it, *and he will*, bacteria invade the moist and often broken skin and cause inflammation and infection. This is a "hot spot," which is a raw, open and often oozing sore. Without medical attention the infection can spread and quickly become severe. The veterinarian will cut away the fur to allow airflow, clean and disinfect the area and prescribe antibiotic and anti-inflammatory medication as needed to treat the hot spot and the underlying condition. Fido may have to wear an Elizabethan collar to prevent him from reaching the hot spot while it heals.

Over the years, I've found some horrible hot spots on my clients. A while back, a big, beautiful long-haired Old English Sheepdog came in for his haircut. To my horror, during the prebath inspection I found a huge hot spot (about four inches square) around his left ear. I knew that the hot spot had been there a while, based on its size and the fact that it had already scabbed over. Moreover, the spot smelled rancid and the fur around it was matted and embedded in the scabs. The poor dog was incredibly relieved when I cleaned up the area and removed all the mess.

I wasn't going to let the owner off the hook for ignoring his dog's uncomfortable and probably painful skin condition. So I put everything I'd shaved and cut off into a clear plastic baggy. When the owner arrived for pickup, I presented him with the bag. He responded, "Oh, the dog was scratching, but we figured he had some type of ear infection. We kept looking in his ears and didn't see anything." Clearly, this guy had *never* bothered to examine *around* the ear area and *never* parted the long hair to inspect the skin. To this day, I still don't understand how anyone could miss a hot spot *that* big or why anyone wouldn't investigate if a dog was manically scratching. The moral of this sad story is: always take the time to pet, touch and inspect your dog regularly and actually look at his skin. Moreover, if the symptoms don't clear up, visit the veterinarian.

Diagnosis

Veterinarians have a variety of diagnostic tools at their disposal. The doctor will examine your dog and discuss your home observations. She may order blood tests to look for certain antibodies that indicate the immune system is overreacting to specific allergens. The doctor may also order skin tests, in which small areas of the skin are exposed to various allergens so she can gauge the reactions. An elimination diet is frequently used to diagnose food allergies. The suspected allergens are systematically removed from the dog's diet over eight to twelve weeks. After the symptoms disappear, the suspected allergen is reintroduced. If it causes a reaction, then that food is permanently eliminated from the diet.

Remember that you are your dog's loudest advocate. Ask questions and visit specialists to obtain a second opinion if necessary.

Treatment

Once diagnosed, Fido can begin treatment. Never treat an allergy without veterinary guidance. I cannot stress enough the danger of diagnosing and treating *any* canine symptom or illness on your own. For dramatic emphasis, imagine that I'm in Times Square on New Year's Eve straddling the famous ball that is seconds away from plunging. I'm gripping a huge sign restating the admonition in massive red flashing letters. I'm risking life and limb and this stunt is excluded from my life insurance policy, so please pay attention! Reading about a treatment in a book (even mine) or on the Internet is no substitute for proper veterinary care. Home remedies, mysterious formulas, herbs and oils may aggravate the allergic reaction or an underlying illness, interact with other medications and supplements or damage Fido's skin and coat.

Allergies can't be "cured," but they can be controlled and the symptoms diminished. Sometimes, simply avoiding the allergen is effective. For instance, if Fido is allergic to dust mites, wash his bedding in hot water at least every week, forgo stuffed toys, remove carpeting where he hangs out and run the air conditioner. Your veterinarian can help develop a strategy to help Fido avoid any problematic allergens.

If Fido is allergic to substances he absorbs through his skin, frequent (and proper) bathing may help, since you'll wash away the allergens before they cause problems. Veterinarians often prescribe special shampoos with colloidal oatmeal and other anti-itch ingredients or topical creams, sprays or salves. Don't use any topical treatment without veterinary approval. Fido could lick the medicine and get sick.

Fatty acid supplements help many canine allergy sufferers. Omega-3 fatty acids from fish oil and flaxseeds sometimes reduce allergic reactions by minimizing inflammation. But don't just grab a bottle of fish oil from the grocery store and pop a pill in Fido's mouth. The veterinarian must prescribe the appropriate dose and formulation.

With more severe allergies, prescription and over-the-counter drugs, such as corticosteroids and antihistamines, are often used to reduce symptoms. Many of these drugs are the same ones used to treat allergies in humans. Because they aren't approved or dosed for canine use, however, never administer them unless directed by your veterinarian. Moreover, all drugs can have side effects. Be sure that you fully understand how the particular drug works and the associated risks before you leave the veterinarian's office. Carefully read and follow the directions. Call the veterinarian immediately if your dog has any reaction to the drug.

Allergy shots, or "immunotherapy," are often employed if the symptoms occur for several months and other remedies fail. Immunotherapy desensitizes the dog's immune system over time through regular injections of small amounts of the allergen. Allergy shots are extremely effective, but patience is required. Improvement is slow and may take six months to a year.

Pernicious Parasites

Parasites are uncomfortable and often dangerous. Fleas, ticks, mosquitoes, mites and other creepy-crawlies cause skin irritations at best, and at worst cause serious, life-threatening illnesses, including Lyme disease, bubonic plague, West Nile virus and heartworm, just to name a few. The average well-cared-for house dog faces several prevalent parasitic threats: fleas, ticks, mosquitoes and, more rarely, mites. Internal parasites are also problematic and some are contagious to people. Report unusual bowel movements, weight loss or change in eating habits to your veterinarian and bring in stool samples for analysis at least twice a year to detect and diagnose tapeworms, hookworms, whipworms, roundworms and other internal creepy-crawlies.

Preventing and eliminating parasites is a critical aspect of caring for your beloved furry friend. Common sense, veterinary assistance and persistence will help your dog live a more comfortable, healthier life and decrease the opportunity for parasites to harm your best friend.

Safety Rules for Parasite-Control Products

Your dog's safety is always my first concern. Pest control involves chemical treatments. So we'll study the relevant safety rules before we get into the nitty-gritty details of parasite prevention and removal.

1. Consult your veterinarian before using *any* flea, tick or other insecticide products on your dog, including medicated shampoos, over-the-counter and prescription treatments and natural or herbal products. These products may interact with other medications, supplements and treatments or aggravate existing conditions.

2. Choosing the appropriate parasite preventative requires a veterinarian's expertise. A self-proclaimed expert pontificating on the Internet, in a book or at the watercooler is no substitute. The vet will choose the correct parasite-control product based on the climate and your dog's breed, health, age, home environment and lifestyle. Notify the vet if your household includes other pets, children, older or sick adults, pregnant women or asthmatics.

3. Purchase all medication and parasite-control products from reputable sources, such as your animal hospital. Unscrupulous merchants sell counterfeit products that can seriously endanger

your pet, or products that haven't been stored properly and become useless.

4. Treat all the pets in your household with species-specific products. Many dog products are lethal to cats.

5. Never apply any parasite preventative to very young, elderly, pregnant or sick animals unless directed by a veterinarian.

6. Carefully read the package. Study the ingredient list and follow the use and dosing instructions. Heed the warnings on the package too. Discard any expired product. Store all medications out of reach of children and animals.

7. Preventatives work only if you remember to use them. Mark your calendar to remind yourself when to administer the medication and check it off to keep track. If you skip a treatment, contact your veterinarian right away.

8. If Fido has a reaction to any parasite-control product, call the veterinarian immediately and begin first aid. Danger signs include: vomiting, diarrhea, drooling, swelling, redness, itchiness, rash, seizure or collapse. (See "Allergic Reactions" in chapter 19, "Home Dog-Care Safety and Basic First Aid.")

9. Wash your hands immediately after applying or using pest-control product.

10. If you are confused or have questions, talk to your veterinarian before you do anything rash.

Foul Fleas

Fleas make Fido uncomfortable and miserable. Fleas can even cause anemia and transmit tapeworm, an internal parasite. As we discussed above, flea-bite dermatitis is also a problem. To make matters worse, fleas like humans too. Flea season varies by geographic region, climate, temperature and humidity. Depending on your location, flea season runs from early spring through December, or all year round.

Thankfully, fleas leave us obvious clues. Brush your dog over a white cloth or paper towel and look for small dark flecks, which are flea feces. Moisten the flecks and if they turn reddish brown, you'll know you've got a problem. When you examine Fido's skin and coat, look for brown or black crusty residue or teeny tiny white flea eggs. The most obvious sign of fleas, however, is your dog's persistent scratching, biting or chewing on himself. Look for hair loss, scabs and hot spots too. Fleas like to hang out near the base of the tail and rear, around the head, behind the ears and on the neck, armpits and undercarriage. Like many of us, fleas like the warm spots.

Unfortunately, fleas are sneaky—and hardy. Fido can pick up a flea from another infested animal or anywhere in the environment. One flea can start a whole colony. Indeed, if you see one, it's usually safe to assume that an entire flea circus has moved in, and Fido's not getting a cut of the box office take.

Adult fleas rarely leave their host, whether human or animal. Flea eggs, babies and teenyboppers, however, are constantly falling off Fido and finding their way onto furniture, upholstery and bedding and all over your yard, where they mature and start the cycle over again. You may even see one of those little buggers jumping or crawling around. Your poor pooch is suffering as the fleas feed on his blood, and it's up to you to evict the free-loaders.

Prevention Is Your Best Weapon

Prevention and quick action the moment an infestation occurs are the keys to a flea-free lifestyle. Fleas are harder to get rid of than cockroaches, especially in warm climates. Once fleas take up residence, clearing them out requires time and effort. Depending on the severity of the infestation, fleas may live on for days, weeks or months after you've treated your dog, home and yard. Be persistent and patient. The fleas must contact and absorb the insecticide before they die.

Treat the Dog
Back in the day, we had to walk seventeen miles in the snow and blustery wind to school wearing hand-me-down flip-flops *and* use flea powder, bombs, foggers, collars, dips and sprays. Of course, nowadays, these products are shunned because they contain chemicals that many experts consider dangerous to humans, pets and the environment. I remember years ago dipping Ivan, my Giant Schnauzer, in flea-killing chemicals every two weeks. During the summer, he smelled like a pine tree. This wasn't an

ideal solution, but at the time, it was the best option. Thankfully, safer and more-effective remedies are now readily available.

Modern prescription preventatives and treatments contain chemicals that kill fleas when they land on Fido's body even before they bite. The best formulations also kill fleas at every life-cycle stage, combat ticks and are waterproof. I swear by the monthly "spot-on" topical treatment I use on my dogs. It's so easy to use, safe for most dogs and extremely effective.

Your veterinarian can also prescribe sprays, dips, medicated shampoos and collars. Carefully read the labels before you decide to use these products. Many require special handling or must be applied in well-ventilated areas. Frankly, I'm nervous about using products on a live animal that require such extreme precautions. Think about my Ivan and then think twice about which flea products you use.

|||||||||||||||||||||||||||||||||||||||||||||||||||||||||||||||||||||||||||||||||||||||||||||||||||||

Problems with Over-the-Counter Flea and Tick Products

Certain chemicals—organophosphates (OPs) and carbamates—used in many over-the-counter flea and tick products have recently come under fire for their harmful effects on pets and children. The Environmental Protection Agency has only recently begun reviewing pet-product safety. As expected, changes are extraordinarily slow and many products with potentially harmful chemicals are still for sale.

Before purchasing and using any over-the-counter products, carefully read the entire label and talk to your veterinarian and medical doctor. Until we know more, avoid products that list these chemicals as "active ingredients":

- **OPs: chlorpyrifos, dichlorvos, phosmet, naled, diazinon, malathion or tetrachlorvinphos**
- **Carbamates: carbaryl and propoxur**

Most of these OPs have been removed from products for sale in the United States. If you have older products, throw them away. Unfortunately, the OP tetrachlorvinphos and the carbamates carbaryl and propoxur are still used. With so many less-hazardous choices available, there's no reason to risk harming your pet or your family.

|||||||||||||||||||||||||||||||||||||||||||||||||||||||||||||||||||||||||||||||||||||||||||||||||||||

Following your usual home dog-care routine helps prevent and terminate flea and other parasite problems. Regular visits to the professional groomer are also important, since an extra set of expert eyes will be examining your dog. During flea season inspect all your pets as often as you can. Remember, a few minutes devoted to inspection each day keeps the fleas away.

In addition, brush and bathe Fido regularly. If you have a Uniform Fur dog, follow up all brushing sessions with a flea comb during flea season. If you have a Multilength Fur dog, use the comb on the shorter parts of the coat. For Hair dogs and the longer fur on a Multilength Fur dog, use the white towel method to check for black specks (a flea comb will break off fur that's longer than a half inch).

The teeth on a flea comb are extremely close together and lift fleas and eggs off the skin and coat. Work the comb to the skin and move the comb through the fur all over Fido's body. Use the flea comb outside, since it may cause fleas to jump off. If you are stuck inside, work in the bathtub so you can quickly wash fleas down the drain. In addition to the comb, you'll need a container of soapy water to drown the fleas as you comb. After each stroke through the coat, dunk and clean off the comb (and any caught fur) in the soapy water. Continue this procedure until the entire pet has been combed. Discard the dirty water down the drain. Although it's time-consuming, this procedure involves no chemicals and is safe for every dog.

Treat Your Home

Vacuuming sucks up eggs and immature and mature fleas. So vacuum, vacuum and then vacuum some more. Vacuum the top and bottom of your mattresses, lift up the couch cushions and use that tentacle-like attachment to reach under the furniture and curtains and into every crack, crevice and molding. Don't place mothballs or flea-control products in the vacuum, as this may spread toxic fumes.

After each vacuuming session, remove the bag, seal it with tape and place it in a plastic bag, because fleas can survive suction. Immediately deposit the bag in an outdoor garbage can. If you have a bagless vacuum, go outside to empty the contents into a plastic bag and then separate the collection bin from the machine and rinse it with soap and hot water. Dry the bin thoroughly before reattaching it to the vacuum. If your machine's collection bin doesn't detach, contact the manufacturer for washing directions.

In multipet households or if the infestation is particularly severe, you may need to call in a professional exterminator. Inquire about less harmful or nontoxic insecticides. Ask your veterinarian about safe carpet powders, sprays and foggers too. In addition, take all your curtains down and have them professionally cleaned. Don't rehang them until you're fully certain that the infestation is over.

Nonchemical flea traps are also effective and inexpensive. Traps are widely available at stores and on the Internet. They use an incandescent lightbulb to attract the fleas, which then become caught on sticky paper.

During flea season, frequently wash your furry friend's clothing, bedding, blankets, crate and stuffed toys with hot water. Many people forget to treat the other areas used by their pets. Vacuum your car and anywhere else your dog hangs out.

Treat Your Yard

Fleas like to hide out in long grass and moist or shady spots. Mow your lawn; remove weeds; clean up grass clippings, old leaves and other yard waste and remove all standing water. In addition, eliminate extraneous dirt, sand and gravel piles, which attract fleas. Ask your veterinarian to recommend nontoxic products to treat your yard.

||||||||||||||||||||||||||||||||||||||||||||||||||||||||||||||||||||||||||||||||||||||||||||||||||||||||||||||||||

Going Green With Parasite Control

With all the concern over synthetic chemicals and pesticides, many people are using natural or herbal remedies to fight fleas, ticks and other parasites. These products often use oils and herbs, such as eucalyptus, citrus, citronella, lavender, brewer's yeast or garlic. Just because something is natural, however, *doesn't* mean that it's safe or even effective. For example, we know that garlic is dangerous for dogs; ergo, garlic pesticide pills are a no-no. Save your garlic for pasta and vampire attacks.

Before using any natural flea remedy, contact either a traditional or holistic veterinarian. Like their synthetic counterparts, natural products can be harmful if misused or improperly dosed and may react with other medications and treatments.

Also, visit a reputable and knowledgeable home and garden center to discuss safe, natural products to kill fleas living in your yard. Many people successfully use pest-killing worms like nematodes, or diatomaceous earth, which is the fossilized remains of microscopic shells.

||||||||||||||||||||||||||||||||||||||||||||||||||||||||||||||||||||||||||||||||||||||||||||||||||||||

Terrible Ticks

Ticks are bad news for dogs, people and just about any mammal in your home. Ticks often carry and transmit dreadful diseases, such as Lyme, Rocky Mountain spotted fever, canine anaplasmosis, babesiosis, canine ehrlichiosis and tick paralysis. Fortunately, you can minimize tick risk with a two-pronged plan of attack: prevention and removal.

Tick season varies by climate and geographic region. Ticks live in warm climates year-round. In other areas, tick season runs from early spring though late fall. Many ticks can survive cold weather. For example, adult deer ticks, which carry Lyme disease, flourish in October and November. Check with your veterinarian to determine the length of tick season where you live. Before traveling, research the tick activity in the area and take appropriate preventative precautions.

Ticks don't jump or fly. Rather, they wait on vegetation for an animal to pass by and make contact. Then, they happily attach to the animal and mosey down to the skin. Once there, ticks insert their mouthparts into the skin and begin feasting on blood. While it's eating, an infected tick transmits disease-causing bacteria into the host's bloodstream.

Prevention Essentials

As with fleas, successful tick control means treating your pooch, your home and the environment.

Treat the Dog

Talk in detail with your veterinarian about tick-borne illnesses, their symptoms and tick activity where you live and vacation. Your veterinarian should prescribe the safest preventative based on your dog's age, breed, health, environment and lifestyle. Ask whether your pooch is a candidate for the Lyme disease vaccination. Remember, though, even if Fido is vaccinated, he's still susceptible to other tick-borne diseases. In addition to your inspections, have your vet look for ticks during every visit and remind your groomer to check too.

Your veterinarian may suggest additional tick-control products, including shampoos, powders, dips or collars. Some of these products may contain chemicals dangerous to your pooch, you and your family. Before using these products, talk to your family doctor and do your own research.

Treat Your Home

If ticks appear in your home, consult with your veterinarian and a trusted professional exterminator. Examine and wash Fido's clothing, bedding, blankets, crate, plush toys and sleeping area more often during tick season.

Treat Your Yard

A clean and manicured yard controls ticks too. Mow the lawn, remove plant litter and standing water and cut back any weeds, brush and tall grass around the home, at the edges of the garden and near open stone walls. In addition, elevate stacked woodpiles and store in a dry location. Be sure to clean up any leaf piles in the fall because ticks keep warm here during cold weather. Hire a reputable, licensed professional to spray your yard. Keep kids and pets away during pesticide treatments.

Avoid Tick-Infested Areas

Although Fido (or you) can pick up a tick anywhere, try to steer clear of known tick-infested areas. Ticks like moist and humid environments, tall grass, bushes, shrubbery and leaf piles. They're found in open fields, city parks, grassy areas and the woods. When hiking, walk in the center of trails.

Immediate Inspection and
Rapid Removal

During tick season, inspect Fido daily. The minute Fido returns from an outdoor jaunt, check him for ticks and remove them promptly. Postponing the removal because you're too busy or waiting for the groomer to do it unnecessarily endangers your pal and drastically increases the likelihood that he'll contract a tick-borne illness. Don't assume the prescription tick killer will take care of it for you either. The insecticide doesn't kill instantly; it has to be absorbed into the body, which takes time. In general, a tick must be attached to a dog (or person) for about twenty-four to seventy-two hours before it begins transmitting disease. So if you act fast, you significantly reduce the chances that your furry friend will get sick.

A casual inspection won't do; you must devote adequate time to inspect every square inch of your dog. Remember that if you find ticks on your pooch, you may have some too. After you examine the dog, check yourself and wash your clothing in hot water.

Recently a client brought in his Portuguese Water Dog for a bath after a long weekend in the country. The owner reported that he'd *already* checked the dog and removed two ticks. I inspected the dog and found close to forty-five more, most of which were engorged and feeding, and the rest of which were moving rather quickly up my arm as I systematically eliminated them all and reached for the nearest barf bag.

If possible, inspect your pooch outside or in the garage to prevent ticks from falling off in your home. Use a magnifying glass! Ticks range in size from the head of a pin to a fingernail if fully engorged with blood. Ticks are generally black or dark brown and sometimes the legs are visible.

Painstakingly examine Fido's skin and coat. Some ticks may be sitting on the fur and some may already be feasting. Pay extra-close attention in

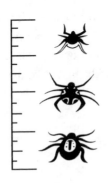

folds and crevices, such as the armpits, face, ear flaps, head, neck, genitals and paws. If you feel a bump, part the fur to identify it. Unlike fleas, which run away faster than a speeding bullet, feeding ticks don't move and might resemble a small mole, growth or tumor.

Removing a tick is actually not that difficult once you're over the heebie-jeebies factor. Start by ignoring anyone, especially the purported experts, who advise you to treat a tick with a beauty product, chemical solvent or household cleaner. I agree with the Centers for Disease Control: never use nail polish, a lit match, petroleum jelly or rubbing alcohol to remove a tick. These outdated tricks won't force the tick out, but will harm your dog's delicate skin and often cause the tick to expel its bacteria into the dog's bloodstream.

Safe Tick Removal

1. Don't panic. The horror and nausea will subside if you take a deep breath. Besides, not every tick is infected with a disease. If you act quickly, Fido should be fine. Gather the necessary tools:

   ✓ Canine shampoo
   ✓ Clean and sanitized fine-tipped tweezers. Choose high-quality tweezers with flat, unetched edges that fit tightly together.
   ✓ Covered jar filled with fresh isopropyl alcohol. (If you're in the field, use any alcoholic beverage.)
   ✓ Disposable gloves
   ✓ Dog-safe antibiotic ointment
   ✓ Magnifying glass
   ✓ Sealable plastic bag

2. Place Fido in a well-lit area, preferably outside or in your garage. Don your gloves because tick bacteria can transmit an illness if you're bare-handed.

3. To remove the ticks off the fur, carefully pluck them off with the tweezers, but *don't* squish them. Releasing the disease-causing bacteria onto your hand is a bad idea. Place the ticks in the jar

filled with isopropyl alcohol to guarantee death. Keep the lid closed.

4. Ticks that have attached their mouthparts into the skin are more difficult to remove. Using the tweezers, grasp the tick *as close to the dog's skin as possible*, which is where you'll find the embedded mouthparts.

DO NOT grasp the tick by the body. Use firm pressure but avoid crushing the tick, which will release the disease-causing bacteria into Fido's bloodstream. With a steady motion, pull the tick's body outward and away from the skin. Don't jerk or twist the tweezers as you're pulling. Try to remove the tick in one piece, but don't fret if you leave the tick's mouthparts in the skin, because once separated from the body, they can't transmit disease. The leftovers usually fall out, but watch the area for signs of infection, such as redness, swelling or irritation around the bite site.

5. Place the tick in the jar. Repeat until all ticks are removed. Alert your vet about the engorged ticks you have removed. The doctor may want to test the dead ticks for disease or inspect your dog.

6. Clean the area around the bite with shampoo and rinse thoroughly. Follow up with a small amount of dog-safe antibiotic ointment from your pet first-aid kit.

7. Place the disposable gloves in a sealed plastic bag and into a covered trash can immediately. Wash your hands thoroughly with hot soap and water. Disinfect the tweezers.

8. Generously reward Fido for his cooperation during this critical dog-care activity.

Early detection and treatment of a tick-borne disease is Fido's best chance for recovery. If you have even the slightest inkling that something is wrong, contact your veterinarian immediately. Mention you have removed engorged ticks. Often, an infected dog exhibits few or no symptoms until the disease is quite advanced. Watch for these common signs of tick-borne illnesses:

- Difficulty walking or lameness
- Fever
- Lethargy or depression
- Loss of appetite or weight loss
- Muscle and joint soreness, pain, swelling
- Neurological abnormalities, such as neck or back pain or seizures
- Rashes
- Unusual discharge or sores
- Vomiting or diarrhea

Malicious Mosquitoes

As we all know, mosquitoes are bad, very bad. These insects transmit some of the world's deadliest illnesses to humans and animals alike. Mosquito-borne diseases, such as heartworm and West Nile virus, are genuine threats to your dog.

Horrible Heartworm

Heartworm is a horrible disease that can kill your dog, no matter where you live. An infected mosquito transmits the disease when it bites a dog. The disease causes worms to grow inside the heart and pulmonary vessels and wreak havoc. Typically, dogs don't show signs of the disease until it is advanced, when treatment is difficult and expensive. Indeed, sometimes dogs don't survive the medication or surgery. Be on the lookout for these common heartworm symptoms:

- Abnormal heart or lung sounds
- Dark, bloody or coffee-colored urine
- Decreased appetite or weight loss
- Difficulty exercising
- Difficulty breathing
- Pale gums
- Persistent cough
- Swelling of the abdomen

Thankfully, heartworm is preventable! Your veterinarian will prescribe a preventive medication that suits your dog's age, health and lifestyle. The American Heartworm Society and most veterinarians recommend that dogs use heartworm preventatives year-round regardless of geographic region. As an added benefit, many preventatives also kill certain intestinal parasites, including hookworms and roundworms. Preventatives are available as pills, monthly topical treatments or an injection that provides six months of protection.

Use Heartworm Preventatives Safely

Fido must be tested annually, usually in the spring, *before* he begins taking any heartworm preventatives. Administering this medication to a dog with heartworm is extremely dangerous and can be fatal.

Wicked West Nile Virus

The West Nile virus has spread far and wide since it was first identified in Africa in 1937. Now it's slowly making its way across North America. Mosquitoes become infected when they feed on diseased birds and then they transmit the virus when they bite humans and animals.

Although it's still rare in dogs, the number of reported cases is growing and researchers are still learning about this relatively new disease. West Nile virus doesn't usually cause severe illness, but young and old dogs and those with compromised immune systems are at higher risk. Contact the veterinarian promptly if you observe these symptoms: decreased coordination, depression, difficulty walking, tremors, abnormal head posture, circling and convulsions. Currently, no specific West Nile virus treatment exists. The veterinarian treats the infected dog with antiviral medication and manages the symptoms.

Scientists have much to learn about this disease. In the meantime, preventing mosquito bites is the best way to protect your beloved furry friend, you and your family.

Mosquito Safety

Follow these safety rules in addition to using preventatives prescribed by your veterinarian.

- Keep pets indoors during peak mosquito hours: dawn, dusk and early evening.
- Remove all standing water around your yard. Mosquitoes can breed in a puddle in only four days.
- Mosquitoes hang out on weeds, so mow the lawn and clean up your garden.

- Maintain door and window screens and promptly patch rips to stop mosquitoes from entering your home.
- Ask your veterinarian and reputable exterminator to suggest a pet-safe yard insecticide.
- Avoid dead birds and dead animals, since they may have died from West Nile virus.
- Never use a human mosquito repellent on your dog or any animals. Ask your veterinarian to recommend a dog-safe product. DEET-based repellent should **never** be used on dogs, since they're likely to lick themselves and ingest the chemical.

Mean Mites

Fido always has many parasites happily living in harmony on his body. This usually isn't a problem—you have them too. Occasionally, though, the *demodex* mite, one of these freeloaders living in Fido's hair follicles, gets out of control. This can happen when Fido experiences stress, or his immune system is weakened. Young puppies with undeveloped immune systems are at risk too. Often a demodectic mange outbreak indicates a more troubling systemic issue, such as immune disorders. Demodex mites cause flaky, scaly, crusty or greasy skin, lesions, rashes, pustules or hair loss. Hair loss often begins around the snout, eyes and head, but spreads all over. Demodex mites must be treated and controlled quickly. Demodex mites are transmitted only by a mother to her puppies soon after birth, but then can lie dormant for years before an outbreak.

Otodectes mites attack canine ears. They leave a telltale brown or black crust in or around the ears. In addition, you'll probably see Fido scratching at his ears or shaking or tilting his head. Ear mites are extremely contagious, so treat all pets in your household with the products prescribed by your veterinarian and keep Fido away from other animals until the mites are gone. (Not all ear infections, however, are caused by mites.)

Sarcoptes mites cause scabies (sarcoptic mange). These mites are highly contagious, incredibly uncomfortable and totally gross, especially since they can affect you too. Scabies mites burrow into Fido's skin and secrete allergens in the tunnels, which produce crazed itching. Other symptoms include hair loss, rash and scaly or crusty skin. Scabies commonly appears on the ears, face, belly, elbows, legs and tail.

All mite infestations require prompt veterinary intervention. The intense itching means that Fido is at risk of developing a secondary infection from all the scratching, chewing and licking. Moreover, responsible pet owners should do everything they can to prevent passing contagious diseases to others. The veterinarian will prescribe medication, topical treatments and insecticidal shampoos as well as antibiotics to control any secondary infection. Don't use any over-the-counter medicine, home remedy or herbal treatment unless directed by your veterinarian. Wash all Fido's clothing, bedding and stuffed toys in hot water. Better yet, discard everything in a sealed plastic bag and start fresh after Fido recovers.

11.

Planning Your
Dog-Care Routine

F ido requires a full-blown home grooming session every month in which you'll clean him from head to toe. As a kind and loving dog owner, you'll supplement these complete grooming sessions with additional daily, weekly and monthly tasks. You have a few semiannual and annual responsibilities too.

Yearly Dog-Care Calendar and Planner

Daily Tasks

- Ideally, brush your dog every day or, *at a minimum*, a few times a week.
- Ideally, brush your dog's teeth every day or, *at a minimum*, a few times a week.
- Every morning inspect and carefully clean your dog's eyes and lashes.
- Play with your dog, exercise him, pet him, praise him and hang out with him for at least sixty minutes each day. Don't fret if you're busy; feel free to play in smaller time increments. Just be sure to spend quality time with Fido *each day*.
- Wash food and water bowls every day or *at least* a few times a week. Wash all utensils after each use and clean food and treat containers each time you refill.

Weekly Tasks

- If you truly cannot brush your dog every day or a few times a week, do it weekly.
- If you truly cannot brush your dog's teeth every day or a few times a week, do it weekly.
- Inspect your dog's body and be sure to check the skin and coat too.

If she has wrinkles, folds or flaps on her neck, body or tail, inspect, clean and dry them.

- Inspect and clean your dog's head, mouth and nose. If her face has flews, flaps, folds or wrinkles, inspect, clean and dry them too.
- Inspect your dog's ears. Clean inside the ears only when it's dirty in there.
- Inspect and clean paws, rear and genitals.
- Formally scout your home every week for dangerous objects, chemicals and other hazards that your dog may discover. In addition, be constantly on the lookout as you go about your daily business—especially if your roommates are careless or messy.
- Take an elderly, busy or homebound neighbor's dog for a walk.
- Plan a playdate or dog-park visit, *at least* once a week, to teach your dog proper social skills.

Monthly Tasks

- Treat your dog to a bath and full home grooming session *at least* once a month, but spot wash as necessary.
- Administer parasite preventatives. (Note: some medication might require daily, weekly or other dosing. Mark your calendar accordingly.)
- If your dog is chewing his rear or scooting on his butt, take him to the veterinarian or the groomer to empty his anal sacs or do it yourself if you are extraordinarily brave.
- Take your dog to the veterinarian or the groomer for a professional nail trim or, if you categorically insist, do it yourself after studying my instructions.
- Take your dog to the veterinarian or the groomer for professional ear-hair removal *if necessary*. If you absolutely must do it yourself, first discuss the procedure with your veterinarian or professional groomer.
- Inspect and wash all toys and chews for excessive wear and tear *at least* once a month, but more often if Fido is a power chewer. Dispose of anything that is dangerous, broken or just too gross.
- Inspect and wash all Fido's clothing, bedding, crates, blankets and

sleeping accessories *at least* once a month, but more often during flea and tick season. Replace anything worn or dangerous.

- Volunteer at a local animal-welfare organization or donate money or services.
- Congratulate yourself for all the effort and care you have devoted to your dog.

Semiannual Tasks

- Take your dog to the veterinarian for a checkup twice a year, especially if she's a senior citizen (about eight to ten years old depending on size and breed).
- Review your pet first-aid manual *at least* every six months.
- Check and replenish your pet first-aid kit and pet emergency and disaster supplies after every use and every six months. Discard and replace any expired items.

Annual Tasks

- Update your dog's identification, microchip information and license *at least* once a year and each time your information changes. Replace tags if they are no longer legible.
- Update the Emergency Information Card *at least* once a year and each time the information changes.
- Affix new stickers to all exterior doors to alert firemen and other emergency personnel about your pets. Replace more often if the stickers become illegible.
- Review and update plans for Fido's care in the event of your death, illness or incapacitation.
- In the spring, take your dog to the veterinarian for a heartworm check.
- Take your dog for his annual vaccinations.
- Schedule a professional dental cleaning.
- Enroll your dog in an obedience or agility course to maintain her positive attitude and good personality.
- Celebrate your dog's birthday or adoption day by throwing a party.

Professional Grooming Schedule:
Mandatory Minimums

- Hairless: every four to eight weeks
- Hair dogs: every four to six weeks
- Multilength Fur dogs: every six to twelve weeks
- Uniform Fur dogs: every twelve to sixteen weeks
- All dogs: as needed for nail trim, ear-hair removal and anal-sac expression
- Hair and Multilength Fur dogs: immediately go to a professional if you notice a profusion of mats on your dog.

NOTE: puppies should not visit a professional groomer, or anywhere else populated by many dogs, until they're fully vaccinated at approximately four months old. They are too vulnerable to diseases. Until then, wash, brush, play with and care for your puppy at home. Allow young Fido to recover from the spay or neuter procedure for ten days before bathing.

Special Occasions and Holidays

Your pooch enjoys celebrating holidays just as much as you do. Here are some suggestions to celebrate throughout the year.

JANUARY:

January is Bath Safety Month. Review the proper and prudent way to bathe your pooch.

1st: Start the New Year off on the right paw by resolving to pamper your pooch with regular home grooming, using my fail-safe techniques and suggestions.

5th: Treat your dog to an extra-long stroll to celebrate the day Snoopy first walked on two legs in the *Peanuts* cartoon (1956).

8th: It's Elvis' birthday. Even if he's not a hound dog, take your pooch for a spin!

15th: Celebrate the anniversary of Super Bowl I by playing catch with your dog.

21st: Observe National Hugging Day. Embrace every dog you see today.

27th: Today is famous toilet entrepreneur Thomas Crapper's birthday. Honor this important man by picking up leftover dog . . . well, um, you know . . . in your neighborhood.

FEBRUARY:

February is National Pet Oral Care Month. Celebrate by brushing your dog's teeth every day this month! If needed, schedule a professional teeth cleaning with your veterinarian.

February is also National Single and Searching Month. Allow a *responsible* single friend to walk your dog—dogs are date-magnets.

4th: Today is Thank a Mailman Day. Have your dog greet your mail carrier with a big kiss to make amends for the alleged historical pain and suffering purportedly inflicted by other canines.

7th: Make an extra effort to say hello to people as you walk your dog around your 'hood for Greet Your Neighbor Day.

14th: Buy your dog a special Valentine's Day treat, but absolutely no chocolate or sweets!

20th: Celebrate Love Your Pet Day. Treat your beloved pooch to a doggy massage to demonstrate the depths of your affection.

23rd: It's National Dog Biscuit Day. Take your pooch out to a fancy dog boutique for a gourmet dog biscuit or make some from scratch using Chef Art Smith's tasty recipe on pages 82–83.

MARCH:

March is American Red Cross Month. Purchase a Red Cross pet first-aid manual or review the one you already have.

March is also Poison Prevention Month. Refresh your knowledge about dangerous chemicals, plants, food, and poisons by reviewing chapter 6, "Keeping Fido Safe and Sound at Home," and by visiting the ASPCA's Poison Control Center Web site at www.aspca.org.

1st: Show your porcine pride and buy your pooch a new pig's ear for National Pig Day.

Second Sunday: Daylight saving time begins today. Set your clocks forward one hour, but don't subtract the lost hour from playtime with your dog!

17th: Kiss your dog even if he's not an Irish Setter; it's Saint Patrick's Day.

22nd: Today is National Goof Off Day. Forget your chores, reschedule meetings and ignore anything you are required to do today. Instead, take your dog to the park and enjoy being silly together.

22nd: The first public college of veterinary medicine in the United States was founded in 1858 at Iowa State University. Thank your veterinarian for caring for your pooch.

31st: Celebrate the 1889 inauguration of the Eiffel Tower by hugging a Poodle today. If no Poodle is available, hug your dog instead.

April:

April is a significant month for pets: April is Animal Cruelty Prevention Month, National Pet First-Aid Awareness Month and Pets Are Wonderful Month. Celebrate these initiatives by volunteering at an animal shelter, taking a pet CPR class and reminding your pooch daily how fabulous he is.

10th: Celebrate the founding of the ASPCA in 1866 by donating time, money or supplies to a local animal shelter or the ASPCA.

15th: It's Tax Day. Put your tax refund to good use and buy your dog a new toy.

22nd: Pitch in on Earth Day and help clean up your favorite dog park.

Last Friday: Observe National Arbor Day. Treat your pooch to a picnic under a tree at a local park, but don't let him lift his leg near the trunk.

May:

May is National Physical Fitness and Sports Month. Make an extra effort to exercise both yourself and your dog this month.

While you are exercising, remember that May is also Skin Cancer Awareness Month. Avoid exercising during hours of peak sun, dress both of you in protective clothing and slather on the sunscreen, human and canine.

First full week in May: Since 1915, the American Humane Association has sponsored Be Kind to Animals Week. Be kind to your pooch by pampering her with an extra full home grooming session and then be kind to a shelter animal by sending a donation or volunteering.

2nd: Treat your pal to dog-safe fruit for International Scurvy Awareness Day. (See chapter 6, "Keeping Fido Safe and Sound at Home," for ideas.)

5th: It's Cinco de Mayo. Even if you don't have a Mexican Hairless, a Peruvian Inca Orchid or a Chihuahua, kiss your pooch.

26th: Celebrate Neighbor Day by taking an elderly, busy or homebound neighbor's dog for a long walk.

Last Monday: Observe a moment of silence to remember the bravery, dedication and sacrifice of our fallen human and canine soldiers on Memorial Day.

JUNE:

June is National Trails Month, a perfect excuse for you and your pooch to go hiking and spend quality time together.

8th: It's Best Friend's Day. Treat your best friend to an extra-long walk and a new toy.

Friday Following Father's Day: Dress up the dog in a business suit, pack his briefcase and show him what you do all day on Take Your Dog to Work Day.

26th: The bristle toothbrush was invented today in 1498. Brush your dog's teeth, especially if you've been negligent with your canine dental duties.

27th: Happy birthday, Helen Keller. To honor this brave activist who also introduced the Akita to the United States, donate time, money or supplies to a shelter for disabled animals.

JULY:

July is National Hot Dog Month. Send a donation to a Dachshund rescue.

3rd: The Dog Days of summer begin today. Take your dog to romp in the water.

4th: Keep your pal safe on Independence Day. (See chapter 6, "Keeping Fido Safe and Sound at Home.")

10th: It's Hot Diggity Dog Day. Keep your dog cool and play catch inside.

AUGUST:

August is National Immunization Awareness Month. Verify that your dog's vaccinations are current. If not, promptly schedule a veterinarian appointment.

14th: David N. Mullany invented the Wiffle ball today in 1953. Grab a ball and practice fielding with your pooch.

15th: It's National Relaxation Day. Kick back with your canine.

Third Saturday: Today is National Homeless Animals Day. Visit an animal shelter and use your new grooming skills to help these dogs find their forever homes.

22nd: In honor of National Tooth Fairy Day, commit to brushing your dog's teeth every other day for the rest of the year. We both know you've been slacking off lately.

25th: Curl up on the couch with your pooch and watch Toto steal the show in *The Wizard of Oz*, which was released in the United States on this day in 1939.

SEPTEMBER:

September is National Pet Wellness Month. Review your dog's lifestyle and implement positive changes, such as increased exercise, less snacking and more teeth brushing. September is also National Hunger Awareness Month. Donate food to a local animal shelter.

4th: In 1888, George Eastman, the founder of Kodak, received a patent for the first roll-film camera. Use your new home-grooming skills to primp your dog and then snap his photo.

8th: Turn your dog into a beauty queen by treating her to an extra full home-grooming session or an appointment with a professional groomer to commemorate the first Miss America Pageant in 1921.

11th: Observe 9/11 Heroes Day. Pause for a moment of silence to remember the humans and canines who bravely assisted others on this day in 2001.

17th: Even if your pooch isn't a show dog, make him look like one with an extra-long bath and brushing session to commemorate the anniversary of the American Kennel Club, which was founded in 1884.

19th: Be extra silly with your favorite four-legged scallywag on International Talk Like a Pirate Day.

28th: Celebrate longtime animal rights activist Brigitte Bardot's birthday by volunteering at an animal shelter. In the evening, curl up with your pooch and watch one of her movies.

OCTOBER:

October is National Good Nutrition Month. Review your dog's diet and nutritional requirements with your veterinarian. Then, purchase nutritious food and treats.

Early October: Attend a Blessing of the Animals event in honor of Saint Francis of Assisi, patron saint of animals and ecology. Many churches offer nondenominational ceremonies.

5th: Play catch with your dog to celebrate the first radio broadcast of the World Series in 1921.

7th: Commemorate the 1943 premiere of *Lassie Come Home* by cuddling on the couch and watching the movie with your furry friend.

31st: Plan your Halloween activities with your dog's safety in mind. (See chapter 6, "Keeping Fido Safe and Sound at Home.")

NOVEMBER:

November is Adoption Awareness Month. Volunteer at a local animal shelter's adoption event or primp the dogs beforehand.

First Sunday: Daylight saving time ends today. Set your clocks back one hour and play or cuddle with your pooch for an extra sixty minutes.

5th: Remember, remember the Fifth of November. . . . Today is Guy Fawkes Day in England. Forgo the fireworks; light a fire in your fireplace and curl up with a dog of English heritage or, if one is not conveniently located, any pooch will do.

11th: Celebrate Veterans Day. Observe a moment of silence to honor our canine soldiers who bravely served their country alongside the heroic human troops.

12th: Mark the anniversary of the first professional football game in 1892, when the Allegheny Athletic Association defeated the Pittsburgh Athletic Club 4–0. Enjoy the fall weather and toss a doggy football with your pooch.

13th: Observe World Kindness Day. Be kind to an elderly or busy neighbor and take her dog along on your daily walk.

15th Today is America Recycles Day. Gather plastic grocery-store bags and bring them to a shelter for poop cleanup.

Third Thursday: It's the Great American Smokeout. Stop smoking and protect your pooch from the perils of secondhand smoke.

Fourth Thursday: Give thanks for your canine pal as you celebrate Thanksgiving. Keep your pooch away from the garbage and turkey bones. At least make some effort to minimize his people-food intake.

DECEMBER:

December is Safe Toys and Gifts Month. Inspect your dog's toys and chews for wear and tear. Purchase safe replacements. Review the holiday safety rules in chapter 6, "Keeping Fido Safe and Sound at Home."

5th: Lend a hand at a local animal shelter for International Volunteer Day.

12th: Celebrate animal rights activist Bob Barker's birthday. Be like Bob and advise everyone you encounter today about the benefits of spaying or neutering their pets.

25th: Celebrate a safe and fun Christmas with your furry friends.

29th: The first Y.M.C.A. in the United States opened in Boston in 1851. Exercise with your dog while listening to "Y.M.C.A." by the Village People. Feel free to dress up as my favorite, the construction worker.

12.
Helpful Hints for Home Dog-Care Success

Know Thy Dog

Caring for your dog is not a one-size-fits-all proposition. Rather, it requires you to tailor the experience to fit your dog's *particular* body, mind and spirit. It's fairly straightforward to recognize Fido's physical features and fine-tune his care accordingly. Dogs range in size from tiny to huge, and we've already separated coats into Hair, Uniform Fur and Multilength Fur categories (see chapter 3, "Why and When to Care for Your Dog"). Understanding Fido's natural predisposition, personality and mental state, however, is trickier, but fascinating. You must see Fido for who he *is*, not who you want him to be.

Contemplate Fido's age, breed, health, life history, stage of life, attitude and exposure to grooming. Moreover, consider how he responds to new situations and his physical fitness too. He'll have to stand, sit, get up, turn around, be still, lie on his side and tolerate poking and prodding all over his body. Once you understand Fido's personality and capabilities, it's easy to develop and maintain a dog-care routine that maximizes everyone's fun and enjoyment while keeping Fido clean, healthy and pampered.

To complete this task, there's no need to dust off your twenty-three-volume set of *The Standard Edition of the Complete Psychological Works of Sigmund Freud*. We're relying on a more authoritative source: Walt Disney. To understand Fido's personality, imagine your pooch as Snow White or one of the Seven Dwarfs.

Easygoing

Perhaps the grooming gods have been good to you and your furry pal is a Snow White rather than a Grumpy. Like Snow White, your dog is easygoing and adaptable no matter how strange or uncomfortable the circumstance. It's unlikely that Fido will be required to scrub the kitchen floors, but he will have to tolerate having his rear end cleaned, his genitals manhandled and his ear canal swabbed.

While you care for him, do everything in your power to maintain Fido's positive attitude and generous cooperation. If you accidentally shoot water up his nose or pull too hard on a mat, don't make a huge fuss. Instead, take a break and distract the dog with praise and treats. Then, pick up where you left off.

Occasionally, an easy dog will decide that he no longer enjoys being groomed. Often, the change occurs for no discernible reason. Your pooch is not being difficult or exacting his revenge because you cut his last play session short. Rather, he's probably acting out of fear. Think back: did you accidentally contact a sensitive area one too many times when you brushed him? Did you or someone else forget to monitor the water temperature during his last bath? Perhaps the Poodle at the park told him the truth about what's happening to his anal glands.

Whatever the reason, if your pooch suffers a grooming setback, **never** discipline or scare him. Instead, gather every ounce of patience you can muster and enter grooming rehab. Slowly reintroduce the problematic task over a few sessions and be extra-careful and considerate. Remember back when you taught your pooch to love grooming the first time. Rehab can be frustrating, especially when Fido's grooming tolerance changes inexplicably. But I know you can do it, since you have Fido's best interests at heart. In no time, your pooch's tail will wag when it's time for grooming.

Dogs with Physical Limitations

Dopey looks and acts different from other dwarfs. He's mute and beardless. He shuffles his feet, stumbles and has trouble keeping up. And he's always the last in line. Despite his name, Dopey is not dim-witted at all. Rather, he's misunderstood and doing the best he can, just like a dog with physical limitations.

Physically challenged dogs require the same care and maintenance as any other dog—just with a bit of special handling to meet their special needs. Consider how Fido's bodily limitations affect his ability to endure the physical demands of grooming, such as standing, sitting and balancing. Then, modify each task to make him feel less vulnerable and more comfortable and confident. For instance, if Fido has three legs, climb into the tub with him so he can sit during his bath. In addition, brush him and clean his eyes and ears while he's reclining.

Blind dogs are extra sensitive to sound, so choose air-drying over blow-drying. Talk continuously in a soothing tone to calm a blind dog because he can't see what you're doing. If Fido is deaf, position yourself in his line of sight at all times so he's never startled by your appearance or sudden movements. With forethought and planning, your physically challenged dog will trust you and truly enjoy the physical and emotional benefits of grooming.

Puppy

Like Happy, your puppy is cheerful, bubbly, silly, energetic and hungry for fun. He's a clean slate with no negative experiences to overcome. Indeed, he's at a grooming crossroads. It's as if he's standing at the fateful, dusty intersection of U.S. 61 and U.S. 49 in rural Mississippi, where Robert Johnson sold his soul to the devil to become the greatest blues guitar player ever. Unlike Robert Johnson, however, your pup is standing in your home grooming station waiting for you to decide which grooming road he'll travel.

It is the rare puppy that will begin his grooming career by sitting still and cooperating the entire time you're working with him. He'd rather be playing. Thus, the manner in which you introduce each task will determine his lifelong attitude toward grooming, or any other activity for that matter. If his early experiences are scary, stressful and painful, your pup will quickly learn to hate and fear grooming. If, however, he associates grooming with pleasure, treats and your positive attention, he'll flourish and enjoy a lifetime of grooming. Carefully heed my advice and you'll lead your puppy down the right path in grooming and in all aspects of his life.

||||||||||||||||||||||||||||||||||||||||||||||||||||||||||||||||||||||||||||||||||||||||||||||||||||||||||||||||||||||||||||||||||||||||

Puppy-Coat Primer

Your new puppy sure is cute—right down to his fuzzy coat. Although puppy coats don't shed or mat much, now is the time to introduce grooming. When a puppy's coat matures at about nine to twelve months, it undergoes a drastic change. For some puppies, the transformation seemingly occurs overnight. For others, the changes to the texture, length and fullness are gradual and barely noticeable.

Waiting for the mature coat before you initiate grooming is irresponsible *and* foolish. (And in some places this type of behavior warrants thirty days in the public stocks.) If you've failed to establish a regular grooming routine or haven't even bothered to introduce your pup to a brush or a bath, you, my friend, are in for a rude awakening. Once the coat changes, your pup will be uncomfortable and embarrassed by his uneven, unsightly coat. Moreover, if Fido is a Hair or Multilength Fur dog, his new coat will mat and tangle in no time flat. All too often, I have puppies come in for a haircut and leave with a complete shave down because their owners failed to prepare for the coat change.

Your pup will be wearing his adult coat before you can blink. Slowly introduce all grooming tasks and establish an adult grooming routine as soon as possible. In addition, once he's fully vaccinated at about four months old, schedule your puppy's first professional grooming appointment. By the time his coat is mature, he'll already love being groomed.

||||||||||||||||||||||||||||||||||||||||||||||||||||||||||||||||||||||||||||||||||||||||||||||||||||||||

Older Dogs

Your older dog has been around the block a few times and he's beginning to show signs of wear and tear. He tires easily, and like Sleepy, he'd rather be snoozing than standing in a bathtub. Like the bespectacled Doc, elderly dogs experience vision changes and are easily confused. Your older dog may also begin to resemble Doc with a scraggly gray beard.

Senior Fido desperately needs your help. After all, there's no AARP for dogs and you made a lifelong commitment to him. His age-related infirmities aren't insurmountable obstacles that permit you to slack off. Instead, adjust your grooming routine to accommodate Senior Fido's physical and emotional changes. If Fido's joints are stiff, turn up the heat before you bathe him, and support his back as you assist him in and out of the tub. Allow him to rest as you work, since he tires easily and he may no longer have the stamina to stand for extended grooming sessions. Allocate extra time to account for Fido's slower pace. Rather than placing him on an elevated surface, brush him while he's lying on his bed or the floor.

Senior Fido's coat becomes sparse, dry and brittle and his skin becomes thinner as he ages, so use moisturizing shampoo and wield grooming tools with extra care. He may develop tumors and growths seemingly overnight, so inspect him more often. Senior Fido is less active and his nails are less likely to wear down, so you'll have to schedule additional pedicure appointments. If his hearing is failing, stand so he can see you.

Meet with your veterinarian and discuss strategies to keep Senior Fido comfortable, happy, active and healthy as he ages. Proper grooming is but one element of a larger plan to increase Fido's quality of life as he enters his golden years. The doctor may suggest additional tactics, such as dietary changes, orthopedic bedding or medication that can slow or control the effects of aging.

Inexperienced, Abused or Neglected Dogs

Perhaps Fido has been around long before you began reading my book and learned the importance of grooming. Maybe your newly rescued dog has an uncertain history that rendered him afraid of intimate contact. Whatever the reason, if Fido has minimal grooming experience or has been abused or neglected, he'll need extra care and you'll need extra patience. Like Bashful, Fido is scared, nervous, shy and uncertain how to act when attention is paid to him, especially in the grooming context. Don't expect a dog with limited grooming exposure to behave like a veteran.

Observe Fido carefully and learn what makes him bashful like Bashful. Fido may tremble when he hears running water or cower at the sight of a brush or an open hand. Once you discover the cause, rehabilitate him with a slow and extended introduction that demonstrates that grooming is pleasant and fun. Let Fido sniff the toothbrush or play in the water—just for fun. If he's afraid of physical contact, work with him over days or weeks by touching him gently throughout the day. Over time, Fido will feel less vulnerable and begin to trust you. If, despite your valiant efforts, Fido cannot overcome his past, talk to your veterinarian about other options, such as professional rehabilitation with an animal behaviorist.

Recently, a local dog rescue brought a ten-year-old black terrier to my shop. We knew nothing about her other than that she'd been picked up as a stray. By the looks of her scruffy, moth-eaten coat, she had rarely if ever received any care.

Because of her uncertain history, I knew I must be especially gentle and slow. While I worked, I constantly praised her, lovingly stroked her and spoke with a soothing voice. Had I not been mindful of her past, she might have bitten, cowered, flopped around like a fish out of water or even lost control of her bowels—all things I've seen happen when a groomer is not sensitive to a dog's history. My gentle touch and constant explanation of my actions quickly gained the terrier's trust. She even let me wash her three times in a row. I think she truly enjoyed the massage as I worked in the shampoo. When I was finished, she was relaxed and happy. She knew that she looked good and she certainly felt marvelous. All it took was some extra TLC! This dog is now enjoying life in a wonderful new home and I'm confident she'll look forward to future grooming sessions.

Sick Dogs

Sneezy's uncontrollable bouts of hay fever interfered with his job at the diamond mine. Although Fido's occupation, which in this case is cooperating during grooming, may not be as strenuous as Sneezy's or regulated by OSHA, an illness can impede Fido's ability to satisfy his duties. Whenever Fido is under the weather, modify your home grooming routine. For example, if Fido has an eye infection, you'll have to temporarily alter his daily eye care according to the veterinarian's instructions. If Fido vomits due to a minor stomach bug, spot wash his beard. Save the full bath for when he's feeling better.

If Fido has a chronic or serious illness, talk to your veterinarian. Some illnesses necessitate major alterations to Fido's grooming routine. For example, if Fido has a bleeding disorder, the veterinarian may recommend that Fido visit a professional groomer for nail clipping or ear-hair removal, since these tasks can draw blood if performed improperly. If Fido has a heart condition, he may not be able to withstand long grooming sessions, or he may be less maneuverable if he has hip dysplasia. Therefore, if Fido isn't healthy, *always* discuss your grooming routine with your veterinarian *before* you begin, and check in as Fido's health changes.

Aggressive or Truly Difficult Dogs

Last but not least, we have Grumpy, the easily annoyed, stubborn dwarf who is quick to anger. I won't lie to you—grooming a Grumpy dog is challenging and demanding. In fact, it can be downright dangerous if Fido is a biter. Virtually all dogs, however, can be trained to overcome aggressiveness and other serious behavioral issues if you're willing to devote the necessary time and effort. You promised to care for your furry friend for better or for worse, in sickness and in health, so here's your chance to shine. Besides, if you ignore Fido's grumpiness, you won't groom him and his health and well-being will suffer. He'll be uncomfortable and dirty and his behavior will deteriorate. The sweat equity you invest in helping Fido overcome his grumpiness will return to you tenfold.

Dogs bite when they're scared or in pain. It's an instinctual reaction, not a reflection of your dog's feelings about you. Once Fido has learned to overcome his fear or he's feeling better, the behavioral problem will often cease. If Fido has genuine aggression issues, he'll growl, lift his lips or refuse to break eye contact when you approach him. His fur may even stand on end. If Fido snaps or nips while he's crouching with his tail tucked all the way under his rear end or flattens his ears and averts his eyes, he's afraid but submissive. He's probably not about to attack; he's just trying to escape the situation and telling you to stay away *or else*.

For your own safety and that of the dog, don't force the issue if Fido exhibits any signs of aggression or fear. Respond with a tranquil voice and allow him some breathing room. Don't leave him unattended; just back away. Once he calms down, approach him cautiously and remove him from the grooming area. Call your veterinarian to discuss behavior modification options. Aggressive or overly fearful dogs require professional training and rehabilitation.

Prepare Fido for the Sensations of Grooming

Let's face it. If your only tactile contact with Fido involves an absentminded pat on the head as you race by into the kitchen to grab a snack during a commercial break, Fido won't understand why you're manhandling him during the bath—he won't tolerate it either. From the first moment Fido arrives in your life, begin touching, petting and handling him and allow other people to do the same.

Devote *at least* sixty minutes *over the course* of each day to playing with and handling your dog. This shouldn't be a chore; pampering our dogs and making them happy is our duty. As you play with and pet your dog, specifically handle the areas that are involved in dog care. Use a soft touch, continuous praise and treats. Rub Fido's ears, pet his face, handle his paws, pads and nails and pat his belly, rear end and tail. Run your fingers over his lips, teeth and gums. Desensitizing your dog to contact with his mouth makes dental care and administering pills easier *and* trains him to allow someone to reach in and remove dangerous (or gross) objects. Gently run your fingers through his coat down to the skin like a brush.

Fido will appreciate all the tactile contact and attention, and his trust and bond with you will grow exponentially—especially if you provide praise and treats. And a dog that's comfortable with physical contact in *nongrooming* situations will be cooperative and relaxed while you groom and care for him. He will be so well socialized and accepting of physical contact that visits to the professional groomer and veterinarian will be easy and enjoyable too.

Begin Grooming Immediately, but Slow and Steady Wins the Race

Whether he's a new pup or an elder statesman, Fido's arrival at your home is full of new experiences, people, sights and smells. There's certainly no need to perform every dog-care task on the first day. Certainly, Fido is unlikely to develop the trust, patience and tolerance required for proper grooming overnight. Moreover, home dog care may be new to you too. So no rushing—accidents occur when you rush. Introduce each grooming task s-l-o-w-l-y over days or weeks.

Even if Fido has been in the family for years, there's no time like the present to adopt safe and proper dog-care techniques. You *can* teach an old dog (and owner) new tricks!

Practice Makes Perfect

The more you groom, the easier it becomes. Of course, this is true if you exercise restraint, exhibit monumental patience and follow good grooming practices. Since you're reading my book, you'll have nothing to worry about. Each time your dog enjoys a positive grooming experience, his cooperation and pleasure increase and your job becomes easier.

Similarly, your comfort and confidence grow with each grooming session, especially if you employ my techniques and adhere to my recommendations. Practice *does* make perfect, so lather, rinse, repeat and repeat and repeat. Sure, you'll stumble along the way, but that's no sweat. Your diligence and hard work will make you a home-grooming success story.

Formulate, Establish and Sustain a Grooming Routine

Think of grooming as scheduled quality time with Fido. Except for the full-blown grooming sessions, most of the tasks require only a few minutes and they are fabulous bonding opportunities for you and your pooch. Dogs are creatures of habit. As such, they're less anxious and more comfortable when they know what to expect. If possible, try to set aside the same time every day for grooming, which allows Fido to learn the routine quickly. At home, I care for Zeke and Arthur after dinner, when they are relaxed and a little tired.

There's no need to hang your head in shame if you fall off the grooming wagon. Just apologize to Fido, climb right back on and take up where you left off. Remember, however, that skipping certain tasks, such as brushing, can quickly become huge problems. Mats can materialize faster than green grass through a goose, so don't waste any time fretting about all the missed grooming sessions. If things truly get out of hand, visit a professional, who can usually solve the grooming problem and help you get back on track at home.

Stop in the Name of Love

When Fido revolts during grooming, he's probably not being difficult. He may be hurt, be tired or just need a break. Therefore, **always** cease all grooming activities the moment that Fido exhibits any sign of discomfort or pain like crying, whimpering, flinching or nipping. Likewise, stop if you discover a potential medical problem, such as a wound, growth or skin irritation. Contact your veterinarian before you continue to groom. (See chapter 14, "The Inspection Connection.")

If Fido is under the weather and today is dental-care day, waiting until tomorrow won't cause his teeth to fall out. If he wakes up from his nap and he's bouncing off the walls ready to play, postpone a long brushing session. Forced grooming is always a bad idea. Fido will remember the stress and he's less likely to cooperate the next time. Worse, he'll learn to hate grooming, and as you know, grooming is critical to maintaining your dog's body, mind and spirit.

If Fido is merely rambunctious or antsy, he's usually requesting a rest, so take five at the next convenient break in the action; rinse out the shampoo *before* you stop. In most cases, you'll be able to continue after you assess the situation and allow Fido to calm down. The break may last only a few minutes. If you or Fido woke up on the wrong side of the bed or if either of you is having a bad day, try again tomorrow.

Pushing Fido to his emotional breaking point is immoral and dangerous and often results in injuries, usually to you. Moreover, struggling and fighting cause both you and your pooch to shy away from future grooming. It's better to cease all grooming activities than risk permanent emotional damage.

Your goal is to cultivate Fido's love of grooming. Accordingly, Fido must *never* have any negative associations with dog care. While grooming, or whenever you're dealing with your dog, remain composed even in the face of catastrophe. Never act like a jerk or hit or yell at your dog. Fido isn't complaining to be annoying or misbehaving "on purpose." Something is wrong and he's counting on you to find out what's going on and react accordingly.

|||||||||||||||||||||||||||||||||||||||||||||||||||||||||||||||||||||||||||||||||||||||||||||||||||||||

What Happens Away from Home Matters Too

Unpleasant incidents with his professional staff significantly affect your dog's attitude and behavior during home dog care. So before each appointment, deliver a State of the Dog address. Discuss Fido's current health and personality and alert the veterinarian, trainer, professional groomer or caregiver to any changes. This will ensure that Fido's grooming and dog-care experiences outside the home are also positive and don't spoil all your hard work at home.

|||||||||||||||||||||||||||||||||||||||||||||||||||||||||||||||||||||||||||||||||||||||||||||||||||||||

Take Care of Business Before You Begin

Both you and your dog must be physically comfortable before embarking on any grooming task. Accordingly, Fido must visit the little puppy's room before he enters your home grooming station. Play or exercise with him too so he's tired, but not exhausted. If Fido has ants in the pants, he's unlikely to remain still while you care for him. Refrain from feeding Fido immediately before you begin. Treats will be more persuasive if he's a bit hungry.

Your comfort is important too. Once you begin grooming, leaving Fido unattended is strictly forbidden. So be sure that *you* are fed and watered, are comfortably clothed and have visited the facilities too. Stretch, have a glass of wine or do whatever you need to be relaxed, animated and entertaining.

Be Miss Congeniality

Dogs are highly intuitive and respond to touch, body language and tone of voice. If you radiate stress, impatience or frustration, Fido will react accordingly. Conversely, if you're upbeat, patient and positive, Fido will be ready to join in the grooming merriment. Throughout the grooming session, praise and cuddle your dog. Take a deep breath and relax. Liberally bestowing treats and affection makes your pooch more amenable to grooming. Indeed, he'll quickly learn that it pays to cooperate.

I always talk to the dog while I'm grooming. Speak with a smile on your face. Your upbeat words will engage Fido and distract him. Feel free to share the latest gossip with your dog. I promise you, he'll never repeat what you whisper about your boss!

Add music to the party and Fido may join you when you belt out your favorite tune. Dogs love to be serenaded and they won't complain if you miss the high notes. Please, however, refrain from singing heavy metal; Fido may break into wild head banging and the next thing you know, the walls are soapy and Fido has come back from an all-nighter with multiple body piercings and a naked-cat tattoo.

So, sing, dance or do whatever it takes to keep Fido's tail wagging. You may even burn a few extra calories in the process. Let loose and enjoy yourself. Without a doubt, Fido will be enjoying himself so much that he won't notice that you're cleaning his ears or lifting his tail to remove stinky debris.

Disciplinary Dos and Don'ts

Physical discipline is **never** allowed, no matter what the circumstance. Rather, use positive reinforcement. Dogs crave attention from their pack leader, so use this to your advantage by rewarding all good behavior and ignoring all bad behavior. I don't care how mad you are—if Fido escapes from the tub and shakes the water off on your new rug, or if he nips your hand when you brush too close to his anus, you must be absolutely stoic and unflappable. Dogs' ears are acutely sensitive; they're expert body-language interpreters. So utter no angry sounds and don't allow the smile to fade from your face. Likewise, there's no fist clenching, hand-wringing, swearing under your breath, yelling, screaming, carrying on or adopting a belligerent stance or tone of voice. Some dogs view *any* attention as desirable, even if it's negative.

When Fido is cooperative, acknowledge his good behavior and patience with pats, praise and treats. In addition, offer Fido your undivided attention while you care for him. Grooming is no time for multitasking. Fido is more likely to relax and enjoy himself if you turn off the TV, ignore the phone and focus on him. This one-on-one time enhances your relationship, builds trust and fosters a strong bond.

13.
Setting Up Your Home Grooming Station

Consider yourself enlisted in home-grooming boot camp. Here, you'll learn how to care for every inch of your best pal. There are no push-ups or locker inspections in this brigade, just good, clean sudsy fun. Your first mission is to prepare your grooming station. Reconnoiter your home and inventory the available sinks, bathtubs and showers. Your home grooming station doesn't need to be fancy—a simple basement utility sink will do for bathing and the (clean) floor is fine for brushing and other tasks. What truly matters is the preparation you devote to assembling your grooming station, the products and tools you stock it with and the care and patience you exhibit while using it.

Where, Oh Where, Should I Groom?

Making smart choices for your home grooming station starts the process off on the right paw. First and foremost (and this may sound so obvious that you're surprised I'm even mentioning it, but you'd be doubly surprised to know how many people don't think of it either), select an area that can get wet, such as a bathroom or utility room. And when I say "wet," I mean soaked—hello, typhoon season! Bathing is an extremely soggy procedure: your dog *will* shake, you *will* splash and at least until you perfect your technique, the floor will be soaked. Honey, this is not a job to be performed in your new Prada dress and suede Jimmy Choos. Come prepared for wet conditions. Wear an apron or old clothes (or both), have a pile of clean towels at the ready and move away, far away, any items that are not waterproof. Out of an abundance of caution, remove all electric appliances from the bathing area. Indeed, **never** use a blow-dryer or other electric appliance in or near water. I'm sure you know this, but my coauthor, the lawyer, insists on including disclaimer language.

Aside from cleaning your dog, one of your main goals is to prevent escapes. Nothing tarnishes a positive grooming experience faster than a wet dog rampaging through your home. Thus, be certain that your grooming area can be securely sealed. And when I say "secure," I mean assume that your dog is channeling Harry Houdini. I swear that all dogs possess opposable thumbs that they secrete away until they can be used as an escape aid during bath time. Moreover, confirm the area is well lit so you can see every detail of your dog and detect when he releases those secret thumbs.

Your chosen grooming area should also allow easy access to the dog. Ideally, you'll need to stand easily over your dog, turn him 360 degrees and keep him under control while grooming. If you're short, have a sturdy chair or stool at the ready. If you're tall, use an elevated washing surface. If you'll be on your knees, use a cushion. The tub or shower area must comfortably accommodate your dog. So, contrary to what we've all heard, size *does* matter. For a small dog, a (*very* clean) kitchen sink may be adequate. If, however, Fido resembles an offensive lineman, you may need to outsource to a do-it-yourself dog wash. An enclosed shower stall is another good bathing option as long as you're not too shy to shower with your dog.

An easily accessible water source is another essential consideration. No matter how you slice it, a thorough bath involves water, specifically lots and lots of *clean* water. Pressure and temperature control are also critical.

In addition to the bath portion of your job, you'll need a place to perform all the other daily, weekly and monthly grooming tasks, such as brushing, inspections and eye, ear and paw maintenance. The space must have a flat, nonskid surface that allows you easy access to your dog. You don't need a professional grooming table. Instead, you can use the floor, counters, couches, beds or any other surface that is comfortable for you and your furry pal.

Finally, your home grooming station must include appropriate tools and products. Selecting these items for your particular dog is not easy, and can be overwhelming if you allow it to be. The aisles of pet-supply stores are crammed with grooming products and gadgets, most of which are superfluous. Similarly, beware of charlatans trying to sell you expensive professional tools. These tools are dangerous in an amateur's hands. Later on in this chapter, I'll discuss the tools and products that you *actually* need.

Make it a habit to assess the state of your grooming station *before* you fetch Fido. Once you begin, you can **never** leave Fido unattended. Everything must be cleaned, prepped and easily accessible at the start of each session. Always retain and follow the cleaning instructions for your tools and products. In addition, confirm that you have enough product on hand to complete the job. I can guarantee that Fido will *not* wait patiently in the tub while you fumble for a new bottle of shampoo.

Checklist: Tools and Products

Tool and Equipment Must-Haves
- ✓ Brush
- ✓ Comb
- ✓ Two pairs of blunt-nosed scissors
- ✓ Nontoxic, dog-safe disinfectant
- ✓ Canine nail file
- ✓ Toothbrush
- ✓ Canine toothpaste
- ✓ Ear-wash product
- ✓ Natural cotton balls
- ✓ Natural cotton swabs
- ✓ Sterile eyewash
- ✓ Clean sponges
- ✓ Small container for diluting shampoo
- ✓ Hose with an adjustable sprayer
- ✓ Drain screen
- ✓ Lots of clean towels
- ✓ Rubber mat
- ✓ Pad for knees
- ✓ Blow-dryer
- ✓ Notebook and pen
- ✓ Phone, pet first-aid kit and emergency information
- ✓ Nutritious treats
- ✓ Toothy smile, patience and praise

Grooming Product Must-Haves
- ✓ Hypoallergenic shampoo
- ✓ Specialty shampoo, if desired
- ✓ Conditioner
- ✓ Detangler

Optional Tools and Products

- ✓ Nail-cutting supplies: canine nail clippers with extra blades and a coagulating (styptic) product
- ✓ Ear-hair-removal supplies: two straight-nosed hemostats, dog-safe disinfectant and ear powder
- ✓ Ophthalmic ointment or mineral oil and dropper
- ✓ Bathing noose
- ✓ Grooming table, pole and noose
- ✓ Paw pad moisturizer

Prepare Your Grooming *Mise en Place*

In the culinary world, the French term *mise en place* means "everything in its place." In other words, assembling, preparing and laying out everything you need to cook: ingredients, tools and equipment. At the beginning of each shift, the chef measures, chops, slices and dices all necessary ingredients. He also gathers all the bowls, pots, pans, knives and other tools and equipment required to prepare the meals. This vital initial step allows the chef to work efficiently without having to interrupt his work flow.

Similarly, in grooming, we take ingredients (you and your dog) and equipment (grooming products and tools), and use them according to a recipe (grooming procedures). And, voilà, we achieve the desired result, not a meal, but a clean, gorgeous and delighted dog. Like a chef, before you begin, prepare your home grooming *mise en place*. If you jump right in, you may discover that you're missing a key ingredient at an inopportune time. If you have to leave Fido in the tub while you hunt for a towel, he will not be there when you return.

||||||||||||||||||||||||||||||||||||||||||||||||||||||||||||||||||||||||||||||||||||||||||||||||||||||||

How to Choose Tools and Products: A Quick Lesson

- Take your time.
- Read the labels with an extremely critical eye.
- Be skeptical of extravagant claims and alleged quick fixes.
- Before purchasing, hold the tool in your hand to verify that it's comfortable for *you* to use.

- Check each tool for sharp bristles, teeth or edges.
- If the item is expensive, wait to see if you really need it.
- Don't be afraid to ask questions and consult with your professional groomer and veterinarian.

|||||||||||||||||||||||||||||||||||||||||||||||||||||||||||||||||||||||||||||||||||||||||||||||||||||||

Your Grooming *Mise en Place*: Tools and Equipment

Brush

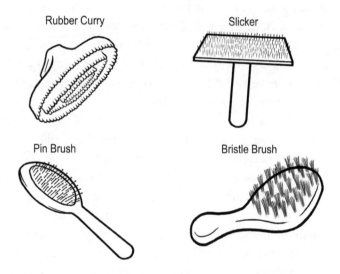

Rubber Curry

Slicker

Pin Brush

Bristle Brush

Brushing is an integral step in grooming, and using the correct brush is critical. Contrary to what consumers are typically told, you *don't* need to purchase multiple or highly specialized brushes in order to successfully care for your dog at home. For most dogs, one brush will do the trick.

One important tip: always replace a brush immediately if you notice bent, broken or missing bristles. A damaged brush will harm your dog's coat or injure her sensitive skin. Moreover, **never brush a wet dog.** Wet canine skin is too pliable and easily injured. We don't want Fido to ever fear the brush or brushing. With that in mind, here are the brushes you have to choose from, and their most useful applications.

Rubber Curry: A rubber curry is used *exclusively* for Uniform Fur dogs with *very* short coats, such as Dalmatians, Dobermans, Weimaraners, Boxers and bully breeds. On longer coats, the curry will pull and damage the fur. The curry's short rubber tips stimulate blood flow to the skin and oil glands and bestow a relaxing massage. It also grabs the dead fur before it can fall off the dog and all over your floors and clothes. A curry works on dry or wet fur, as long as it is very short. A curry is the only brush that you're *ever* permitted to use on wet fur. To clean a curry, rinse it with soapy water and dry it before storing.

Slicker Brush: Yes, at first glance, a slicker resembles a medieval torture device. Despite its intimidating appearance, however, a properly wielded slicker is a grooming workhorse and safe for virtually all dogs. Nonetheless, my persnickety legal team compels me to include the following disclaimer: "If your dog is a Hairless breed, do not use a slicker brush on said dog. Indeed, do not bring said brush within five hundred yards of said dog." A slicker's wire bristles are flexible and designed to move away from the skin. That is, unless you are treating it like a rake and applying excessive pressure or brushing the same spot too many times.

Luckily, high-quality (and safe) versions of the slicker are reasonably priced. Slicker brushes are sold in a variety of head sizes and bristle lengths. A good slicker has a supple rubber pad and densely packed, flexible, fine wire bristles. Before purchasing a slicker, check the bristles on your arm to determine if they are overly sharp or leave scratches. The bigger the dog, the bigger the slicker that you can use. For small dogs and puppies use a small slicker, which has extremely flexible bristles and is the most gentle. Small slickers are also best for Hair dogs with thin, oily or sparse coats, such as Maltese, Yorkshire Terriers and Schnauzers, and for Uniform Fur dogs with very short coats. For all other dogs, purchase a medium-sized slicker. The larger bristles move through the thicker and longer coat more efficiently.

Remove the fur caught in your slicker after *each* use. You may wash your slicker as needed in the dishwasher. Verify that it is thoroughly dry before storage to prevent rust. In addition, slickers are delicate and the bristles can be easily crushed or bent if mishandled. Examine your slicker before each brushing session and throw it away if the bristles are damaged, so you don't scratch Fido's skin or break his fur.

Pin Brush: The bristles resemble metal or plastic pins with or without rubber-tipped ends. The pins are placed far apart on a pliable rubber base, which makes the brush gentle. A pin brush must be used only on a clean, dry coat.

A pin brush is a fine *additional* brush for Hair dogs with extremely long and thin coats, such as the Lhasa Apso, Shih Tzu, Tibetan Terrier or Yorkshire Terrier, because it keeps the coat full and voluminous without weeding out too much hair. Pin brushes, however, cannot remove mats or efficiently brush through other coat types. Therefore, pin brushes are useless for most dogs.

If you use a pin brush, remove the fur after each use. Occasionally rinse the brush with warm soapy water and air-dry before storing.

Bristle Brush: Bristle brushes have tightly packed bristles and resemble a human-hair brush. Although they're ubiquitous at pet shops and grocery stores, I don't use them for anything other than removing fur off my pants and neither should you. The bristles are too soft and too close together to do much good on a dog's coat. Don't waste your money on a bristle brush.

Comb

A comb is used *after* brushing a *dry* dog to check for stray tangles or mats. That's it! I don't ever want to hear that you used a comb to remove a mat or to break up tangles on a wet dog. When pushed to my limits, I quickly turn into Nurse Ratched.

I prefer combs with two different-sized teeth. Use the finer teeth around the face, mouth or other delicate areas and the larger teeth on the rest of the body. I choose stainless steel over plastic because metal combs don't transfer static to the coat. Before you purchase a comb, check the ends of the teeth to determine if they're sharp. Go ahead and test it on your arm to see if it scratches or scrapes. Look for a comb with rounded tips for safety.

After each use, wipe down the comb with a nontoxic, dog-safe disinfectant or wash it with hot, soapy water. Dry the comb before storage. Immediately replace the comb if it has missing or broken teeth.

Two Pairs of Blunt-Nosed Scissors

Scissors are available in so many shapes, sizes, colors and styles, it boggles the mind. Unless you plan on enrolling in grooming school or are studying the geometric aspects of hand-scissoring a Poodle into topiary, you can forgo the expensive "professional" models. Let's be honest: you're probably not qualified to give your dog a full-blown haircut anyway. You will be using scissors for *extremely* limited purposes: removing stubborn debris and small mats not too close to the skin and, in an emergency, trimming around Fido's eyes, ears or paw pads.

I recommend purchasing two pairs of metal scissors with blunt ends and reserving them for grooming use only. Blunt-nosed scissors minimize the chances that you'll shish kebab Fido. Designate one pair to use around the eyes and one pair for use on the rest of the body. Choose stainless steel scissors that won't rust in the wet grooming environment. In addition, your scissors must be small enough to maneuver around delicate areas, including eyes, ears, paws and rears. Many scissors are made with cushioned or ergonomic handles and these are fine unless they're outrageously priced. Hold several pairs to determine the best fit for your hand.

Clean scissors with a wet cloth soaked with nontoxic, dog-safe disinfectant or wash in hot, soapy water. Always thoroughly dry the blades before storing.

Nontoxic Dog-Safe Disinfectant

Keeping your tools and home grooming station clean is an important aspect of proper grooming and helps keep Fido healthy. Use any nontoxic, dog-safe disinfectant you like. You can even use plain old soap and hot water as long as you wash for at least thirty seconds. **Never** use the disinfectant *on your dog*.

Nail Tools

Everyone needs a canine nail file to repair the occasional broken or splintered nail. Don't use that old file at the bottom of your purse. Purchase a sturdy canine metal file and clean and dry it after each use.

As we'll discuss later on, I don't want you to trim your dog's nails. It's not that I don't trust you; it's just that nail cutting is a precarious and delicate task. OK, I admit it. I don't trust you—at least not yet. (See chapter 15, "Dirty Deeds Done Dirt Cheap . . . at Home.") In case you nevertheless insist on clipping Fido's nails at home, you will need a few supplies.

Nail clippers come in two basic styles: pliers and guillotine. I prefer the pliers type and find them easier to control. Don't even think about using human nail clippers. They are not made for a dog's thick nails and can inflict physical and emotional pain and suffering on you and Fido.

Whichever style you choose, purchase nail clippers with steel blades for safety and durability. Verify that the nail clippers are comfortable in your hands and that the blades are easy to replace. If the nail clippers don't include extra blades, purchase some. Carefully follow the manufacturer's cleaning instructions.

Home nail clipping also requires coagulating products, such as styptic pads, gel or powder, to stop bleeding when (I mean if) you sever the quick. Always keep your coagulating products tightly sealed. They absorb moisture and swiftly turn into rock if exposed to air.

Dental Kit

Dental care is essential to canine health and we'll discuss it at length in chapter 15, "Dirty Deeds Done Dirt Cheap . . . at Home." Convenience is the key to making doggy dental care a habit. Purchase a complete dental kit or create your own and store it in a plastic, ventilated case.

Fido's dental kit must contain a canine toothbrush and unexpired canine toothpaste. **Never** use human toothpaste on your dog. When swallowed, human toothpaste upsets sensitive canine stomachs and in large amounts fluoride can cause serious medical problems. Besides, why would you want to deprive Fido of liver- or poultry-flavored goo?

As for the brush, choose one that fits your dog's mouth and comfort level. Try a few out until everyone is happy. I prefer a soft-bristled nylon brush. If you have multiple dogs, each dog must have her own toothbrush. Wash and thoroughly air-dry the toothbrush after each session. Most brushes are dishwasher safe, which is a convenient sterilization method.

Ear-Wash Product

Routine ear care is a basic but critical home grooming activity that keeps your pooch healthy and infection free, which of course makes Fido happy, very happy.

I prefer liquid ear wash in squeeze bottles. Talk to your veterinarian or trusted professional groomer to determine which product is best for your dog. You'll use the ear wash before and after bathing and for weekly ear maintenance. I teach you how to clean ears in chapter 15, "Dirty Deeds Done Dirt Cheap . . . at Home."

Ear-Hair-Removal Supplies

It's normal for some dogs, especially Hair and Multilength Fur dogs, to grow hair *inside* their ears.

Ear-hair removal is controversial and canine professionals disagree as to whether it should be done at all. Most professionals, including me, however, agree that ear hair should not be removed at home because it's a difficult and painful procedure. (See chapter 15, "Dirty Deeds Done Dirt Cheap . . . at Home.")

If you are, nonetheless, dead set on removing Fido's aural hair yourself, you'll need a few special tools and products. Ear powder absorbs moisture so you can more easily grip the hair before yanking it out. Your veterinarian may prefer a specific brand or formulation, so inquire before you purchase a product. Carefully read the directions before you begin.

You'll need two hemostats so you don't cross-contaminate if one ear is infected. I prefer straight-jawed hemostats because they are easier to maneuver than the curved version. Your hemostats must be meticulously clean and dry before, during and after each use.

||||||||||||||||||||||||||||||||||||||||||||||||||||||||||||||||||||||||||||||||||||||||||||||||||||||

Billy's Product-Safety Rules and Regulations

- Use only canine products.
- Discard any expired product.
- Discard a product if the packaging is damaged, the product's appearance has changed or it smells rancid.
- Keep applicator tips scrupulously clean.
- Read labels and instructions before each use.
- Discuss products with your veterinarian and professional groomer before using them.

||||||||||||||||||||||||||||||||||||||||||||||||||||||||||||||||||||||||||||||||||||||||||||||||||||||

Natural Cotton Balls

If ears are unprotected during bathing, water collects inside Fido's ear canal and can cause nasty infections. Regular old-fashioned drugstore-variety *natural* cotton balls are an effective, economical water barrier. This is red Magic Marker territory: **always remove the cotton balls from Fido's ears when you conclude the bath**.

Natural cotton balls are also handy product applicators. Never use synthetic cotton, as the material easily frays and leaves behind irritating fiber residue.

Natural Cotton Swabs

Cotton swabs are **not** for canine ears. The temptation to push the swab too deep into the ear is difficult to overcome and you can quite easily damage your dog's eardrum. You'll use swabs *exclusively* to wash and dry inside any wrinkles, folds or flaps on your pooch's body and head. Never use synthetic swabs as they shed fibers.

Sterile Eyewash and Ophthalmic Ointment

You'll use sterile eyewash daily and in emergencies to clean Fido's eyes. Many different sterile eyewash formulations are available, so ask your veterinarian or professional groomer to recommend a preferred product.

Veterinarians often recommend that you treat a dog's eyes with an ophthalmic ointment or mineral oil (applied with a clean dropper) before bathing. These products create an invisible film barrier and protect the eyes from stray grooming products. I've been washing dogs for decades and I am well practiced, so I don't personally use these products. They are, however, available and safe to use provided that you are mindful of expiration dates, keep the applicator tip meticulously clean and vigilantly follow the directions. Immediately discard the product if the applicator or dropper touches anything, including the dog's eye.

Clean Sponges

I use sponges to apply shampoo. It is my trademark, and until today it was a closely held secret known only by my canine clients (I knew they'd keep it on the Q.T.). I use regular dish sponges *without* a scrubbing pad. They are available on the cheap at the grocery store.

Resist the temptation to grab the sponge from your kitchen sink; Fido does not want or need any additional dirt on his skin and coat. Likewise, once you've cleaned your dog's rear, use a fresh sponge for the rest of his body and never use the same sponge on multiple dogs.

I wash my sponges in the washing machine with bleach and hot water to ensure that they're disinfected. Once your sponges are clean, and I mean so clean that you would eat off them, dry them thoroughly. Whether you air-dry the sponges or pop them into a clothes dryer is irrelevant. What matters is that the sponges are hygienic and dry as a bone before storage. Sponges are cheap, so replace them often.

Small Container for Diluting Shampoo

As part of my signature sponge technique, I also use a small container to dilute shampoo before I apply it on the dog. The container doesn't need to be anything special. I actually cut the bottom off gallon milk jugs, leaving the sides about four inches tall, or wrist height. The container must be deep enough for you to dunk the entire sponge and wide enough to comfortably accommodate your hand. If you're crafting your own container, be mindful of sharp edges as you dunk.

Hose with an Adjustable Sprayer

A hose with an adjustable sprayer is an indispensable grooming tool. I use one at my shop and at home. The sprayer makes it easy to control water pressure and, thus, prevents you from power washing your dog. The sprayer also allows you to maneuver the water into every nook and cranny and rinse Fido's coat easily and thoroughly. As you'll learn, a meticulous rinse is crucial to proper grooming. If your budget is limited, this is the one extra accessory you should splurge on and it's fairly inexpensive. Of course, a bucket, quick hands and strong arms will work too.

Before Fido arrives in the tub, verify that the hose easily and securely attaches to your faucet and is long enough to reach all around him.

Drain Screen

Purchase and install a drain screen to catch the fur that washes off your pooch so your pipes don't clog. In a pinch, stuff soap-free steel wool into the drain.

Lots of Clean Towels

Bathing your dog is a wet activity, so be prepared. I always have at least five or six large clean towels and a few smaller ones at my grooming station. I use several for drying the dog, one for drying me and a few for drying the floor. No matter how pampered your pooch is, the towels need not match or be in pristine condition. They must, however, be clean and dry to start. Accordingly, resist the urge to grab the towel you used for your morning shower. The idea is to clean the dog, not have him smell like a used towel.

Rubber Mat

Slippery surfaces and wet dogs don't mix. Even the most seasoned dog squirms occasionally during her bath. To prevent any slips and falls, place a rubber mat on the washing surface. The Beagle around the corner could be a personal-injury attorney and I presume that you've never checked whether your homeowner's insurance would indemnify you under these circumstances. Moreover, your dog is more likely to enjoy the bath and remain calm if he has secure footing. Dry the mat after each use to prevent mold.

Pad for Knees

I want you to be comfortable too. Purchase a gardening pad or a stadium seat to protect your knees while grooming. These items are typically water-resistant and stand up to years of bathing. A rolled-up towel works fine too. Just protect your knees. You'll be hard-pressed to maintain Fido's cooperation and properly groom him if your knees are numb and stiff. If you're standing, knee protection is not necessary, at least not for the bath.

Blow-Dryer

Professional blow-dryers are expensive and superfluous, since most home groomers air-dry their dogs. Unless you have an unlimited grooming budget, your human hair dryer will work just fine as long as it has a *functioning* low-heat or no-heat setting.

Bathing Noose

There's no typographic error; you did just read the word "noose." Contrary to the rumors being spread by the neighbor's cat, Fido has nothing to fear, as you'll not use the noose for any nefarious purposes. A bathing noose is a useful tool if your dog will not stand or needs an additional incentive to stay in place. Trust me, you'll know right away if your dog requires supplemental restraint in the tub.

A noose is inexpensive and safe *if used correctly*. Under no circumstances should you use a choke collar and leash to restrain a disorderly dog in the bath. I had one client who refused to follow this advice for her nervous and extremely willful 120-pound German Shepherd. She fitted her dog with a choke collar and wrapped the leash around her bathtub faucet. Needless to say, the dog became agitated, the choke collar gripped his neck and he desperately tried to free himself. During the struggle, he actually tore the faucet clean off the wall and damaged the water pipes. My client spent hundreds of dollars on a plumber. *Sigh*—if only she had read my book!

A bathing noose resembles an adjustable collar and leash with either a hook or suction cup on the end. Unless you have purchased a grooming tub or installed a ring on your wall, you'll have no place to attach the hook. So, purchase a waterproof model with a suction cup. Moreover, if your dog struggles too hard, the noose will detach and choking injuries are less likely. **That said, never, and I mean not even for a split second, leave your dog unattended while in a noose.**

To use the bathing noose, place the "collar" portion around your dog's neck. Use the slide to tighten the noose, but it should never strain the neck. I find that a noose discourages bad bath behavior even when left extremely loose. Remember, the noose is a deterrent, not a punishment.

After the bath, hang the noose dry and put it away immediately, especially if you have small children. If you're gentle and loving while you groom, eventually your dog will actually like the bath and you'll retire the noose.

Grooming Table, Pole and Noose

I'll be the first to admit that a grooming table is useful, convenient and easy on the back and knees. I am, however, a professional and spend at least twelve hours a day caring for dogs. Do not forgo professional grooming or other essentials just to afford a grooming table. If, however, you have room in your grooming budget, feel free to purchase one. A grooming table provides a comfortable work space, especially if your dog requires extensive brushing, she is prone to mats or her coat is a debris magnet. The table requires a noose and a telescoping pole as well. The entire setup is a pricey proposition, so wait to see if you actually need it before spending the money.

Tables are useless for bathing and occupy a good deal of space. As we speak, your home offers many acceptable substitutes: floors, counters, couches, desks, tables and beds. Remember, though, **never leave your dog**

unattended on any elevated surface, whether it's your computer desk or a grooming table. Your pooch can seriously injure himself jumping off, especially while restrained in a noose. Again, this is red Magic Marker territory—underline this rule and memorize it.

Notebook and Pen

Use a dedicated notebook and pen to record information from all dog-care activities. Date each entry so you can easily compare the results over time and track subtle changes that may reveal serious medical problems. As you groom, jot down anything you want to remember for the next session or tell your vet. Bring your notebook to every veterinary appointment, as it contains precious health information.

Phone, Pet First-Aid Kit and Emergency Information

Keep a phone, first-aid kit and emergency information with you while you care for your dog in case a crisis arises. You cannot leave Fido unattended while you fetch a phone to call the veterinarian or look for your first-aid supplies.

Nutritious Dog Treats

I have consulted my lawyers and they solemnly swear that you will not be prosecuted for bribery under the narrow circumstances of home grooming. The idea here is to have fun, and dogs view food as fun (don't we all?). Therefore, dispense plenty of *nutritious* bite-sized treats while you care for your pooch. Do not, however, go hog wild and use an entire bag of snacks in one session. If you overindulge your dog, you may have to bathe her a second time due to the resulting gastric distress.

Toothy Smile, Patience and Praise

I cannot overemphasize the importance of bringing your biggest and best toothy smile and your happiest face to the grooming station. Dogs have an uncanny ability to sense mood and decipher the emotions relayed by our tone of voice and body language. If you're good-humored, patient, relaxed and cheerful, Fido will follow your lead. So pack your smiles in your grooming kit and heap tons of praise throughout the process.

Tool Don'ts

Grooming books, infomercials, shop owners and other so-called experts often tout rakes, splitters and blades as essential home grooming tools. Luckily, you're reading *my* book and won't be hoodwinked—you know that if you brush your dog regularly with a properly wielded slicker brush, these tools are unnecessary.

Consider it a red flag if a product name contains a menacing word, such as "rake," "razor," "breaker," "stripper" or "blade." Most of these tools are meant for *professional* groomers and can be downright dangerous in unpracticed hands. At first glance, these tools appear to offer easy solutions to aggravating grooming issues like shedding or matting. As Mom always said, "If it seems too good to be true, it probably is." These tools are easy to misuse and a poor substitute for frequent, correct brushing—not to mention sharp and dangerous if brandished with too much speed or pressure.

For instance, traditional shedding blades are just plain damaging. They are essentially a saw blade formed into an arch and attached to a handle—a design that's good for woodshop but bad for home grooming. In the park, I regularly see people vigorously wielding their shedding blade against the grain of the coat. This cuts the top of the coat clean off rather than merely thinning it. Besides, the saw blade is sharp and can wreak havoc on a dog that squirms or moves.

Although I'm forbidding *you* from hand-stripping Fido's coat or removing his undercoat ("carding"), Fido's professional groomer may occasionally perform these tasks. I want you to know what to look for when Fido visits your groomer. When hand stripping or carding, the groomer must move the tool *with the grain* of the coat. (See "Brush with the Grain" in chapter 15.) This allows the coat to lie flat and tight against the body. If Fido comes home looking like a Chia Pet with his coat sticking up in all directions, have a talk with your groomer.

I don't forbid deshedding tools, which are advertised to remove the dead fur trapped in a dog's coat, but I never employ them myself. They are harmful if overused or improperly employed, which is easy to do. In addition, these tools can easily break off or cut longer fur. You must, therefore, conscientiously follow the manufacturer's instructions. Rather than waste your money and worry about harming Fido's coat, do what I do: use your slicker brush, because it does essentially the same thing if you brush regularly and properly.

Now that I am on a roll, let's discuss professional grooming clippers, which are now marketed directly to dog owners. Even though most books aimed at the home groomer provide instructions purporting to show how simple it is to clipper your pooch into fancy breed hairdos, *I won't*. It's impossible to learn correct and safe clipping techniques by reading a few paragraphs and reviewing a few illustrations. Moreover, these haircuts require extensive expertise with scissors too. Even experienced groomers may refuse to execute these clips because they are so complex and time-consuming and require the use of advanced geometry. Don't try these elaborate clips (or even the simple ones) at home!

Moreover, in unpracticed hands, clippers can scratch, cut or burn skin, damage the coat or render your dog bald. I'm not being a snob; it takes countless hours of instruction and practice to wield clippers safely and effectively. I doubt that Fido will patiently wait while you fumble with your clippers and change blades just to shave a pom-pom on his butt. In reality, dogs twitch, move or just stretch out to see what you're doing. Contrary to what other books claim, sculpting your pooch into a work of art is *much* more involved than inserting a specific blade into the clippers and wrapping the legs in special nonstick veterinary tape.

A while back, a client brought in her sweet little white Poodle. The owner had watched the Westminster Dog Show and wanted her little Muffin to look exactly like the winner, who of course wore a fancy show cut. Figuring that clippers and a book were all she needed, she bought a pair and went to town. It was a fiasco and she left her poor Muffin shaved, red and swollen. The owner had dragged the clippers repeatedly over the same area, scraped up Muffin's skin and left her covered with clipper burns, which are red bumps like on a man's beard. Dogs, however, cannot use aftershave to clear up the reaction. Instead, dogs tend to exacerbate the clipper burn by licking, scratching or chewing.

I said to the owner, "Next time, call for help when you need to shave your Muffin." I sent Muffin and her owner directly to the veterinarian because Muffin's skin was in such dire shape. The owner never tried to shave her Muffin again.

If, despite my warnings, you decide to use any of the above-mentioned or similar tools, visit your professional groomer or veterinarian for chastisement and private instruction before you subject your dog to such hazards.

||||||||||||||||||||||||||||||||||||||||||||||||||||||||||||||||||||||||||||||||||||||||||||||||||||||||

Clipper Safety

Until Congress passes a constitutional amendment banning clipper use by anyone but a highly trained professional, I expect that some of you may be tempted. If you are one of those sorry souls who cannot resist the lure of the clippers, keep these safety tips in mind:

- Blades quickly become hot during use, so change them frequently and use a blade coolant or lubricant.
- Continually stop and check the temperature of the blade on your hand. Turn the clippers off first!
- Immediately stop using and discard dull, damaged or broken blades.
- Keep your hand moving and apply only gentle pressure to prevent pulling hair, raking the skin or abrasions.
- If your pet exhibits any sign of pain, turn off your clippers immediately and begin first aid.
- One injury and Fido will swear off clippers for life. The next time you grab the clippers, prepare for a fight as Fido will be afraid and home grooming will quickly turn into a nightmare. It's not worth it!

||||||||||||||||||||||||||||||||||||||||||||||||||||||||||||||||||||||||||||||||||||||||||||||||||||||||

Navigating the Vast Universe of Grooming Products

Oh boy, where do I start? Today, it seems like every Tom, Dick and Harriet has a line of canine-grooming products. Labels are bursting with claims of "essential," "organic" or "secret" ingredients. Product purveyors lead you to believe that you "must have" numerous shampoos on hand, one for each doggy dirt situation. Others claim to provide "spalike" experiences. The reality is that there is little governmental regulation of these claims. Thus, many purveyors of pet-grooming products have become quite imaginative.

I'm not forbidding you from using the latest canine spa or organic products. I'll be the first to admit that it's fun to use a grooming product that brightens a white dog or adds shimmer to the coat. All I'm saying is that these fancy, expensive extras are not *required* for proper, effective grooming. I would rather that you spend your grooming dollars more wisely, such as on having your dog's nails professionally trimmed.

Use Only Canine Products

Regardless of which grooming products you choose, **never use any human products on your dog.** If I could, I would shout this admonition from every rooftop! Human products contain ingredients that are too harsh for a dog's delicate skin and coat. All too often, an otherwise healthy dog arrives at my salon with mysteriously dry, irritated skin. Inevitably, I discover that the dog was washed with human shampoo.

Grooming products use acids and alkalies to cause physical changes to skin and hair. The pH measures the acid and alkaline levels in a substance. Grooming products are formulated or "balanced" for the species-specific pH level. The skin and hair on humans and dogs have different pH requirements. For this reason, most human shampoos dry out a dog's coat or irritate his delicate skin.

Many people wash their dogs with baby shampoo, believing that it's tearless and gentle. Like all human shampoos used on a dog, baby shampoo strips oil from the coat and quickly renders it dry, dull and brittle. Moreover, baby shampoo often causes dandruff and extreme itchiness.

Several years ago, a client brought in her cute little Lhasa Apso mix. The pooch looked like he had been dipped in a combination of Crisco and bacon grease. He smelled like it too. I can still hear the owner naively declaring, "Rover had flaky skin. I tried to put oil in his food just like the vet said, but Rover wouldn't eat it. So I soaked him in baby oil." Let's review: baby oil is a human product and as such is **never** to be used on a dog. It took twelve baths with heavy-duty degreasing shampoo and an undue amount of *my* elbow grease to clean Rover. Even so, he smelled like baby oil for months.

If you're polishing your dog's nails, use a product specifically formulated for canines. Human nail polish is toxic if ingested. I can tell you from experience, your dog will lick or chew her painted nails.

Actually, just to be sure everyone understands, right here and now I'm expanding the human-product prohibition to include all household and industrial products, chemicals and any other substance not specifically made for topical use on dogs.

Leave No Product Behind

Dogs have sensitive skin and anything left on the skin for an extended time is potentially irritating. Moreover, leave-in products often attract dirt and quickly render the coat dull. Unless you're directed by your veterinarian, never use a product that is meant to remain on the coat. I recommend that you forgo any product that has the term "leave in" or "do not rinse" on the label.

The Wide World of Grooming Products

Shampoos and Conditioners

Shampoo is a cleaning agent. It opens the cuticle and breaks down and lifts dirt off the skin and coat. While it's removing dirt and unwanted grime, shampoo can also strip some of the natural oil necessary to maintain a healthy coat. Moreover, some shampoo residue remains regardless of how thoroughly you rinse. This is where the conditioner comes into play.

Conditioner cuts through shampoo residue, seals the cuticle and moisturizes the skin. Conditioner also softens the coat, adds shine and reduces static and tangles, which makes brushing easier. Besides, a conditioned coat actually repels dirt more effectively than a coat treated with shampoo alone, because the dirt clings to the unsealed cuticle. Therefore, **never** skip the conditioner; it's essential to good grooming.

Resist the temptation to save time by using a "conditioning shampoo." Quite simply, these pathetic products don't work, or at least not very well. In order for shampoo and conditioner to be most effective, they must be separate. Shampoo and conditioner work at cross-purposes; shampoo opens the cuticle and removes dirt, while conditioner seals the cuticle and coats the hair shaft. Because these products perform opposite tasks, they cancel each other out if used simultaneously. Moreover, the combined product is unlikely to contain enough conditioner to actually do anything useful.

Similarly, deep conditioners are unnecessary unless you *really* want to spend the extra money. You can achieve similar results by merely applying your regular conditioner and waiting a few extra minutes before rinsing.

Hypoallergenic Shampoo

Always read product labels carefully. True hypoallergenic products never contain fragrances or dyes. Although formulated to be gentle, many puppy shampoos actually contain scent and color!

Think of the hypoallergenic shampoo as a paint primer. Its sole job is to prepare the canvas for painting. In this case, your dog is the canvas and you'll be grooming rather than painting. The primer shampoo removes dirt, odor and debris and renders your dog's coat a pristine painting surface.

Specialty Shampoo

Once he's primed, Fido is ready to be "painted" with the specialty shampoo. Instead of choosing a particular color, you're going to pick a shampoo with a specific quality: fragrance, odor remover, color enhancer, brightener or deep cleaner. These specialty shampoos, though, are often not the best cleaners. Use them only to add grooming bells and whistles. If Fido has sensitive skin, definitely skip the specialty shampoo. Just use the hypoallergenic shampoo.

If your dog has skin or coat issues, such as parasites, allergies or itchy or overly sensitive skin, you may need a medicated shampoo. Never use a medicated product without your veterinarian's approval and follow all label directions. Medicated shampoos or products with strong active ingredients can be harmful if not used properly. For example, tar-based and sulfur-based shampoos are **fatal** to cats.

Conditioner

I prefer basic hypoallergenic, scent-free conditioners. I won't scowl if you succumb to cute packaging or fancy ingredients as long as you don't skimp on required grooming products. Nonetheless, if your shampoo of choice has a matching conditioner, feel free to layer the scent as long as Fido's skin is not sensitive.

Dry and Waterless Shampoos

Manufacturers market dry and waterless shampoos as convenient time-savers. Typically, you are directed to apply the product, massage it into the coat, wipe it off or brush it out and voilà, Fido is "clean." What, no rinsing? If the words "no rinsing required" fail to trigger a Scarlett O'Hara–style fainting spell, then immediately review chapter 16, "Every Dog Must Have His Day . . . in the Bath."

It's one thing if you're hiking in the mountains, days away from the closest ranger station, and your dog rolls in yak poop. Then, yes, I agree that you desperately need a quick cleanup and you may employ a dry or waterless shampoo. Under any and all other circumstances, take the time to provide your beloved pal with a proper bath and rinse every drop of product from his coat. In my professional opinion, dry or waterless shampoos are useless and no substitute for a regular bath. After all the unconditional love and loyalty Fido provides you, he deserves a few minutes with water and effective cleaning products.

Many companies claim that dry or waterless shampoos are a perfect solution for dogs that fear water or bathing. I say, let's determine why the dog is afraid and work to overcome the hang-up. A dry bath is a cop-out. Spend your money on a canine therapist rather than settling for the quick fix.

Between-Wash Products: Friend or Foe?
Products for use between baths crowd store shelves. I have seen everything from doggy deodorant to canine perfume. My opinion? If Fido smells, just wash him. These products will merely mask the odor and Fido will remain dirty.

Tearstain and General-Stain Removers
White or light-colored dogs often have visible brownish tearstains around their eyes. Usually, these stains are normal and nothing to fret about. If, however, the stains become excessive or are accompanied by discharge, contact your veterinarian promptly to rule out infections, tear-duct blockages or other problems.

Many owners are desperate to make tearstains disappear. It seems that I see a new tearstain remover on the market every month. These products all claim to be effective and safe and I'm sure that *some* are, as long as you don't get even one drop in the eyes. You may also hear rumors about homemade stain-removing potions. Steer clear of them all! They usually contain extremely harsh chemicals, such as hydrogen peroxide, that have no business being near canine eyes.

I never use tearstain removers because I don't mind the stains; after all, they're natural. More importantly, I don't like to use any unnecessary chemicals around a dog's fragile eyes, especially products that are labeled DO NOT USE DIRECTLY IN EYES. No one, not even a seasoned expert like me, can be 110 percent sure that absolutely none of the product will get into the eyes. So why risk injuring your pooch for purely cosmetic reasons?

White and light-colored dogs also appear to "rust" around the mouth, beard, paws and privates. This discoloration is a natural by-product of saliva, and let's face it: dogs lick and drool *a lot*. For all the above reasons, I never use a general-stain remover and neither should you. It's never a good idea to subject your dog to superfluous chemicals.

If you insist on ignoring my advice and throw common sense to the wind, at least do me the favor of discussing stain-removing products with your veterinarian before use.

Detangler

Detangling products are useful for all dogs except those with very short coats or none at all. A light misting of detangler lubricates and protects fur from breaking while you brush or remove mats from a dry (**never** wet) coat. Always thoroughly rinse out the product during the bath and skip any "leave-in" detanglers.

You are hereby put on notice to use a detangler solely *before* the bath. As you know, it violates my moral and ethical principles to leave any grooming product on a dog's skin and coat. After all your hard work, it would be a shame if your dog walked around with itchy skin or a lackluster coat.

Paw Pad Moisturizer

Some dogs, especially those living in colder climates, experience cracked or dry paw pads. Moisturizer made especially for dogs will help heal the pads safely. Never use human moisturizer on Fido's paws because he will lick and ingest the product.

Do-It-Yourself Dog Washes

Although I agree with Dorothy that "there's no place like home," do-it-yourself dog-wash establishments are handy. For example, your Saint Bernard may be too big for your bathtub, or your diminutive Yorkshire Terrier may be too unruly for home bathing. Likewise, you may not have a convenient bathing space or you just might not want to wash at home. If you go out to wash, remember that all my home-grooming rules and regulations remain in effect. You never know when I may walk by and see you violating my "never brush a wet dog" rule. Let's just say I'll show no mercy!

Choose an establishment that is clean, maintains its tools and equipment and employs knowledgeable, helpful staff. Confirm that you understand the shop's procedures and payment options *before* you begin. Even if the shop provides certain tools, always BYOB—bring your own brushes and any other tools that are subject to cross-contamination, such as combs, scissors, sponges and anything else you wouldn't want to share. Likewise, forgo any products left over from a previous dog. You never know who she is or where she's been.

Before you position your pooch, study all the tools and equipment and verify that you can work everything. You don't want to be fiddling with the faucet and accidentally scald your dog or blow him across the room with a high-pressure hose. Most importantly, set up your grooming *mise en place* so that all the requisite tools, equipment and products are at your fingertips *before* you put Fido in the tub. Do not expect Fido to wait patiently and safely as you run to the front of the store to buy conditioner. Just like at home, you can **never** leave your dog unattended even for a moment while he is in the bath, on a grooming table or on any elevated surface. If it's the middle of winter or chilly, your pooch must be bone-dry before leaving the shop.

Final Words to the Wise

Carefully read the label before you purchase and use any product. Confirm that you understand the directions, as some products require dilution. Indeed, when using any product or tool, always follow the directions with painstaking exactitude. If any product irritates your dog's skin or causes any discomfort or negative reaction, stop using it immediately, thoroughly rinse it off and try another brand. If the reaction is severe, promptly call the vet and begin first aid.

If you're still overwhelmed by the myriad products for sale or suspect that your pooch has allergies, sensitive skin or other conditions, ask your veterinarian and professional groomer for advice.

14.
The Inspection
Connection

Why Inspect

My grandmother always said, "You've got nothin' without your health." Alas, Fido can't tell you if he's under the weather or uncomfortably dirty. An inspection, therefore, is actually a critical whole-dog wellness assessment. It allows you to track, monitor and assess the state of your dog's health and cleanliness in a systematic and thorough manner. Inspections uncover injuries, abnormalities and subtle clues about underlying medical conditions. Moreover, inspections reveal grooming troubles before they become big, painful, complicated, traumatic and expensive problems.

Routine inspections also encourage you to spend quality time with your pooch. This quiet time together has the added benefit of relaxing your dog and teaching her that grooming and the associated manhandling are pleasant. She'll quickly learn that cooperation brings positive attention, praise and treats.

Unfortunately, many perfectly good dog owners are clueless about the value of inspections and never take a close visual, tactile and olfactory look at their beloved pals. I know this for a fact because I've found a wide array of items on my clients, some outrageous and some humorous, but all things the owner should have noticed well before the dog arrived on my grooming table. Not once, but twice, I've found a condom protruding from a dog's rectum, which proves that dogs will eat anything. Once the chuckling and blushing subsided, I strongly admonished the owners to secure their garbage because these items can cause serious and deadly internal damage. I've also found ringworm, very large and very small tumors, hemorrhoids, oozing eye and ear infections, puncture wounds, bites, animal feces, paint, gum, clumps of burs, sticks and even a gaping, oozing scabby hole the size of a dime. My paw-pad perusals have uncovered glass, staples, huge chunks of mud, pebbles, ripped and missing nails and severe cracks and tears. Those poor dogs had been suffering with every step. So, please, for Fido's sake, commit to inspecting him.

When to Inspect

At a minimum, plan on performing a complete once-over each week. Fido's eyes, however, require daily attention. If you see or sense trouble brewing, never hesitate to carry out additional inspections. For example, check the area if your dog has been licking, scratching or biting.

Use the handy chart below to track and organize your work. Fido has a lot of areas to be checked, but many tasks can be easily integrated into regular bonding activities, such as petting, brushing and cuddling. Feel free to break up the inspection duties over the week so both you and Fido don't get antsy or overwhelmed. Moreover, most of the inspections can be performed in a matter of minutes. If you really think about it, you unconsciously inspect yourself every day. Since Fido lacks the ability, it's up to you to help him.

After a few sessions you'll be able to complete your inspection in a shorter time. Never rush, though; I want you to be fast but accurate. Your dog's health and well-being are at stake—and not just his quality of life, but also the quantity.

Remember, though, your inspections supplement but don't replace yearly or semiannual veterinarian appointments.

How to Inspect

During the inspection, touch, feel, scrutinize and smell every square inch of your dog. Run your fingers through his coat and over his skin, and check every accessible external organ. In addition, observe his mood, behavior and reactions. Note the details if your dog displays any signs of discomfort or pain. While you work, talk to your dog continuously, praise him and reassure him so that he remains cooperative.

|||||||||||||||||||||||||||||||||||||||||||||||||||||||||||||||||||||||||||||||||||||||||||||||||||||||||||||||||||||||||||||||||||||||

How Do I Know If Fido Is in Pain?

Fido can't tell you if he's in pain. Indeed, he's hardwired to conceal his pain from predators even though he no longer lives in the wild. If you're paying attention, however, you'll notice subtle changes in his habits or behavior that indicate a problem.

If you observe any of these changes, contact your veterinarian immediately:

- **Abnormal chewing while eating.** If Fido's mouth is painful, he may chew on only one side.
- **Dramatic weight loss or gain.** Pain may cause your dog to lose his appetite or he may eat less because bending down to his food bowl hurts.
- **Avoiding affection or touch.** If Fido winces, yelps or hides when you want to cuddle him or if he snaps when you try to handle him, he's not being aloof; he's probably in pain.
- **Decreased exercise or movement.** Pain may cause your normally active dog to become a couch potato. Likewise, if Fido is limping or refusing to jump or walk up the stairs, he isn't well.
- **Having accidents in the house.** Pain can cause a sudden change in Fido's bathroom habits. He may begin pooping or peeing in inappropriate places or be unable to hold it like he used to.

||||||||||||||||||||||||||||||||||||||||||||||||||||||||||||||||||||||||||||||||||||||||||||||||||||

Use your grooming notebook to record a baseline map of your dog's skin and body and log how your dog looks, acts and feels from week to week. Always note any area that is particularly dirty, smelly, tangled, matted, debris-ridden or in need of additional attention at subsequent grooming sessions. All this information assists you over time in assessing your dog's well-being and provides crucial information to your veterinarian and professional groomer.

||||||||||||||||||||||||||||||||||||||||||||||||||||||||||||||||||||||||||||||||||||||||||||||||||||

When to Contact the Vet

If you've uncovered something new, unusual, scary or confusing, promptly call your veterinarian. It's always better to be safe than sorry. Indeed, every veterinarian should encourage client questions. Many veterinary offices and emergency animal hospitals employ veterinary technicians who field questions from concerned owners and offer advice and instructions all day long. Don't be embarrassed to call and don't wait until a minor problem becomes major. If your gut tells you something isn't right or you're not sure what to do, call.

||||||||||||||||||||||||||||||||||||||||||||||||||||||||||||||||||||||||||||||||||||||||||||||||||||

Inspection Checklist

AREA	DIRTY	MATS	SPECIAL CONCERNS (medical red flags)	COMMENTS Changes/Pain/Injuries
Date:				
Skin				
Coat				
Nose				
Whiskers				
Head				
Face				
Snout				
Mouth				
Teeth				
Gums				
Tongue				
Lips				
Flaps, Folds, Flews				
Eyes				
Lashes				
Inside Ears				
Ear Area				
Neck				
Back				
Body: Right Side				
Body: Left Side				
Legs				
Armpits				
Paws				
Nails and Dewclaws				
Chest				
Belly				

AREA	DIRTY	MATS	SPECIAL CONCERNS (medical red flags)	COMMENTS Changes/Pain/Injuries
Genitals				
Rear End				
Tail				
Anal Sacs				
Behavior				
Mood				
Eating Habits				
Bathroom Habits				

What and Where to Inspect

Skin and Coat

Your pooch is covered in skin and fur that can hide all kinds of medical and grooming troubles. As you inspect each specific area, your eyes and fingers must work through the coat all the way down to the skin. Be sure you actually see and feel the skin. This is easier with a Uniform Fur dog because she has shorter fur. With Hair and Multilength Fur dogs, take your time and make your way carefully through the coat so you don't pull or tug. Regular brushing will make the inspection easier because mats and tangles won't impede your progress.

A quick once-over of the skin and coat won't do. The inspection must be careful and systematic. Every week, I have to remind my clients to examine their pooch's skin and coat. All summer long, I surprise owners by displaying multiple engorged ticks or masses of inflamed fleabites. A while back, I uncovered a syringe with a broken-off needle lodged under a mat on the leg of a big shaggy dog. When I presented the syringe with obvious horror on my face, the owner casually remarked, "Oh, we find a lot of stuff in his fur." It took all my self-control not to slap the guy and say, "Of course you do, your dog is covered in mats and he's clearly not receiving adequate home care."

Scrutinize each area on your dog's skin and coat looking for any changes or abnormalities:

- Hair loss, bald spots or thinning coat
- Dull, dry or brittle coat
- Greasy or oily skin or coat
- Stinky skin or coat
- Color changes to skin or coat
- Debris, dirt, burs, plants, sticks and any foreign matter that has no business being attached to a dog
- Hot spots
- Swelling
- Cuts, scratches, wounds, bruises and injuries
- Scabs, sores, pustules, dandruff, flakiness and rashes
- Crusty, dry or thickened skin
- Lumps, tumors, growths or masses
- Bites from insects, parasites, dogs or other animals
- Ticks, fleas or other parasites

In addition, search the skin and coat for dirt accumulation, mats and tangles. Note their location and magnitude for later removal. If, however, the mats are large, numerous or close to the skin, take Fido to a professional groomer ASAP before the situation becomes dire and the only solution is a complete shave down. Carefully remove any debris, but don't yank or tear it out. If you are using scissors, place your finger between the skin and the scissors before you cut. (See "Scissor Safety" in chapter 15.)

Nose
Look for injuries, discharge, dryness, crustiness, debris and changes in color or texture.

Whiskers
Determine if the whiskers need to be trimmed.

Head, Face and Snout
Run your fingers through the fur and over the skin on Fido's head, face and snout. Be on the lookout for grooming problems, hidden debris, skin

abnormalities and any medical red flags, such as lumps or injuries. If Fido is sensitive while you touch or inspect this area, it may indicate an acute oral situation, such as a tooth abscess, severe gingivitis or embedded debris.

Mouth—Inside and Out

Be brave! Gently open Fido's mouth, peek inside and sniff. Offensive or particularly strong odors often signal decay, infections, gum disease or other oral troubles. Check for trapped food or debris. Search for broken, loose, missing, discolored or decayed teeth and plaque and tartar buildup, which appears as yellowish brown stains near the gum line. If left unchecked, tartar causes gum disease and can lead to tooth loss and serious heart, liver and kidney disorders. If you see lumps or swelling around a tooth, Fido has a serious dental problem requiring a prompt visit to the veterinarian.

Move your fingers along the gum line checking for raised bumps, growths, discoloration, redness, sensitivity, soreness and inflammation. Note whether Fido winces in pain or his gums bleed during the inspection.

Inspect the top and bottom of Fido's tongue. Check for embedded debris, growths, injuries, swelling and any change in texture. If your pooch has a spotted tongue, watch for changes in color, texture and size of the spots, which can indicate disease. Reach under the tongue and move it out of the way for a better view. Foreign objects love to hide here.

Use your finger to search the lips and any and all facial flaps, flews and folds for dryness, injuries or bumps. Dirt and debris often lurk here, so get your fingers inside and really check.

Eyes and Lashes

Gaze into Fido's eyes. Some dogs dislike eye contact, so don't take it personally or force the issue. It may take a while for your dog to be comfortable with the eye inspection. Get up close, but **never** touch the eyeball. If your dog has been pawing at her eyes, be on the lookout for infections or injuries.

Healthy eyes are moist, bright, wide open and alert. Often, the eyes of older dogs appear cloudy or hazy, which is usually normal but an issue to discuss with your veterinarian. Also, alert the doctor if you see excessive stains or tearing, since this can indicate a blocked tear duct. Droopy eyelids, uneven eyes, separation of the eyeball from the socket, swelling, cloudiness, redness, squinting and unusual or colored discharge are all trouble. In addition, look for debris in and around the eyes and for signs of injury, trauma or pain.

Next, examine the eyelashes. Lashes should grow out and away from the eye. If you notice an ingrown lash, do not touch it, and call your vet. A small amount of crusty debris on the lashes is normal and can be washed away with sterile eye solution or in the bath. If the crust prevents Fido from opening his eye, you've probably discovered an infection. Eye infections are often contagious and quickly spread to the other eye and other dogs.

Finally, note whether the fur around Fido's eyes or his eyelashes require a trim.

Ears

Whisper sweet nothings into Fido's ears as you examine in and around each ear. And I mean truly whisper; a dog's ears are many times more sensitive than ours. If Fido's been scratching or rubbing his ears on the ground or furniture or tilting or shaking his head, he may have an ear infection or parasite infestation.

First, scrutinize the flap and external area of each ear for redness, swelling, abrasions, injuries, sores, rashes or anything unusual. Be sure to feel behind and around the outside of the ears too. Mats, debris and parasites love to lurk here.

Next, look inside. If your dog has Drop ears, gently pull the ear flap up and out of the way to allow full access. A *small* amount of brownish wax is normal. Excess wax, debris, crusty or colored discharge or strong or musty odors indicate ear problems and require veterinary attention.

While you're perusing inside the ear, evaluate the amount of ear hair for potential removal, preferably by a professional. Pay close attention to determine whether your dog winces or exhibits any signs of pain during the examination.

|||||||||||||||||||||||||||||||||||||||||||||||||||||||||||||||||||||||||||||||||||||||||||||||||||||||||||||||||||

Seasonal Inspection Additions

In the summer look for sunburn; skin rashes and ear infections from swimming in chlorinated pools or dirty water; parasites and plant debris; and paw-pad burns from hot asphalt or other playing surfaces.

In the winter look for chapped skin all over the body (especially on the nose, lips and undercarriage). Also, check paw pads for cracks, embedded winter debris like snow, ice and rock salt and burns from winter chemicals.

||||||||||||||||||||||||||||||||||||||||||||||||||||||||||||||||||||||||||||||||||||||||||||||||||||||||||||

Neck, Back and Body

Systematically move down the neck, back and sides of the body searching for debris, grooming issues, skin abnormalities and sensitivity or pain. Look carefully for parasites, lesions, hot spots, rashes and any other signs of trouble. Run your fingers over the area looking for bumps, bites, cuts, injuries and tumors. If applicable, assess the state of the wrinkles and loose pendulous skin folds in the area and flag for extra attention in the bath.

Legs and Armpits

Run your hands up and down each leg searching for skin abnormalities, injury, swelling, tenderness, pain, bumps, bites or debris. Check the stopper pad, which is located on the back of each front leg a few inches above the paw, for abrasions and injuries. If Fido's coat is thick or long, you may have to search a minute to uncover these pads.

Remember to visually assess and feel all four armpits, as they tend to collect dead fur, produce mats and tangles and conceal debris.

Paws, Nails and Dewclaws

Many dogs are not used to having their paws handled and may try to pull away. Be patient and reward heavily. Scrutinize the top and bottom of each paw. Palpate each toe and check each of the five pads. Gently spread the toes to see and feel between the pads. Search for trapped debris, injuries, masses, dryness and mats. Note whether the paw-pad fur is sticking out and requires a trim.

Examine each of Fido's nails to determine if he needs a pet-i-cure. (I've been saving that joke for years!) Search for long, broken, splintered, chipped or torn nails. Don't forget to inspect the dewclaws if Fido still has them. Verify that they're intact and determine if they need a trim.

Undercarriage: Chest, Belly and Genitals

Now brace yourself and concentrate. We are now inspecting the undercarriage, which includes the genitals. Stop blushing. Your dog's well-being is at stake, so modesty (either yours or Fido's) is no excuse for skipping this vital step.

For the inspection, lay your dog on her back or side. Feel free to offer a treat to bribe her into position and keep her there. This is a sensitive area, so use a soft touch. Start at the chest and move toward the rear. Use your hands and eyes to search for mats, trapped debris, sores, injuries, rashes, masses and anything that's new or unusual. If your dog cries or exhibits signs of pain or tenderness in the belly or genital area, make an urgent call to the veterinarian.

On both males and females, a *small* amount of dried urine or colorless discharge on the genitals is normal and can be washed away along with dirt and grime. Strong odors, excessive or colored discharge, blood or pus, sensitivity and swelling are not normal and warrant a prompt call to the veterinarian. Dogs have fur "down there," which means trapped debris, tangles and mats that must be noted and removed. Scan the nipples to verify that they're not swollen, crusty or changed in any manner. Search for foreign matter trapped in skin folds or in and around the vulva or penis and the scrotum, which really shouldn't be there because responsible owners neuter.

||||||||||||||||||||||||||||||||||||||||||||||||||||||||||||||||||||||||||||||||||||||||||||||||||||||

Genital Goings-On

Occasionally, you may observe your pooch licking his or her genitals. Why? you ask. Three reasons: (1) because he or she can, (2) to self-clean and (3) to relieve pain, itch or pressure caused by a medical problem. Excessive licking, chewing or scratching in the area, unusual or odoriferous discharge, straining while urinating or defecating, blood or pus in the urine or stool or sudden incontinence frequently indicates an underlying infection or illness that requires veterinary attention. Calling the veterinarian at first onset of any of these symptoms will help you help your pooch.

||||||||||||||||||||||||||||||||||||||||||||||||||||||||||||||||||||||||||||||||||||||||||||||||||||||

Rear End and Tail

Before we go any further, let's get one thing out into the open. Properly caring for your dog means getting up close and personal with his *every* nook and cranny. Whether you call it a tushie, behind, rear end, backside, bottom or seat, I bet that this isn't your favorite part of your dog. No matter how you slice it, however, you must touch your dog's private (often extra smelly and dirty) areas to get him truly clean. If *you* don't, who will? Fido should not have to go elsewhere to feel clean and fresh. After all, who knows where the neighbor's cat has been?

Let's begin: move to the back of the bus and check your dog's rear end. First, inspect the tail itself for skin abnormalities, injuries, debris, tangles and mats. Then, carefully lift the tail to access Fido's rectum and peruse the area for parasites, redness, swelling, blood, strong odor, pus, discharge or injuries. In addition, look for mats and trapped detritus from, *ahem*, previous trips to the bathroom.

If you've seen Fido biting or nipping at his butt or scooting it across the floor or you notice a particularly rancid odor, he probably needs his anal sacs expressed.

Mind and Spirit

Think back over the week and evaluate Fido's demeanor. Fido's mood, behavior, appetite and level of activity are usually indicative of his physical health. Sudden or drastic changes often hint at underlying medical conditions that require veterinary attention.

Praise and Pet

Once you've concluded your inspection, liberally confer kisses, treats and pats on the head so Fido understands that you appreciated his cooperation and patient assistance.

15.
Dirty Deeds Done Dirt
Cheap . . . at Home

The Game Plan

I magine that I'm your coach (minus the high-waisted Sansabelt® slacks, shiny whistle and huge headset, but I'll keep the locker-room pass, thank you very much). This is your playbook. Our sport is Canine Wellness. Fido is the star of the team and you're the rookie defensive back. We're playing our archrival, Dirt and Disease, and we're going for a touchdown every time and the yearly Canine Good Health Trophy.

I'll coach you through all the important plays so you'll be prepared when you enter the grooming stadium. Our playbook covers brushing; mats; ear, eye, dental and anal-sac care; nail clipping and skin-fold cleaning. Remember, however, practice makes perfect. Be patient and don't get frustrated. Your skills will be in tip-top shape in no time.

The Rule Book

Like any rookie, before setting foot on the field, you must learn and understand a few ground rules.

1. Hygiene is *crucial*. All the surfaces, tools, and equipment you use, including your hands, must be thoroughly washed and dried before, during and after each task.
2. Start every task on the same side to minimize confusion over what you've completed. I'm right-handed, so I begin on the right side. If you take a break or are interrupted, record where you left off in your grooming notebook.
3. Tailor the grooming session to Fido's *current* personality, tolerances and mood (see chapter 12, "Helpful Hints for Home Dog-Care Success"). Never use excessive force, a loud voice, intimidating body language, scare tactics or threats to keep Fido in line while

you work. If Fido's not in the mood, don't force him. Take breaks as needed.

4. Consider Fido's current health before performing difficult tasks yourself, such as nail clipping, removing ear hair and expressing anal sacs, which can draw blood and/or induce stress. If your pooch has a serious medical problem, such as a heart condition, a bleeding disorder, epilepsy or an autoimmune disease, talk to your veterinarian before you begin home grooming.

5. Don't groom or brush a dog with an active skin infection or injury until you visit the veterinarian. Likewise, stop and call the vet if you discover an active infection, an open wound, a growth, sores, swelling or anything new or unusual. Stop immediately if your dog exhibits any sign of pain or discomfort.

6. Report any serious grooming accident to your veterinarian. Many eye and ear injuries require urgent veterinary attention.

7. Record any interesting or troubling aspects about the tasks in your grooming notebook for discussion with your vet.

8. Generously bestow praise, hugs and treats and have fun! We want your dog to love having his body maintained.

The Playbook: All Dogs Must Be Brushed and Brushed and Brushed

Most people believe that only "fancy" dogs like Poodles require extensive upkeep. Well, as I've said many times before, and I'll keep saying it until no dog remains unbrushed, *all dogs except for the truly Hairless require frequent brushing regardless of coat type.* If you take nothing else away from this book, know that frequent (meaning daily or a few times a week) and correct brushing is fundamental to your dog's health and happiness.

How is brushing important? Let me count the ways. Brushing stimulates the skin by removing dead skin flakes, encourages natural oil production, removes irritating debris and encourages blood flow to the skin. Brushing also clears out dead fur, distributes the oil—which makes the coat shine—loosens and lifts dirt, breaks up mats and tangles and prevents new ones. What is more, brushing uncovers skin and coat troubles, such as dandruff, parasites or dry or brittle fur, which may indicate that your pooch is ill. Perhaps most importantly, brushing makes Fido feel and look good. Brushing is like a massage on steroids: you're touching your dog, the bristles are kneading his skin and he's earning treats just by sitting and enjoying himself.

Brushing 101

TOOLS

- **Hair and Multilength Fur dogs**
  - ✓ slicker brush
  - ✓ comb
  - ✓ detangler (for mats)
  - ✓ blunt-nosed scissors
  - ✓ treats
- **Uniform Fur dogs**
  - ✓ rubber curry or slicker brush
  - ✓ treats

Before you begin, inspect the tools and verify that the bristles, rubber tips or tines are intact. If any are broken, bent or sharp, discard the tool. As you work, clean the brush or curry as soon as it fills with fur. Use your fingers or a comb to lift the fur off the bristles.

FREQUENCY

If you have a Hair or Multilength Fur dog, brushing every day is ideal, but a few times a week is fine too. If you have a Uniform Fur dog, brush at least once a week, but feel free to pamper your pooch more often. Establish a routine and brush at the same time each day. The more often you brush, the easier and more enjoyable it becomes.

In addition, brush your dog *before* every bath. Once Fido is wet, move the brush away so you're not tempted. Don't pick up the brush again until Fido is *thoroughly* dry.

NEVER BRUSH A WET DOG!

Why am I making such a fuss? A dog's skin is delicate, much more so than a human's—that is why the skin is covered with fur. When wet, a dog's skin becomes soft and pliable, and the nerve endings and blood vessels are closer to the surface. Accordingly, if you brush a wet dog, you're likely to injure or scratch him or leave a brush burn. Your dog will also curse you under her breath and run away when she sees the brush. So please just don't do it—ever.

|||||||||||||||||||||||||||||||||||||||||||||||||||||||||||||||||||||||||||||||||||||||||||||||||||

Procedural Basics

Comfort

Everyone must be comfortable during a brushing session. Experiment until you find a position that makes you and Fido happy, relaxed and cooperative. I recommend that you start on the floor or a bed and try a few different positions. Some people find it easier to have the dog standing for the entire session, while others like to have him lie down on his side. It's really up to you and your dog. Once you find the optimal position, it will become habit for your dog and brushing will be smooth sailing. Arthur loves to be brushed so much that he lies down and relaxes while I brush, and won't move until I flip him over.

Develop a System

Develop and stick with a methodical system that allows you to efficiently work your way around the dog and ensure that you brush every area. I always start brushing at the back right leg and move counterclockwise around the dog. This is my own quirky system. Feel free to change it, but *always* brush the head last. It's the most difficult and sensitive area to brush and the one most likely to cause Fido to complain.

My apologies to the old wives, but despite what tales you may have heard or read, every part of your pooch that's covered with fur requires brushing. Just because the fur is short or sparse is no reason to skip over it, especially if you're extra gentle and careful. For instance, the fur on Fido's chest or ears may be short, but his chest and ears are *still covered in fur*. As such, they require brushing. There are no shortcuts here.

Brushing an entire dog in one sitting may be difficult at first. Both you and Fido will need a few sessions to get comfortable with the new positions and sensations (especially in delicate areas). It's OK to take breaks as you work or spread the brushing out over a few days. Always note where you left off in your grooming notebook.

|||||||||||||||||||||||||||||||||||||||||||||||||||||||||||||||||||||||||||||||||||||||||||||||||||||||||

Divide and Conquer: Brushing Longer Coats

If you visit a human hair salon and watch a stylist working on long hair, you'll see the stylist divide the hair into smaller, manageable sections. The stylist works on one section and places the remaining hair out of the way in a clip and then methodically moves around the head.

This divide-and-conquer technique works well on a dog with a long or thick coat because it allows you to work without tangling fur in the brush. Start at the bottom of the first section of the body. Make a horizontal part, flip up the hair above the part and use your free hand to keep it out of the way. Brush the hair below the part. Be sure the bristles are working down to the skin and moving *with the grain* of the coat. (See "Brush with the Grain" on page 276.) Move up the dog in small increments until you reach the top of the area. Then, start the next area, working your way around the dog.

|||||||||||||||||||||||||||||||||||||||||||||||||||||||||||||||||||||||||||||||||||||||||||||||||||||||||

Proper Strokes

A few whirls with a brush on the top layer of Fido's coat won't do. The brush must work all the way down to the skin, where dead fur and debris loiter.

With longer fur, run the brush to the end of the strands to avoid tangling it in the brush. Test the pressure on your hand first. Use a gentle, light touch with slow, controlled strokes to prevent skin injuries. Keep the brush moving and don't slap the brush onto your dog with every stroke. Rake your yard, not your dog's coat.

Every dog has bald areas on his body, such as the nose, lips and inside the ear flaps, and a few exceptionally sensitive areas like the rectum and genitals. Due to their fragility, the brush must never touch these areas. Not surprisingly, Fido will be hard-pressed to forgive any inadvertent brush stroke on his penis. To avoid accidental "brushes" with injury *no matter* where you are brushing, place your fingers as a protective barrier between the sensitive area and the brush.

Brush with the Grain

Regardless of the coat type, **always** brush *with the grain*. Start at the roots and brush in the natural direction of the fur. Brushing with the grain allows you to smoothly and easily remove dead fur at the root.

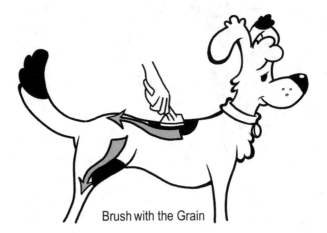

Brush with the Grain

Brushing against the grain means that the brush stroke pulls the fur up in the opposite direction of how it normally lies on the body. When you brush against the grain, it's much harder for the brush to reach the roots and the dead fur. Moreover, excessive brushing against the grain can confuse the hair follicle and your straight-coated pooch may end up with waves and bumps in his coat.

Brush Against the Grain

If you have a Hair dog with a wavy or curly coat, however, one extremely limited exception applies. Brushing against the grain leaves a Hair dog's coat extra fluffy because it helps removes any wave or curl and makes the fur stand on end.

||||||||||||||||||||||||||||||||||||||||||||||||||||||||||||||||||||||||||||||||||||||||||||||||||

Scissor Safety

While you brush, you may notice that Fido has some long fur that needs a simple trim or some debris that *needs* to go. Even your blunt-nosed scissors can injure your pooch, so safety is critical. Never cut without protecting the skin; your fingers will be the barrier. Place your fingers (from your nondominant hand) on the skin and allow the fur to come through your fingers. Place the scissors on top of your fingers and cut with your dominant hand. Point the scissors away from the body. If this isn't possible, hold the scissors parallel to the body and keep the scissors from touching the skin as you cut.

||||||||||||||||||||||||||||||||||||||||||||||||||||||||

Time Frame

The length of a brushing session varies with your patience, how often you brush and Fido's mood, tolerance and coat type. As you become more adept, the sessions will become shorter and easier. You're striving for progress, not absolute perfection. No one, not even a seasoned pro like me, can remove every single strand of dead fur in one session. Fido would mutiny and your carpal tunnel would kick in.

If Fido is a Hair or Multilength Fur dog, stop when you see a dramatic reduction of fur in the brush head. If Fido is a Uniform Fur dog, begin the brushing session by rubbing your hand over his coat, which releases a flurry of fur. This also establishes a baseline measure of how much fur is ready to come off. When the brush or curry is no longer overflowing with fur, rub your hand over Fido's coat. If the amount of fur is greatly reduced compared with the earlier rub, you're through. Smile and pat yourself (and Fido) on the back for a job well-done!

Introducing Brushing to Puppies and New Arrivals

With a puppy or other dog that has little or traumatic prior brushing experience, it's important to start slowly and not force the issue. Don't expect to brush this dog from head to toe on your first try. Everyone's a winner if you introduce brushing in a slow and gradual manner that respects Fido's personality and life history. Most dogs need a slow and steady introduction.

To start, show your dog the brush, tell him what it's for (yes, Fido speaks your language) and let him sniff and investigate—but not bite—it. Give him a treat. Repeat that for a few days and then, show Fido the brush again and make a few strokes on his back, which is not a sensitive area. Give him a treat. Repeat for a few more days. Then, brush a little more each session, but avoid any sensitive areas, such as the head, tail or genital region. As you brush, talk and soothe the dog. Keep the treats coming. Once your dog is enjoying the sessions, add in one new sensitive area every few days and dispense extra treats. Eventually, you'll be brushing your entire dog and she'll be craving the attention.

Gentle Home Groomers,
Start Your Brushes

Remove Debris

At the start of every brushing session, peruse Fido from head to toe looking for debris and dirt. If the gunk is ordinary mud, sand or grime, break it up with your fingers. Carefully remove any larger pieces of debris with your fingers or the brush, but don't pull or use excessive force. Some dirt, like burs, wax, gum or paint, is more difficult and requires special removal techniques, which I discuss in chapter 17, "Dirt Emergencies." While you're looking around, watch for injuries, irritations, growths, masses and anything unusual that might require veterinary attention.

Begin Brushing

Once Fido is debris free, begin to brush. I've listed the body parts from back to front, which is the way I work. Brush according to your preferred routine, but work on the head last. If Fido is a Hair or Multilength Fur dog, before you move to the next area, run a comb through the coat to ensure all tangles and mats are removed.

Rear End and Tail

Fido's rear end is tricky, potentially stinky and *definitely* sensitive—isn't yours? Use treats, praise and extremely gentle and controlled brush strokes in the area. Hold Fido's tail up and out of the way. Carefully remove or trim out any debris or crust around his rectum with your blunt-nosed scissors, positioning your fingers between the skin and the scissors before cutting. Then, begin brushing—cautiously. This is a delicate region. Use your fingers to protect the rectum and exposed skin from the bristles. Before moving on, give Fido a big hug for allowing you to work here.

The tail is delicate too, so use extra-gentle pressure. As you brush, place your fingers over the rectum to protect it from the bristles. Don't panic— you can wash your hands afterward or wear disposable gloves. If the tail is long enough, place it in your open palm for support and steadiness as you brush. For short tails, gently grasp the tail to hold it in place. Work from the

base to the tip. If the tail fur is long, place your fingers between the edge of the tailbone and the brush to protect it from the bristles.

BONE

Legs and Paws

Always hold the legs and paws in a natural position. A bent leg naturally moves forward or back; never pull it out to the side like you're yanking on a wishbone. Likewise, do not bend the paws backward or twist them into strange, uncomfortable positions. The idea is to limit movement, support the leg or paw and preserve Fido's comfort. If you're doing this correctly, Fido won't complain.

Fido can stand normally while you brush the top portion of his leg. To brush the lower leg and paw, bend the leg and hold it in place so it doesn't flail with every brush stroke. I like to rest the paw in my open palm while I brush it. The toes are sensitive, so brush lightly. Use your fingers to protect the pads from the bristles. Never brush the fur growing between the paw pads. If this fur is sticking out beyond the pad, trim it away. Place your blunt-nosed scissors parallel to the pad and carefully trim, avoiding the pad itself. Don't point the scissors toward the pad. For safety's sake, if you discover mats or stubborn debris between his toes or pads, take Fido to your professional groomer. Apply dog-safe moisturizer if the pads are dry or cracked.

Armpits

The armpits are tricky. The skin is extremely thin and mats and tangles grow exponentially with the friction generated by Fido's every step. To reach the front armpits, bend the leg as if Fido were walking and gently push it forward just enough to expose the area. To reach the back armpits, bend the leg as if Fido were walking and carefully push it backward. The rear armpits are perilously close to the genitals, so use your hand as a protective barrier.

Back and Sides of the Body

Most dogs enjoy the massage from the brush along their backs and sides. Start at the base of the back of the neck and work backward. Then, brush down the right side and then the left side of the body.

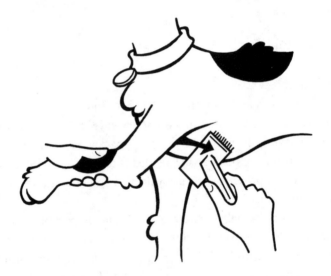

Undercarriage (Chest, Belly, Genitals)

The entire undercarriage is a delicate area. If Fido has a thick coat on his chest, use a firmer brush stroke. On most dogs, however, the coat on the belly and genital area is sparse and requires light brush strokes. For sanitary reasons, I recommend that the genital area be trimmed short or shaved on all dogs. This also helps prevent mats and exposes the area to air, which, as we all know, is a freeing feeling. Don't attempt to cut or shave this area yourself. This requires the expert hand of a professional groomer.

To reach the undercarriage, if he's not too big hold your dog so he's standing on his hind legs. Some people prefer to place the dog on his side or back or have him stand on all fours and work underneath. Experiment until you find a comfortable position. While you brush, *vigilantly* protect the genitals with your hand. If the area has little or no fur, brush with extra-gentle and slow strokes or run your fingers over the area to check for debris or mats.

Neck

This is a sensitive area, so use gentle pressure and keep Fido distracted with praise and treats. Remove Fido's collar. Place your hand under his chin and guide his head up so that his neck is fully extended and his nose is pointed up. You may lightly grasp Fido's snout and hold a treat near his nose so he'll remain still as you brush. Replace Fido's collar before you move along.

Head and Face

The entire head is a delicate area and Fido will be on high alert when he sees the brush. Use your fingers to erect a barrier around the eyes, ears, nose and lips. Brush with slow, soft strokes and talk to Fido as you work. It's fine to hold Fido's snout in place as long as his nostrils aren't blocked. Brace the head with your free hand so Fido can't move while you brush in the eye area. Use the corner of the brush for extra control and avoid the eyeballs at all costs. While brushing the ears, hold the flap in your free hand so it doesn't move around with each stroke. Many dogs have fur inside the flap around the edges. Carefully brush this fur, but not the bare skin. Don't worry about the whiskers as you brush the snout. They require no special attention. Exercise *extreme caution* around the mouth and beard to avoid poking or pulling the lips.

Give Thanks

Wow, Fido looks fabulous! Thank Fido for his cooperation, slip him a few extra treats and give him a big hug. Fido is now ready for his bath or a walk around town to show off his fancy fur coat.

Of Mats and Men

If you have a Uniform Fur dog, there are no mats in your life and this section doesn't apply. Feel free to read it anyway, since it's exceptionally interesting, pithy and well written. Those of you with Hair or Multilength Fur dogs are unfortunately all too familiar with mats. But what exactly is a "mat" and where does it come from?

On a Uniform Fur dog, the dead fur falls right through the short coat and off the dog. Although messy, this problem is easily solved with a vacuum and lint roller. Things aren't so simple for Hair and Multilength Fur dogs. The dead strands on these dogs rarely fall off the dog. Instead, they become trapped in the healthy coat. The dead and healthy strands interlock and resemble a ball made of felt or cotton. Through friction or moisture, the ball continues to tighten into one obstinate mass. This mass is a mat. As you might imagine, removing a mat isn't easy; it hurts and sometimes requires shaving.

To illustrate, imagine washing a wool sweater. Before you place it in the washer, the sweater is fluffy and the individual fibers and stitches are flexible and easily discernible. After you remove the sweater from the washer, everything has changed. The sweater has shrunk drastically and the wool looks and feels thicker. You can no longer distinguish the individual stitches because the wool fibers have fused together. After the sweater dries, the wool is tight, unyielding and stiff. Your wool sweater now resembles a piece of felt—or the mats on your dog.

As you brush your Hair or Multilength Fur dog, you're drawing the old dead fur away from the healthy fur and out of the coat and, thus, preventing mats. Mat removal is also important to your dog's health. Mats block airflow and trap moisture, debris and (yuck!) fecal material next to the skin, which breeds bacteria and infections. Mats also hide sores, injuries and skin conditions. In addition, mats pull the skin, making each step painful for your pooch. The pain and irritation may cause Fido to lick or chew at the area, which usually leads to hot spots. Don't wait for a small mat to grow. The faster it's gone, the more comfortable and happy your dog will be.

In my early professional years, I worked at a kennel that—let's just say—"collected" dogs. Sadly, many of these poor pooches were rarely touched or examined. One day I was called upon to groom a big shaggy dog.

I knew something was amiss the moment I approached his crate. The dog smelled like an armpit smothered in sour cream and left out in the July sun. As I ran my fingers through his coat, I discovered that he was so matted around his rear that his anus had been matted shut. No one had touched this poor guy in so long that the mats had trapped countless poops against his skin. I nearly fainted when I cut away the mats and discovered a slew of live maggots and rotten skin underneath. Ultimately, after many hours toiling away, I was able to clean the dog and he received the appropriate veterinary care. In addition to grossing you out, I hope this anecdote has driven my point home: regardless of how often you bathe your dog, you must brush and demat him frequently. Besides saving him from the fate of that unfortunate shaggy dog, regular brushing makes the entire grooming process easier and more pleasant.

Shaving Grace

When mats are at the skin, are plentiful, form a webbing or resemble a pelt, the dog *must* be shaved. Using a brush to remove such severe matting is downright cruel and unusual punishment and I *never* advocate violations of the Eighth Amendment. I'm really not joking around either. Brushing out serious matting is *so* painful and damaging to the skin that it genuinely borders on torture. It's also extremely time-consuming and stressful for you and the dog. Fido isn't motivated by vanity, and he doesn't understand why you're ripping his fur out, yanking on his skin and forcing him to sit for hours. Besides, one painful dematting session is enough to permanently destroy Fido's love of grooming that you worked so hard to foster. It's not worth it. If Fido has severe mats, have your professional groomer shave him. Buck up, cowboy—Fido's fur always grows back. And I suggest that when it does, you brush him regularly so this doesn't happen again.

TOOLS

- ✓ Slicker brush
- ✓ Detangler
- ✓ Comb

✓ Patience
✓ Blunt-nosed scissors, to be used in extremely limited cases
✓ Treats

FREQUENCY

As soon as you discover a mat, remove it. Mats multiply like rabbits and quickly become serious.

PROCEDURE

You're not at Muscle Beach and the gym adage "no pain, no gain" doesn't apply. Mat removal is an art and requires tremendous patience from you and your dog. Treats, praise, treats, kisses and more treats distract and calm him while you perform this tricky task. Just a reminder: remove mats *only* when your dog is dry!

1. Assess the mat: if the mat is large, part of a huge web of mats, touching the skin, one of many mats or in a delicate area like between the paw pads or near the genitals, stop and put down your brush. Pick up the phone and make an urgent appointment with your groomer. Severe matting requires professional care. Begin preparing yourself mentally for a possible shave down.
2. If you find only a few mats and they are no larger than a half-dollar and are not close to the skin, proceed with immediate mat removal. Have heaps of treats at the ready and use them.
3. Tackle mats one at a time. Spray a light mist of detangler on the mat. If the mat is on or near the face, don't spray the mat. Instead, soak a cloth with the detangler and gently dab it on the mat.
4. Place your finger between the mat and the skin. The mat should be in front of your finger. If you're in the correct position, the brush bristles will hit your hand, not the dog's skin. If possible, hold the mat steady at the root or above the mat so Fido's skin doesn't pull with every brush stroke.
5. With a slicker brush, make short, rapid but light-pressured strokes over the mat to release the dead fur caught inside. Don't pull or rip the mat. Be patient. The mat should *begin* to loosen up

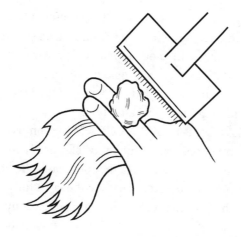

after about fifteen to twenty brush strokes. Continue to brush in the same manner until the mat is fully broken up and disappears. It may take ten to fifteen minutes to break up a large or stubborn mat completely.

6. If after fifteen to twenty strokes the mat has not started to loosen up *at all*, then put down the brush. Try loosening the mat by hand. Never pull at the root or at the top of the mat. If you wield too much force, you may rip right through the mat *and* the skin.

Hold the mat erect between the fingers of both hands, with thumbs toward you in a pincer grip. Your pinkie fingers will touch the skin and hold the mat still so it can't pull skin as you

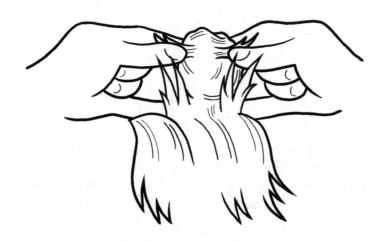

work. Using your thumb and index finger, pull out horizontally from the middle section of the mat. Your fingers should be pulling parallel to the skin, not perpendicular. Work all the way around the mat, but always pulling out from the middle section. If this technique fails, take Fido to your professional groomer. This mat requires professional attention.

7. **NEVER USE A COMB TO BREAK UP A MAT.** Combs don't work and cause tremendous pain. Unlike the slicker brush, the tines on a comb aren't flexible. As such, the comb pulls the healthy fur out from the root and doesn't penetrate the dead fur in the mat. Use your comb only after all the mats are gone. Comb through the coat down to the skin and check for any stray mats. The moment the comb hits a mat, put it down and use your slicker brush to remove the mat.

8. Avoid the temptation to cut out a mat. If the mat is close to or on the skin, don't even think about grabbing your scissors. It's way too easy to slice Fido open because mats often impede your ability to see where the mat stops and the skin begins.

You are authorized to cut out a mat in one extremely limited and restricted situation: if you can position the scissors underneath the mat, if you can place your fingers as a barrier between the skin and the bottom of the mat so the scissor blades rest on top of your fingers and if you can cut parallel to the dog. **Never** cut *through* the mat.

9. Once the mat is removed, inspect the newly exposed skin for redness, swelling, infections, growths, parasites, sores, irritations and injuries. If you discover anything, contact the veterinarian.

10. Praise Fido! He will be more willing to forget what just happened if he receives extra treats, hugs and kisses.

|||||||||||||||||||||||||||||||||||||||||||||||||||||||||||||||||||||||||||||||||||||||||||||||||||||

Mat-Alert Zones
Hair and Multilength Fur dogs often become tangled and matted in these areas:

- Behind the ears
- Under the collar
- In the armpits
- Under the tail around the rectum
- On the belly and chest if the coat is long and close to the ground. The fur is often wet and picks up debris as Fido walks around.

Mat Origins

- Failing to brush regularly
- Failing to remove debris from the coat
- Failing to brush the coat after it has been wet
- Blowing coat
- Failing to thoroughly remove shampoo, conditioner or other products from the coat
- Failing to use conditioner

|||||||||||||||||||||||||||||||||||||||||||||||||||||||||||||||||||||||||||||||||||||||||||||||||||||

Ears to You

Keeping Fido's ears and the surrounding area clean is important. Clean ears are less likely to become infected. This is especially true for dogs with Drop ears, since the floppy flaps (also a new band from Manchester, UK) prevent air circulation and trap moisture, dirt and heat inside. Wax left to build up can travel down the ear canal and cause a wide variety of painful and chronic infections, which sometimes require corrective surgery.

From time to time, you'll be called upon to insert tools and products in and around your dog's ears. The canine ear canal is delicate, and therefore you must never push anything in too far. I once found a piece of the stem from a cotton swab lodged deep inside a dog's ear. When I showed the owner, she sheepishly replied, "Oh, a few months ago, I was cleaning Ginger's ears and I accidentally broke off the end of the Qtip and couldn't find it anywhere." One can only imagine the pain the dog endured due to her owner's carelessness. Without exception, always account for everything that goes into the ears—if the item doesn't exit intact, immediately locate all the pieces. If a piece is missing, take your dog to the veterinarian right away. The same goes for products. For example, ear powder can build up inside the ear and resemble cement if not thoroughly removed.

As long as your pal cooperates and you refrain from shoving anything down the canal, ear cleaning is straightforward. If your pooch is used to having his ears touched in nongrooming situations, your job will be a heck of a lot easier. This is why I've been drilling you on the importance of spending time petting your dog!

TOOLS

- ✓ Unexpired canine ear-wash solution
- ✓ Natural cotton balls
- ✓ Blunt-nosed scissors
- ✓ Treats

FREQUENCY

Inspect Fido's ears each week. Clean *inside* the ear only when you see dirt, wax or debris. If Fido's ears look clear, leave them be because overcleaning can also cause problems. If your dog swims clean more often. Home ear care supplements but never replaces yearly or semiannual veterinary exams.

PROCEDURE

1. Wash your hands thoroughly with soap and hot water.
2. Read the label to verify that you're holding canine ear wash and study the directions. Check the expiration date and throw away the product if it's old—even by one day.
3. Start with the right ear.

   If your pooch has Drop ears, lift the flap up and gently turn it inside out against his head. Hold the flap in place with your free hand. The flaps on dogs with Erect and Semi-drop ears allow easy access. Never tug or pull on the ear flap.

4. Look inside the ear and assess the area. If you've found nothing alarming, begin cleaning. With most liquid cleaners, you'll be directed to squirt the solution inside the ears. Then, lightly massage the base of the ear canal for at least fifteen to twenty seconds and allow Fido to shake his head to distribute the liquid and break down and loosen the wax. Using as many clean cotton balls as necessary, carefully wipe away the wax on the inside of the ear canal opening, but only as far down as you can see.

   Clean the inside of the ear flap too. Keep working until the entire area is sparkling. Once you've used a cotton ball, throw it away. Refrain from ramming anything down into the ear canal,

especially a Q-tip or your finger. Use common sense, people: if you're in past your first knuckle or your dog is howling, you're in too far. Stop immediately if Fido cries, bites or exhibits any sign of pain, like wincing or yelping.

5. Keeping the area around the ear trimmed encourages airflow. Although I prefer that you leave *all* trimming to a professional, if you are exceedingly cautious and your dog is relaxed and cooperative, use your blunt-nosed scissors and my safe trimming technique (see page 277) and trim any fur *around* the ear opening, but *not inside* the ear. Always point the scissors away from the head and protect the ear flap in case your dog moves. Scissors inside the ear are simply not allowed because sharp objects inside small spaces cause serious injuries.

6. Now repeat the procedure for the left ear.

7. If you're bathing Fido, protect his ears from the water. *Gently* place a fresh cotton ball into each ear as a barrier. The cotton balls should be in only far enough to remain in place and should cause no pain or discomfort. The cotton balls may fall out during the bath, especially if your pooch shakes. So keep extras handy. As soon as the bath is over, remove the cotton balls. Confirm that you've recovered both balls and that they're intact.

8. Reward Fido with treats and a hug to remind him that you appreciate his assistance.

|||||||||||||||||||||||||||||||||||||||||||||||||||||||||||||||||||||||||||||||||||||||||||||||||||||||

No Unsanitary Multitasking

Canine eyes and ears are delicate and prone to infection. Moreover, they are easily cross-contaminated if you're not careful. Cotton balls are cheap, so use a fresh ball after each eye and ear. Also, clean, disinfect and dry scissors and other tools after you finish with one eye or ear and *before* you start on the other side.

Reserve one pair of scissors for trimming around the eyes and face. Use the second pair for the rest of the dog. I'm afraid that experience has taught me that I still have to remind everyone: do not trim around Fido's delicate eyes with the same scissors you just used to cut off the poop stuck to his butt. Likewise, never use your grooming scissors for anything other than grooming. Verify that everyone else in your household understands that these scissors are off-limits for crafts and coupon clipping.

|||||||||||||||||||||||||||||||||||||||||||||||||||||||||||||||||||||||||||||||||||||||||||||||||||||||

The Ear-Hair Conundrum

Many dogs grow hair inside their ear canal, especially Hair dogs. Just look inside Fido's ears and you'll know immediately if this section applies. Some people, like me, believe that aural hair creates an inner-ear environment that encourages infection. Others believe that removing the hair causes more wax and increases the risk of infection. In any event, routine removal of this hair is no longer standard practice and a matter for you and Fido's professional staff to decide.

Sometimes, the hair is so deeply rooted that a dog will literally scream and bite as you work and the ear may become inflamed. Regardless of your dog's pain tolerance, he won't sit calmly as you rip out his ear hair. I, therefore, robustly urge and beg you to skip *home* ear-hair removal. This service is usually inexpensive at most grooming salons and veterinary offices.

Despite my recommendation, you may insist on removing the ear hair at home. For your dog's sake, I'm providing instructions for the proper and safe procedure. Truly, I hope that once you read the instructions, you'll understand why this task is best left to skilled professionals.

Wait to Wash

If you're removing ear hair, do it *before* you wash the inside of the ear with cleaning solution. The ear powder absorbs the natural oil, wax and moisture on the ear hair so the hemostats can effectively grip. If you use the ear wash and then the ear powder, Fido's ear canal will be a soupy mess.

|||||||||||||||||||||||||||||||||||||||||||||||||||||||||||||||||||||||||||||||||||||||||||||||||||||

TOOLS

✓ Clean hands
✓ Ear powder
✓ Two clean and dry straight-jawed hemostats
✓ Unexpired canine ear-wash solution
✓ Natural cotton balls
✓ Treats

FREQUENCY

Depending on the dog and the hairiness of his ear canals, you may end up performing this task every few weeks. You are inspecting the ears weekly, so you'll see when it's time.

PROCEDURE

1. Wash your hands thoroughly with soap and hot water.
2. Confirm that the bottle in your hand is actually canine ear powder.
3. Assess the ear area. If everything looks healthy, begin. Read and follow the instructions on the powder bottle. In general, you'll be directed to squeeze the powder into the ear, which dries the area and allows you to have a firm grip on the hair.
4. Clean the hemostats again with soap and hot water or dog-safe disinfectant and dry them thoroughly. It pays to be extra hygienic, since hair removal can inflame the ears and lead to infection.
5. Start on the right ear. Using your clean fingers or the first pair of hemostats, clasp the hair as close to the outside of the ear as possible without entering the canal.

Never aim the hemostats into the ear canal or push them inside. Gingerly pull the hair out from inside the canal. Make sure that the hair you are pulling is actually coming from *inside* the canal and *not* growing on the ear flap or around the canal. Keep going until the majority of the hair is gone or Fido has chewed off your arm.

6. Depending on your dog, you may be able to remove only a few hairs at one sitting. Furthermore, the ear hair on some dogs is so deeply rooted that it requires a veterinarian to remove it. On most dogs, however, the hair comes out fairly easily but often painfully.

7. If your arm is still intact, work on the left ear with the second pair of hemostats. Wash and dry your hands before you begin on this ear.

8. Check inside each ear for bleeding or inflammation. If the ear is bleeding, call the veterinarian immediately and begin first aid.

9. Confirm that no powder remains in the ears. Anything left there is hazardous, builds up over time and often triggers infections. Use ear-wash solution and clean cotton balls to remove all remaining powder.

10. Clean and dry the equipment.
11. Bestow extra treats, praise and hugs, since this was *not* fun for Fido.

Eye Love You

Dirty eyes often become infected. So removing goo, dirt, debris and other crust that collect in the eye area and on the lashes is crucial to maintaining eye health. Safety is of the essence here. *Never* use any product in the eyes without securing your vet's permission.

You'll do fine as long as you're patient and meticulous. Your pooch may not be gung ho at the beginning unless he is used to having his face touched. Use treats and praise to boost Fido's cooperation while you work. Before you know it, he'll be batting his lashes at you as you clean.

TOOLS

✓ Unexpired canine sterile eyewash or clean warm water
✓ Natural cotton balls
✓ Blunt-nosed scissors
✓ Unexpired ophthalmic ointment or mineral oil and a clean dropper
✓ Treats

||||||||||||||||||||||||||||||||||||||||||||||||||||||||||||||||||||||||||||||||||||||||||

Read the Label Every Time

Always take a moment to read the label and the directions *each time* you pick up a product *before* using it. Many labels and bottles appear similar at first glance. Early in my career, I worked at a pet shop. The senior groomer's assistant was charged with washing the infected eyes of a sweet little kitten available for sale. For several days, the assistant treated the kitten's eyes without seeing any improvement. I happened to look at the bottle and saw that the idiot had been pouring ear-mite remover into the kitten's eyes. The poor kitten was probably going blind because the assistant failed to read the label. By the way, once the kitten's eyes were treated with the actual medicated eyewash, the infection cleared up.

||||||||||||||||||||||||||||||||||||||||||||||||||||||||||||||||||||||||||||||||||||||||||

FREQUENCY

Inspect and clean the eyes, lashes and surrounding area every day. Home eye-care complements but does not replace regular veterinary care. Contact the veterinarian promptly if you ever think something is wrong with your pooch's eyes.

PROCEDURE

1. Wash your hands thoroughly with soap and hot water for at least thirty seconds. Dry them.
2. Peruse the eye area and ascertain whether everything appears healthy. Call the veterinarian if you find embedded debris or any sign of infections or injuries.
3. If you're using sterile eyewash, check, recheck and re-recheck that the bottle in your clean hand is actually the correct product. Review the directions and verify that the product has not expired, even by one day. In addition, squirt out a small amount and check that the liquid isn't cloudy, discolored or foul smelling. If it is, throw the bottle away, even if it's new.
4. Read the product's instructions. Typically, you'll be directed to moisten a fresh, clean natural cotton ball with the eyewash.

Don't touch the bottle tip to the cotton, your dog's eye or anything else. Every product or tool used on or around the eyes must be exceedingly clean. I don't care how much you spent on Fido's designer, organic, all-natural eyewash in the handblown ergonomic glass bottle—if the tip touched anything, discard it. If you don't, your dog may acquire a painful and expensive eye infection.

5. Start at the inside corner of the first eye and wipe toward the outside corner. Delicately, slowly and cautiously wipe the moistened cotton ball *around*, but *not in or across*, the eye. If you wipe across the eye, you'll push the dirt into the eye. Be extra careful and precise with your motion to avoid touching the delicate eyeball itself. Don't rush or Fido may need an urgent trip to the veterinarian for a scratched cornea. Be sure that you've removed all the gunk *around* Fido's eye. Use as many cotton balls as necessary. Reusing cotton balls is foolish. The eyes are not an area to economize in, as you could spread germs to the second eye.

6. Now clean the second eye.

7. If you're using clean water instead of sterile eyewash, check and recheck the water temperature before you soak each fresh cotton ball. **Never** direct the water stream into Fido's eyes.

8. On Hair and some Multilength Fur dogs, hair in the eye area occasionally grows long enough to irritate the eye, collect debris or possibly scratch the cornea. I hesitate to tell you to bring scissors anywhere near Fido's eyes and truly prefer that you *always* leave this task to a professional. If, however, you haven't consumed too much caffeine and Fido is calm *and* extremely cooperative, go ahead, but only if you promise to leave the lashes for your groomer. Always use scrupulously clean blunt-nosed scissors. Hold the scissors parallel to the eye. **Never** point the scissors toward the eye, and protect the eye with your meticulously clean finger as you trim.

9. If you're about to bathe Fido, you may treat each eye with either ophthalmic ointment or mineral oil to protect the eyes from accidental contact with shampoo or conditioner. Before you apply the product, wash your hands thoroughly again. Confirm that you're holding the appropriate product and check the expiration date. Avoid touching the applicator or dropper to the eye or anything else for that matter. To apply, follow the product's direc-

tions. For most products, you'll be directed to squeeze a thin strip of the ointment into the eyes or squeeze a few drops of mineral oil via a scrupulously clean dropper into each eye. Then, you'll gently close the eyelid to distribute the product.

10. Now thank Fido for his assistance. He should never feel as though you're taking him for granted.

||||||||||||||||||||||||||||||||||||||||||||||||||||||||||||||||||||||||||||||||||||||||||||||||||||

Big Eye-deas

Most dogs have recessed or flush eyeballs. Some dogs, however, like the Chihuahua, Lhasa Apso, Pekingese, Pug and Shih Tzu, have big protruding eyes that require special attention. Although adorable, these eyes are less protected because they're raised from the socket. Protruding eyes are always at risk of popping out of the socket. This can occur if the dog receives trauma to the face or eye area, plays too roughly, is choking or is just plain stressed-out.

If you have a big-eyed dog, be extra careful and mindful of her mood while you're grooming to minimize eye injuries. Keep her calm with treats and praise, rather than restraints. Exercise extreme caution while cleaning and brushing in the eye area. In addition, those big beautiful eyes typically require daily moisturizing drops. Talk to your veterinarian before using any product in the eyes.

||||||||||||||||||||||||||||||||||||||||||||||||||||||||||||||||||||||||||||||||||||||||||||||||||||

Clean Choppers

Although dental care is integral to canine health, even the best dog owners neglect it. Tooth decay often leads to serious systemic health problems, so doggy dental care is serious business. Caring for Fido's teeth also goes a long way when he's kissing you good morning at six a.m. Besides, imagine how icky it feels to have the remnants of every meal you've *ever* consumed stuck to your teeth! Following a home dental routine also decreases the frequency of professional deep cleaning. A dog must be anesthetized during veterinary dental procedures. Anesthesia has inherent risks and should not be taken lightly. Therefore, anything we can do to reduce the need for it is good for your dog.

Managing *your* expectations is crucial. Don't expect Fido to run into the bathroom, put his paws up on the counter and open wide the first time you try to brush. Be prepared to take it slowly (I mean over days and weeks) and don't quit no matter what. If you have a puppy or new arrival, start home dental care as soon as you can to establish a positive attitude and a feasible regimen. If your dog is older, it is never too late to start.

Talk to your veterinarian and discuss an appropriate oral-health-care plan before you begin. If your furry friend already has a mouth of horrors, your veterinarian may recommend a professional deep clean so Fido can start with a clean slate.

TOOLS

✓ Clean canine toothbrush
✓ Unexpired canine toothpaste
✓ A few small towels or washcloths
✓ Treats

FREQUENCY

In a perfect world, we'd all brush our dog's teeth every day. In the real world, brushing even once a week is enormously beneficial. If that's still too much, brush Fido's teeth each time you bathe him, and ask your professional groomer to do the same. Indeed, any brushing is better than none at all.

To help fight plaque and tartar, limit soft food, provide safe chew toys and feed hard kibble and crunchy treats. Don't, however, expect food and toys to produce dental miracles. They're meant to supplement, not replace, brushing. Always combine home dental care with regular veterinary check-ups and deep cleanings as needed.

PROCEDURE

The best way to prepare your pooch for home dental care is to start slowly and take a break if you have to wrestle Fido into submission. You don't want to put him off dental care for good. Just be patient.

For the first few days, run your clean finger along Fido's teeth and gums. If you're squeamish, wrap your finger in fresh gauze. Then, for the next few days, let Fido sniff and inspect the toothbrush. After a few more days, gently rub the toothbrush inside his mouth for a few seconds so he'll get an idea of what's to come. Continue this for a few more days and then introduce the toothpaste. Let Fido sniff the toothbrush and lick the yummy poultry- (or steak- or liver-) flavored toothpaste. After a few more practice sessions, slowly begin brushing one small area and gradually over a few days or a few weeks, depending on your pooch, work until Fido allows you to clean his entire mouth. Praise Fido every step of the way and soon he'll be (relatively) eager to open wide.

Once you and your dog get the hang of it, the whole process should take about five minutes. Remember, the more you brush, the easier it gets.

Here's how to do it.

1. **Prepare.** Grab a pile of nutritious bite-sized treats. Wash your hands thoroughly with soap and hot water for at least thirty seconds and dry them.

2. **Relax and inspect.** Don't take your dog down to the cold, damp basement utility room and expect miracles. Play soft music, dim the lights, don your lace pajamas—just create a relaxing, calm atmosphere. Pet your pooch and surreptitiously perform a mini mouth inspection. Contact your vet if you find anything suspicious or smelly.

3. **Disclose.** Before you begin in earnest, let Fido smell and taste the toothpaste.

4. **Brush.** Apply a pea-sized amount of canine toothpaste to the CLEAN AND SANITIZED brush (and, yes, I'm yelling). If your dog allows, flip up her lip so you can see where to place the brush. Otherwise, you'll have to rely on feel. Start in the upper right quadrant and move clockwise. This way, you'll always know where you are if Fido interrupts.

   Brush with circular motions using moderate pressure as if you're brushing your own teeth. Concentrate on the gum line and outer edges of the teeth (facing the lips). Expect some minor bleeding, but anything more necessitates a call to the veterinarian. Unless you're very lucky, your dog will not allow you to brush on the inside of his teeth.

   Brush each quadrant for thirty to sixty seconds or, in reality, as long as you can. Your dog will probably lick the toothpaste as you are brushing, so reapply often. Work through each quadrant, taking breaks to dispense treats, pets and praise. Rinsing is usually not necessary with canine toothpaste, but check the toothpaste label.

5. **Flew patrol.** If applicable, check flews and pendulous lips for trapped food and debris. You never know—you might even find Amelia Earhart in there.

6. **Cleanup.** Always clean toothpaste residue from Fido's face and body before you conclude the dental session. If you're about to bathe your dog, cleanup is a snap, since you can shampoo away all the toothpaste and drool. Otherwise, a spot wash will do.

7. **Celebrate.** Both you and your dog have earned kudos for a job well-done. Lavish Fido with kisses and praise. Positive reinforcement works wonders.

8. **Sanitize.** After each use, thoroughly wash the toothbrush in hot, soapy water and then air-dry on a clean towel or standing in a clean cup. Many brushes are dishwasher safe, so sanitize often. If the toothbrush has seen better days, replace it. I recommend purchasing a new toothbrush every four to six months.

If your pooch will not under any circumstances cooperate, talk to your veterinarian about dental-care alternatives. Inquire about special doggy mouthwashes, oral dental aids and dry food designed to reduce plaque and tartar buildup.

Anal Sac Attack

Did you ever wonder why all of a sudden Fido decides to wax the floor with his rear end? He's not trying to be funny. Rather, he has a potentially serious problem with his anal sacs. When anal sacs become full, they need to be expressed (emptied). This is no laughing matter. It's uncomfortable and if left untreated can turn into an infection or abscesses. So what's an owner to do? You have two choices, and from my vast personal experience expressing anal sacs, I'm vigorously urging you to choose the first option.

Option 1. Take Fido to a professional groomer or the veterinarian to have his anal sacs expressed. Fido will be pleased because the person working on his caboose knows what's what back there. You'll be ecstatic because it's a dirty, stinky job.

Option 2. Do it yourself. If you choose to DIY, read on to learn the procedure. In addition, review your technique with the veterinarian or groomer before trying it out on your dog. It's uncomfortable and embarrassing if not performed correctly.

TOOLS

- ✓ A strong stomach
- ✓ Numerous paper towels
- ✓ Disposable gloves
- ✓ Apron or old clothes
- ✓ Gas mask and Tyvek bodysuit (I'm kidding—well, sort of!)
- ✓ Shower or tub
- ✓ Blunt-nosed scissors
- ✓ Treats

FREQUENCY

On many dogs, the anal sacs properly secrete fluid with every poop. On some dogs, however, the sacs aren't that efficient and they need a helping hand. A dog may need to have his anal sacs emptied every week or every few months.

So how do you figure out when Fido's anal sacs need attention? The best place to turn for the answer is, of course, former U.S. Supreme Court justice Potter Stewart. In his concurring opinion in the obscenity case *Jacobellis v. Ohio*, 378 U.S. 184, 197 (1964), Justice Stewart described his test for determining if something is legally obscene: "I know it when I see it." (Forgive the obscure reference, but I promised my coauthor I'd let her make one law "joke.") The same is true for anal sacs; you'll know it when you see it—"it" being Fido's desperate attempts to relieve the pressure and discomfort: scooting across the floor on his rear, relentlessly licking and biting his rear or maniacally scratching near his tail. Ignore the alleged experts telling you to routinely empty the anal sacs. To avoid inflaming or irritating otherwise healthy sacs, don't empty them until you see the telltale behavior.

A good groomer will perform an anal-sac check every time your dog has an appointment. Be sure to ask when you drop Fido off at the salon.

PROCEDURE

1. This is a messy job. I recommend that you perform the operation in a bathtub or shower. You'll want to hose off the area, the dog and yourself when you're through.
2. Wash your hands thoroughly. Put on disposable gloves if you're squeamish or have open wounds on your hands.
3. Gently lift Fido's tail and peruse the area. First, look for debris or anything that could be causing the problem. As they work their way out, worms and parasites are itchy, which can cause the same

scooting and chewing behavior. Using your blunt-nosed scissors, carefully trim away any debris from the area. Never point the end of the scissors toward the rectum. Place your finger between the skin and the scissors before cutting.

4. With your nondominant hand, gently hold Fido's tail up and out of the way. The anal sacs are right below his rectum at the four and eight o'clock positions. (Have you decided to call a professional yet?) You can't see the sacs, so you'll have to do this by feel. When full, they feel like grapes under the skin. Gently squeeze your thumb and index finger toward each other and at the same time push in and up. Keep your face clear and try to catch the goo with the paper towel.

5. Now I bet you wish you chose Option 1! This is especially true if you get hit with the goo. Once this happens, you'll think a skunk attack smells like a bed of roses.

6. Wash your hands for thirty seconds with hot, soapy water. Dry them.

7. Give Fido treats and a hug to remind him that you appreciate his assistance.

8. Now is a perfect time for a bath. First Fido and then you.

9. If Fido continues to scoot, he exhibits any other symptoms or the sacs were empty, call the veterinarian. Fido's anal sacs may be impacted or infected, which requires veterinary attention.

Paw and Pedicure Procedures

Trimmed toenails help prevent injuries to you, your dog and your furniture. Long nails can become caught, broken or ripped off while a dog plays, walks or moves around in his crate. Additionally, when nails are left uncut, they begin to grow into the pad (ouch!) or cause serious orthopedic problems.

Nail cutting would be a snap if it weren't for the pesky quick. On many dogs, the quick is difficult to discern and easy to sever. A cut quick bleeds and is quite painful. Coagulating products usually stop the bleeding, but it will take Fido a good long while before he'll trust you or anyone else around his paws and nails again.

Blood and coagulants and pain! Oh my! This procedure sure sounds serious and potentially painful. One false move and Fido's going to have a date with a vat of styptic powder and a couple of Doggy Downers. More important, we want Fido to *like* home grooming and look forward to it with his tail up. Why insert the added stress into your life and the life of your beloved pet? This is all so easy to prevent. Rather than struggling at home, please take your dog to a trusted professional groomer or a veterinarian for nail clipping. It's not expensive and Fido will thank you. That said, if Fido cringes when you shake his paw after a professional pedicure, reassess where you outsource doggy nail care. Not all professionals are careful and conscientious.

If you choose to ignore my sound expert advice and cut Fido's nails at home, it's important to be patient. This is a difficult procedure, so don't expect to cut all sixteen toenails and any dewclaws in one sitting. Start slowly and be satisfied if you successfully cut one nail on the first try. At the beginning, you'll have to perform the pedicure over several days and in multiple sessions. If you are patient and careful, eventually, you may be able to trim one paw and then, someday, work up to all four at once. Always stop if a struggle erupts or Fido's stress reaches a fevered pitch.

TOOLS

- ✓ Doggy nail clippers
- ✓ Doggy nail file
- ✓ Coagulating (styptic) product
- ✓ Towel
- ✓ Treats

FREQUENCY

Most dogs need a nail trim about every four weeks. A city dog's nails usually require less-frequent trimming because the sidewalks act as a natural file. Dogs that spend their time walking on soft surfaces like grass or carpet have nails that need trimming more often.

Ideally, canine nails should bear no weight and reach about one-eighth inch above the floor. If Fido sounds like he's tap-dancing across the wood floor, it's time for a nail trim. Dewclaws never contact ground and require frequent trimming to prevent them from growing into the paw pad.

Cut nails after a bath because the water softens the nail.

Occasionally you may need to file Fido's nails in between pedicures. This is relatively easy as long as you are gentle and use a canine nail file.

PROCEDURE

1. Wash your hands thoroughly with soap and hot water for at least thirty seconds. Put on disposable gloves if injuries make you queasy or your hands have open wounds.
2. Work in a well-lit area. If possible, position a desk lamp to shine brightly on your work area. Verify that the clipper blade is sharp and undamaged. Replace the blade if necessary. A dull blade will cause the nails to split, while sharp blades ensure a clean cut.
3. Arrange yourself so that Fido is comfortable, and you can see and hold Fido's leg and paw in a natural position. Ask another person to help restrain or distract the dog while you work. Forgo any elevated surface because Fido *will* jump when you cut the quick— oops, I meant "if."
4. I always start on the back right paw. The back paws are most accessible if Fido is lying on his side or back. Gently grasp the front of the leg directly above the paw with your nondominant hand.

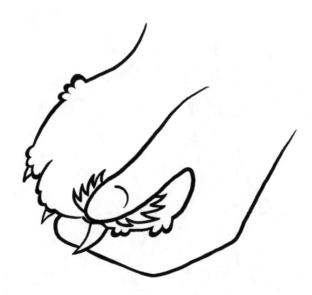

You'll be able to feel Fido's wrist (this is where the leg naturally bends). Hold the wrist so it's still, straight and supported. Simultaneously pull back the fur for a clear view of the nail. Fido's leg should be in a natural position, not pulled out to a ninety-degree angle.

If a dog has long or bushy fur, it can be difficult to see and work on the nails. Gently push Fido's nails through a pair of nylon panty hose. The panty hose keeps the fur safely tucked away and allows you an unobstructed view of the nails.

5. Inspect the paw and nails for any injuries or abnormalities. Check between the paw pads and carefully trim any long fur with blunt-nosed scissors. (Better yet, leave the trimming to your professional groomer.) The scissors must be parallel to the paw. **Never** point the scissors toward the paw or dig them in between the pads.

6. If Fido is calm, start with the rightmost toe and work to the left. Push up on the pad with your finger to move the nail forward and continue to hold the fur out of the area. If your pal has light-colored nails, you'll see the quick through the side of the nail. It usually looks pink or darker than the nail. If your pooch has dark nails, the quick is invisible. I recommend that you put down your clippers and make a pedicure appointment.

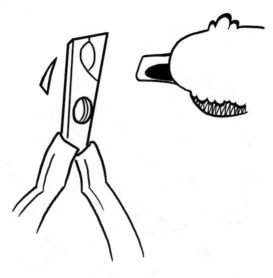

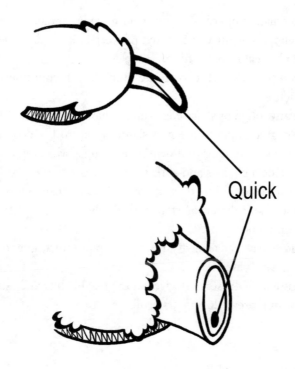

Quick

7. Hold the clipper in your dominant hand perpendicular to the
   nail tip. Make the first cut about one-eighth inch from the tip.
   After each cut, move one-eighth inch farther down the nail. On a
   light nail, locate the quick and stop one-eighth inch before it begins. Since the quick is undetectable through a dark nail, you
   must stop and inspect the underside of the nail after each cut. As
   you get close to the quick, you'll see a dark circle begin to show
   up inside the nail.

   The circle is sometimes subtle, but if you look closely, you'll
   notice that the inside of the nail looks different from the outer
   edges. As soon as you see the circle or even think you glimpse it,
   stop cutting.

8. If you see blood, drop the clippers! You just cut the quick and it
   hurts. Swiftly grab your styptic product and follow the package
   directions and begin first aid. If the bleeding continues after five
   or so minutes or the bleeding is heavy, call the veterinarian

immediately and consult your pet first-aid manual. Don't pick up the clippers again for a few days (if ever). Fido needs some mental and physical recovery time.

9. If you've managed to keep the quick intact, continue with the pedicure.

10. File any rough or sharp edges on the nail. Hold the file at a forty-five-degree angle to the nail slanting *toward* the dog. Work as though you're filing your own nails using a sweeping motion.

11. Give Fido a big kiss and a treat and move on to the next nail.

12. Repeat the procedure on as many nails as you can in this session. If you take a break or stop, record where you left off in your grooming notebook.

13. If Fido's paw pads feel dry, rub a bit of paw moisturizer on as you finish each paw.

14. At the end of the session, give Fido a great big hug and extra treats for sitting pretty during his pedicure.

||||||||||||||||||||||||||||||||||||||||||||||||||||||||||||||||||||||||||||||||||||||||||||||||||

Rotary Clippers

Instead of traditional nail clippers, some people use rotary tools (a.k.a. Dremels). Rather than cut the nails, rotary tools grind them. I never use rotary tools during a pedicure. (Once in a while, I will use a rotary tool to file exceptionally rough edges, such as on an old dog with brittle nails—but that's it, and I'm a trained professional.)

I don't want you to bring a rotary tool anywhere near your dog's paws—ever. These tools move way too fast. Safe nail clipping requires slow, calculated clips. Moreover, these tools obstruct your view of the quick and are difficult to control. One slip and you've sanded Fido's nose.

||||||||||||||||||||||||||||||||||||||||||||||||||||||||||||||||||||||||||||||||||||||||||||||||||

You've Got to Know When to Fold 'Em

Some dogs are wrinkly or full of skin folds or flaps. Fido may have some on his face or neck, all over his body or around his tail. If you have a Shar-Pei, a Pug, a Pekingese, a hound or an overweight pooch, you're very familiar with these nooks and crannies. Because air cannot easily circulate inside, folds hold moisture, harbor bacteria and trap debris, which can lead to nasty skin infections. Keeping the folds clean and dry is your best defense.

TOOLS

✓ Natural cotton swabs
✓ Natural cotton balls
✓ Clean washcloths
✓ Warm water
✓ Treats

FREQUENCY

Inspect and clean all wrinkles, folds and flaps at least once a week and whenever a fold smells. In addition, every time you bathe Fido or brush his teeth, clean and dry these areas.

PROCEDURE

1. Wash your hands thoroughly with soap and hot water for at least thirty seconds.
2. Inspect inside every wrinkle, fold and flap for dirt and debris. You may have to stretch and flatten out the area to see and work inside. Contact the veterinarian if the skin looks irritated, inflamed or sore.
3. For smaller dogs, dampen a natural cotton swab with lukewarm water. If the water is cold, Fido will be unhappy. For medium and larger dogs, natural cotton balls or clean washcloths are more efficient. Slowly run the swab, ball or cloth inside and all around the first wrinkle, fold or flap. Use as many as you need until the area inside is clean. Then, run a new one inside to dry the area thoroughly. Moisture leads to bacteria, which lead to infection.
4. Continue all over the body until every wrinkle, fold and flap shines like the top of the Chrysler Building.
5. Bestow tasty treats and a hug to remind your pal that you appreciate his assistance.

I'm officially designating Fido's wrinkles, folds and flaps as No Powder Zones. Ignore anyone who tells you to use talc, baby powder or cornstarch to clean and freshen these areas. In fact, send them my way and I'll teach them a thing or two. Wrinkles, folds and flaps trap moisture. Powder and moisture mixed together turn into a cementlike sludge, which is difficult to remove, builds up and makes an ideal breeding ground for bacteria. Inserting a powder into the area also runs afoul of my "never use human products on dogs" commandment.

16.
Every Dog Must Have
His Day . . . in the Bath

I magine if you walked on your hands and sat on the ground everywhere, and I mean everywhere, you went. That bathroom break at the gas station just took on a whole new meaning, didn't it? This is Fido's lot in life and he's counting on you to keep him clean and proud. So what's an owner to do? Grab your galoshes—it's time to wash, dry and put the finishing touches on your beautiful pooch.

When to Wash

Odoriferousness alone is not always an indication of doggy dirtiness. All dogs possess a "dog smell"; some are just more subtle than others. Nevertheless, a dog's odor should never be offensive, musty, rancid or unbearably strong. If Fido is foul-smelling, the odor may signal a health problem. Frequently, smelly ears, mouths and rear ends are clues that an infection is present. Bathing your dog only temporarily masks the stench. Take Fido to the veterinarian to treat the underlying health issue before it becomes serious.

For the typical healthy pet dog that spends his time playing in the backyard, running in a park or strolling around the neighborhood, I recommend bathing every two to four weeks unless a dirt emergency arises. (See chapter 17, "Dirt Emergencies.") You may wash your pal more often *if and only if* you adhere to my strict washing techniques and use the appropriate products. If you don't follow my lead, Fido may develop skin problems, regardless of how rarely he's bathed. In addition to your regular bathing and grooming schedule, I also advise you to "spot wash" as necessary.

Dirt happens, of course, and your dog may need a full bath in between her regularly scheduled home or professional grooming sessions. Moreover, weekly baths may ease human and canine allergy symptoms in your household, since your dog's skin and coat produce and trap allergens.

Rome Wasn't Built in a Day

Cleverly named products claiming to abolish the "hassle" of bathing a dog are now flooding the market. Some boldly declare that they eliminate scrubbing or allow a home groomer to wash, rinse and condition an *entire* dog in only three minutes.

Whoa Nelly! Let's pretend we didn't hear the word "hassle" in the same sentence as anything associated with our best friends. What loving dog owner would deem quality time spent with his pal a "hassle"? The entire point of grooming is to pamper, bond with and properly care for your precious pooch. In the immortal words of the celebrated New Age philosopher Céline Dion, "There are no shortcuts to any place worth going." As the wise Ms. Dion teaches in her tuneful hymns, cutting grooming corners leads only to dirty, unhappy, unhealthy and stressed-out dogs (and owners). Grooming is not a race, and indeed, rushing through the process exposes your beloved pal to injury.

Before you get nervous about washing your dog, let me assure you the process is easy and moves along quickly once you learn the basics. Yes, I'll admit, I've broken the process down into ridiculous detail in this chapter, but I *care* about your dog and I want him clean, gorgeous and healthy. Learning to wash a dog properly is like learning to tie your shoes. At first glance, it seems like shoe tying is completed in one smooth motion. However, I could write a minimum of thirty steps instructing you on *exactly* how to perform each detailed movement. That meticulous description would prepare you to succeed at the task, though it might seem a bit daunting at first. At least when you tried tying your shoes for the first time, you'd know exactly what to expect and be able to master it quickly. The *same* is true for washing your dog. I want you to know everything about the process so you won't miss a beat. Anyone who tells you that it's just lather, rinse and repeat is dumber than a bag of hammers and is *certainly* no expert on dog grooming.

Welcome to the Washing Wagon

Even if you've been washing Fido for years, the first trip to the tub using my proper techniques is a learning experience for everyone. So bring your patience, enthusiasm and loads of towels. Many dogs either are afraid of water, have never been exposed to it or just find it distasteful on principle. Don't worry! Even an older dog that refused to bathe without a struggle in the past can be shown the light. Whatever your dog's personality, *gradually* introduce her to the bath. Every dog will respond differently. One dog may jump right in and point to her shampoo of choice; other dogs need to learn to like the bath over days or weeks. The initial bathing sessions should be short, positive experiences. Avoid any struggling, yelling or punishing. Take breaks and stop if you or your pooch becomes stressed-out.

On the first training day, it's show-and-tell! Place Fido in the bath and tell him what's going on. Let him sniff around while you praise him and offer treats. Repeat for a few days.

As you sense that he is becoming more comfortable, place him in the tub and turn on the water. Let him explore and play with the water for a few minutes. Praise him and bestow treats. If he's happy or at least calm, try to wet down an easy area like his back. If he's still hesitant, let him continue to play with the water for a few more days. Work in the tub every day and gradually wet the entire body, except the head, which you'll do last.

Once Fido is accustomed to being wet, start introducing the concept of shampooing, conditioning and rinsing one area at a time. Add a new area during each subsequent bath until you are able to wash Fido's entire body without a struggle. Then, add in the head. Between the water play, your praise, the massage as you apply shampoo and the treats, Fido will be enjoying the bath in no time.

Ready, Set, Go

Gather Your Tools

Before drawing Fido's bath, arrange all tools and supplies within arm's reach of the tub, attach the hose and sprayer and, if necessary, a bathing noose, place a rubber mat in the tub for traction, pop in a drain screen and remove anything that isn't waterproof, such as electric appliances and your grooming notebook. Grab your sponges, dilution container, knee pad and towels. Gather your brush, comb and blow-dryer if applicable. Verify that the bottles contain sufficient shampoo and conditioner for this bathing session. If you're running out, buy more *before* you bathe your dog. If the thought of substituting human products crossed your mind even for a second, shame on you! Stop and reread chapter 13, "Setting Up Your Home Grooming Station," in which I meticulously explain why human products are a Doggy Don't. To reiterate, I'll regale you with a pertinent tale from my real life as a groomer.

Recently, I washed a dog in town on business. I'm serious; this cute, itsy-bitsy Chihuahua was in Chicago to make a personal appearance. Boo Boo even had her own business card and entourage. Boo Boo, however, needed a bath after traveling. The lovely lady who owns Boo Boo forgot to pack doggy shampoo and used the hotel's shampoo instead. Early the next morning, I met Boo Boo to prepare her for her appearance. When I saw that flat and greasy coat, I knew right away that human products were to blame. Thankfully, I had canine degreasing shampoo on hand. After two shampoos and a blow-dry, Boo Boo made her grand entrance, wearing a soft and fluffy coat.

Mandatory Prewash Brush

Brushing is absolutely required before bathing any dog, unless Fido is a hundred percent Hairless breed. Devoting the extra time before the bath to brush actually saves time in the end. Brushing breaks down the dirt, grime and debris and moves it away from the skin so shampoo will clean more effectively. Many dogs also relax due to the massaging action of the bristles, which helps clear away any bad bath attitude.

On a Uniform Fur dog, brushing also removes dead fur that would otherwise end up clogging the drain or attaching to your clothes. Moreover, the bath will be shorter because you won't have to wade through tons of dead fur to work the shampoo or conditioner down to the skin. Brushing Hair and Multilength Fur dogs before the bath removes dead fur and ensures that Fido's coat has no mats or tangles that will shrink and tighten once wet.

The moment you've completed your prewash brush, stow the brush. I don't want you to be tempted to brush your wet dog. After brushing is an ideal time for a bathroom break and a quick spin around the yard or the block to burn off energy before the bath.

Location

Wherever you choose to bathe your dog, it must be clean *before* you begin. This means no unsightly bathtub rings and no wads of hair or mess of bottles on the shower floor. If you're drawing Fido's bath in the kitchen sink, clean and disinfect it before placing him inside. A kitchen sink is the dirtiest place in a home and harbors more germs and bacteria than the inside of a toilet bowl.

||||||||||||||||||||||||||||||||||||||||||||||||||||||||||||||||||||||||||||||||||||||||||||||||||||

No Outdoor Baths

I've heard many hideous rumors about people bathing their dogs with a garden hose. Each time my heart skips a beat when I think of that poor dog being bombarded with icy water in the backyard. No one, whether wearing a fur coat or not, wants to bathe in cold water. Did you ever wonder why Fido struggles during a backyard bath? He's freezing! And if the temperature is below eighty degrees and the sun isn't shining, he can get sick. I never bathe a dog outside. If Fido's too big to pick up, it's the middle of summer *and* his paws are particularly muddy, it's OK to wash his *paws* outside so that he can walk inside to the tub for a proper bath.

||||||||||||||||||||||||||||||||||||||||||||||||||||||||||||||||||||||||||||||||||||||||||||||||||||

Last-Minute Details

If you haven't already, take Fido out for a pit stop and grab a phone before heading to your home grooming station. Close the door and secure the area against escapes. Place Fido in the tub and give him a treat as a sign of things to come. Remove his collar. If you have time, perform all your maintenance tasks on Fido's eyes, ears, teeth and rear so you can wash away the associated mess. If you're starting with the bath, prepare Fido's eyes by applying ophthalmic ointment or mineral oil if you desire.

Finally, if your dog cries, yelps or exhibits any sign of discomfort or agitation, stop immediately. If Fido is particularly anxious, bathe him later or just spot wash the grimy area. Fido should *never* associate grooming with *anything* negative.

Billy's 12 Step Washing Program

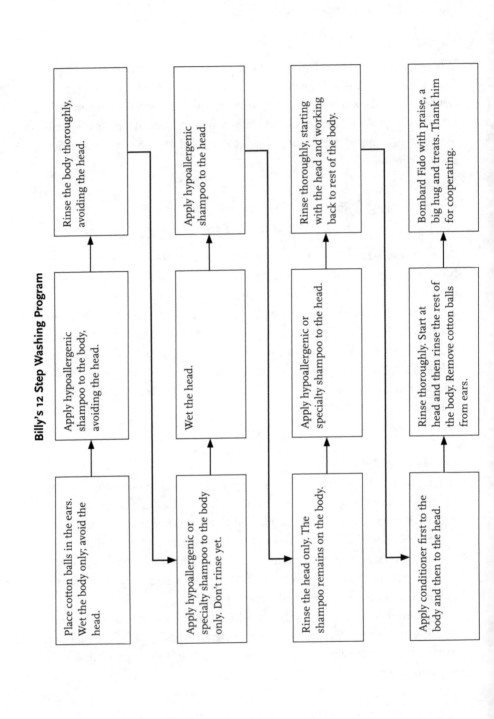

Place cotton balls in the ears. Wet the body only; avoid the head.

Apply hypoallergenic shampoo to the body, avoiding the head.

Rinse the body thoroughly, avoiding the head.

Apply hypoallergenic or specialty shampoo to the body only. Don't rinse yet.

Wet the head.

Apply hypoallergenic shampoo to the head.

Rinse the head only. The shampoo remains on the body.

Apply hypoallergenic or specialty shampoo to the head.

Rinse thoroughly, starting with the head and working back to rest of the body.

Apply conditioner first to the body and then to the head.

Rinse thoroughly. Start at head and then rinse the rest of the body. Remove cotton balls from ears.

Bombard Fido with praise, a big hug and treats. Thank him for cooperating.

Bathing 101

Washing a dog is both an art and a science. If you merely wet your dog, slather on the shampoo and give a quick rinse, you're barely removing the surface oil off the coat and not making a dent on the dirt. I've developed a Twelve-Step Washing Program, and as with all twelve-step programs, *admitting* that your dog *is* dirty is the first step. I've developed this system over the years as a professional groomer. It's tried-and-true and maximizes cleanliness and enjoyment and minimizes stress.

Water Temperature and Pressure

Lukewarm water is best for dogs. To avoid sudden temperature changes, continually monitor the water with your hand. If you scald your dog once, it may take months to rehabilitate her and convince her that bathing is fun.

Ideally you have a hose with an adjustable sprayer. Dogs, even the big ones, are delicate creatures. Use your hand to continually assess the water pressure. It should be strong enough to push the water down to the skin and remove product, but gentle enough to prevent you from removing the enamel off your tub. Never aim the water stream directly into Fido's nose, eyes, ears, genital area or rectum. Use your finger on the nozzle to break up the stream or turn the pressure down very low when in these areas.

Wetting the Body

Once the water temperature and pressure are set, begin the wet-down phase. Don't rush; many canine coats are water-resistant or thick. The water must penetrate the coat and reach the skin in order for shampoo to do its job. Always direct the water and maneuver your hands to move with the grain of the coat. (See "Brush with the Grain" on page 276.) Use your fingers to push the coat around so the water actually contacts the skin. Fido will appreciate the massage too. Aim the water so it saturates every canine crevice, like the armpits, between the paw pads, inside skin folds and flaps and under the tail. To reach the undercarriage, move the sprayer head under the dog and aim up. Be sure to decrease the water pressure if necessary. If you're using a pitcher or cup, use your hand to guide the water across the entire area.

In the early stages of the bath, avoid the head, which is the most difficult area.

The Reach Around

Unlike big dogs, the little guys are more maneuverable in the tub. If your dog is small enough, you can lift and twirl her around rather than lean over her as you work. Anytime you move her, keep her body supported and in a natural position. Place one hand under her rear end between her legs, the other hand under her chest, and lift. With a big dog you'll have to lean over her body unless *she* wants to move.

Shampooing the Body

I firmly believe in a first *and* second shampoo, no matter the doggy dirt level. The first shampoo loosens and lifts dirt from the skin and breaks up grime in the coat. For maximum cleaning, use a hypoallergenic shampoo in the first round, since it deep cleans without the superfluous frills. For the second round, which washes away the dirt, you may use a fancy specialty shampoo. It's up to you and the sky's the limit as long as Fido's skin isn't sensitive. If your veterinarian has prescribed a medicated shampoo, apply it in the second round.

||||||||||||||||||||||||||||||||||||||||||||||||||||||||||||||||||||||||||||||||||||||||

Close the Lid

Close every product as soon as you've used it. At some point, you'll knock over the bottle. I don't want your pooch exposed to the foul language that will inevitably flow from your mouth as the expensive product spills out. Closing the lid also prevents water from entering the bottle and breaking down the product, which causes it to spoil.

||||||||||||||||||||||||||||||||||||||||||||||||||||||||||||||||||||||||||||||||||||||||

Before applying the shampoo, read the label and verify that you're holding the correct bottle. Then, grab your container for diluting shampoo, squeeze in a few dollops and fill with water to make thick suds. Never dilute a product in the original bottle. This breaks down the shampoo and causes it to spoil. Discard the diluted shampoo at the end of the bath.

||||||||||||||||||||||||||||||||||||||||||||||||||||||||||||||||||||||||||||||||||||||||

Mats and Tangles in the Bath

Occasionally, you'll encounter a stray mat or tangle as you wash. Do not grab your brush to remove it while Fido is wet. Rather, make a mental note of its location and remove it using my dematting procedure after your dog is washed and thoroughly dry.

||||||||||||||||||||||||||||||||||||||||||||||||||||||||||||||||||||||||||||||||||||||||

Dunk your sponge and apply the shampoo to every nook and cranny on Fido's body, but avoid the head for now. Always move the sponge with the grain of the coat. If Fido has a particularly dirty area, apply the shampoo here first so it has a few extra minutes to penetrate.

The sponge allows you to efficiently but gently push the shampoo down to the skin. You should see the lather actually contacting the skin. Pay close attention to the more-difficult-to-reach areas, such as the armpits, under the tail, inside wrinkles, flaps and folds and between the toes and paw pads. The sponge is flexible, which allows you maneuver into these tight areas.

Fido, however, is not a washboard. The sponge prevents you from rubbing his skin raw as you lather him up. If you and Fido are in the mood, follow up with your fingers for a pampering massage. Watch Fido for signs of discomfort. If he's desperately trying to escape, nipping at your hand or whimpering, you're rubbing too hard. Be extra gentle in sensitive areas, including the genitals and rectum, but don't skip over these especially grimy areas. Once the sponge touches the rear, grab a fresh one.

Dunk the sponge many times and refill the container with shampoo and water as needed. Continue until Fido looks like he's wearing a lather coat. Take your time. Dogs don't shower every day, so don't skimp on the shampoo—there's a lot of dirt to clean up.

As you apply the shampoo, feel for lumps and growths. I've frequently uncovered masses that the owners never felt. Recently, one of my regular clients came in perfectly healthy and at her next appointment a month later, I found a lump the size of a plum. The owner was dumbfounded when I reported my discovery. I think the owner was just plain dumb, because a tumor that big doesn't pop up overnight. Clearly the owner never touched her dog. Please, touch and pet your dog every day and perform your weekly inspections!

Rinsing the Body

Rinsing is the most critical phase of dog washing. It's also the most time-consuming and requires meticulous attention to detail. On a dog with a thick or dense coat or a larger dog, rinsing may take ten minutes *or more*. Devote as much time as necessary. An inadequate or careless rinse job leaves shampoo or conditioner residue on the skin and coat. The coat will appear dull and the residue acts like a dirt magnet, so you'll be washing again sooner than you'd like. Most importantly, product residue irritates the skin, exacerbates skin allergies and makes the area sore, itchy and flaky. Fido will chew, lick and scratch the area and he will develop hot spots and an infection. So rinse carefully!

Always use *clean* water when you're rinsing. If you have a hose and sprayer, this is easy. If you're using a pitcher or cup, don't reuse the water from the bottom of the tub. As you rinse, bear gravity in mind. Start at the highest point and work down. If you start with the paws, you'll have to re-rinse after the soiled water runs off the top of the dog.

To rinse, push the water across the dog with a flat, open hand like a squeegee so it reaches all the way down to the skin. Always follow the grain of the coat. In smaller areas, use your fingers to direct the water. Be sure to guide water into every wrinkle, fold, crease and difficult-to-reach area. If Fido is on the smaller side, stand him on his hind legs to reach his under-carriage. With bigger dogs, you'll have to direct the water with the hose or your hand and reach under or around.

Catch water rolling off the dog in your hand to check if it's bubbly. Rinsing is not complete until the water running off the dog is *completely* clear. I always rinse for an extra minute or two just to be sure.

Wetting, Shampooing and Rinsing the Head

Washing the head is the most challenging part of bathing. Dogs instinctively shake when water contacts the area, and the ears, eyes and nose are sensitive. Thankfully, your patience and diligence combined with my outstanding instructions make this difficult task a snap. You will use the same technique to wet and rinse Fido's head.

Before you begin wetting or rinsing, verify that the cotton balls in Fido's ears are in place. Decrease the water pressure or break up the stream with your finger and never aim directly into the nose, ears, eyes and mouth. Tilt Fido's head up and hold it stable by placing your hand around his snout.

This minimizes shaking and maximizes control. Shield the nostrils and ear canal with your free hand. Fido will instinctively close his eyes when water is close by. (Thank you, Mother Nature!) Use your fingers to move the water through the fur with the grain of the coat. Verify that the water is reaching the skin. When rinsing, work until the water coming off the dog is clear. Then, rinse for an extra minute or two.

To apply shampoo, sponge it onto the top of the head while using your free hand to protect Fido's eyes. Next, ensure that the cotton balls in the ears are in place and lather up the ear area (notice I didn't say *inside* the ears). If Fido has Erect or Semi-drop ears, lather up the fur while using your hand as a barrier to prevent water and shampoo from leaking into the exposed ear canal. If Fido has Drop ears, lift up the flap and shampoo the fur growing *on* the inside edges of the flap itself, *not* inside the ear.

Move on to the mouth and work the sponge right up to the lip line and inside any folds and flews. Bacteria from food and debris loiter in the lip area and need to be rubbed out. Don't panic if a small amount of lather enters Fido's mouth. Use your clean, wet hand to wipe it away. Thoroughly lather up the beard and neck; this area is constantly wet and dirty from eating and drinking.

Once the rest of the head is lathered, tackle the eye area. Don't use a sponge; the eye area requires precision and a sponge is too big. Hold Fido's head in front of you, positioning your hands around the side like you are holding a basketball and are about to shoot. With your thumbs, pull down shampoo from the top of the head and rub around the eyes to clean the area. The combination of holding Fido's head and the fine control of your thumbs minimizes the opportunity for shampoo to contact Fido's eyes. If this happens, don't panic. Stop and immediately begin rinsing the eyes with copious amounts of fresh tepid water or sterile eyewash. Do not—I'll repeat in case you weren't reading closely—do not aim the water stream directly into Fido's eyes. Rather, use your cupped hand or a cup to pour the water into his eyes *gently*. Rinsing for a few minutes should clear the product from the eyes. Slip Fido a treat and pick up where you left off. If Fido's eyes remain red or irritated, however, call the veterinarian immediately!

Applying Conditioner

Now that Fido's been shampooed and rinsed twice, it's time to condition. Do not skip this step. Without conditioner, Fido's skin may dry out and his coat will be full of static and tangles. Conditioner also seals the cuticle so the coat repels dirt longer.

Apply conditioner first to the entire body and then to the head. Use only your hands and fingers; a sponge is useless, since conditioner is not meant to lather. Methodically work the product through the coat and down to the skin, always working with the grain of the coat. Apply conditioner to every nook and cranny *except* between the eyes. Even on long-haired dogs, the fur here is short and there's no need to risk the conditioner contacting the eyes. Allow the conditioner to soak in a minute or two to exploit the product's moisturizing and detangling effects.

If you've purchased any type of leave-in conditioner, return it to the store and demand your money back. If you want Fido's coat to be softer, let your regular conditioner sit for several extra minutes before you rinse.

The Final Rinse

The final rinse removes the conditioner. This time, start with the head and move down and back. Since this is your final opportunity to remove product residue, double- and triple-check the creases, the folds and all other hard-to-reach areas. No rushing. Wait for the water to run clear all over your pooch. Then, continue rinsing for a few more minutes to be on the safe side.

Spot Washing

Dirty Paws

Most of us were taught to remove our shoes as we enter a home. Even so, many of us (myself included) allow our canine companions to walk all over our homes and beds with the same feet they used to walk all over town. Just think of the filth and residue that may be lurking on Fido's paws: animal feces, human waste, chemicals, car exhaust, mud, pollution and any other gross germ you can imagine. Moreover, when your dog licks his paws, he's ingesting these horrible germs, and when he cuddles up at night, he's bringing them to bed. To keep everyone healthy, I recommend that you clean your dog's paws daily. I'm sure some true germophobes clean their dogs' paws after each and every walk. I wish I could commit to this, but I'm more realistic. So let's all promise to clean Fido's paws at night before bed. More power to you if you can clean more often!

For quick cleanups use a paw wipe or unscented baby wipe. Keep an eye on Fido's paw pads to check for any reaction to the wipes. If Fido's paws are particularly dirty or muddy, spot wash them in the tub or sink. Use your dilution container to wash the paws one by one and remove grime without wetting down your entire dog. Fido will keep his paw in the container as you wash if you lift up the opposite paw. Move his leg in natural positions so he's comfortable. Verify that you've rinsed out all the shampoo and conditioner, especially between his toes and pads. If your pooch is a Hair or Multilength Fur dog, brush the paws before you wash and *after* they dry.

Urine and Poop

If Fido is healthy, his rear and genitals won't need attention after every bathroom break. Occasionally, however, a "situation" will occur that requires you to boldly go where no man has gone before with an unscented baby wipe. A quick, *gentle* rub, and urine and fecal residue will be gone, no transporter or Scottish chief engineer required.

In more-severe cases, you'll need to spot wash with shampoo and conditioner. Allow the shampoo to remain on the dirty area for several minutes to fully penetrate for deep cleaning. Don't try to brush out the dirt. All that scum will end up stuck in your brush and you'll have to bleach it or buy a new one. Instead, brush *after* the area is clean and dry. If you're facing an army of Klingons, use your blunt-nosed scissors to trim the debris out of the fur. If that doesn't work, try the Vulcan Death Grip or your Phaser, but I suspect that's overkill. These procedures may cause both you and Fido to blush, but keeping his rear clean decreases the chance of infection so he can *live long and prosper.* (It also keeps your rugs and furniture clean too.)

Star Trek humor aside, I know what you all are thinking—how much can one person talk about a dog's rear end? Well, I feel compelled to nag because most owners are negligent about canine genital and butt hygiene and it's the dogs that suffer. Imagine if you could *never* wipe after using the restroom. With that in mind, please put your personal issues behind you, so to speak, and pay attention to your dog's private areas.

Facial Filth

If Fido's coat is sparkling, but the kiss he just bestowed smelled like a grease trap in the kitchen of a fast-food restaurant, his face needs cleaning. Chances are, the remnants of his recent meals and snacks are stuck in his fur, lips or flews. Moreover, if Fido has vomited, his face will need some cleaning up. Spot wash the area with a washcloth lathered up with shampoo and then conditioner. Brush after the coat dries. If Fido's face continues to smell, contact the veterinarian. Foul odor often signals a dental problem.

Doggy Drying

After rewarding your sopping dog for her good behavior in the bath, immediately commence the drying phase. Move quickly before Fido shakes, and he will, oh yes, he will. Use a large towel as a tent or hold it between the dog and the rest of the room to catch the water. Now let Fido shake. If the cotton balls have not flown out, remove them from the ears.

Towel Dry

Dry yourself off and then launch into towel drying. For a Uniform Fur dog, feel free to rub energetically and massage, but move with the grain of the coat. On Hair and Multilength Fur dogs, rubbing tangles the coat and un-necessarily complicates the postwash brush. So start at the root, blot and move out along the grain of the coat. Do not terminate towel drying until all excess moisture is absorbed. You may use several towels.

Verify that all wrinkles, skin folds and flaps are completely dry inside. If necessary, run a clean, dry washcloth or a fresh cotton swab or cotton ball inside to mop up any remaining moisture. Look inside Fido's ears and reapply ear wash to clear out any remaining wetness. If you're clipping nails, do it now, or forever gain peace of mind by leaving this difficult task to the professionals.

And now for the fun part—open the door and allow Fido to run around the house like a frenzied maniac. He'll race around with wide, glazed-over eyes, tongue flapping like a flag in a hurricane and legs pumping so fast you'll see only a blur as he passes by. Then, without warning, he'll collapse into a heap, conveniently allowing you time to clean and dry your home grooming station. Dogs absolutely love to run around like this after a bath. I suspect they like to accelerate the air-drying process and celebrate how good they feel after being pampered. Whatever the reason, it's hilarious to watch and it's a fitting reward for good bathing behavior.

Air-Dry or Blow-Dry

You now have a decision: air-drying or blow-drying. Keep in mind that short-snouted dogs are susceptible to overheating and should be blow-dried with extra care. If Fido is afraid of loud noises or particularly restless, do not subject him to a blow-dryer. If you are hell-bent on blow-drying no matter Fido's fears or personality, shame on you. If you insist, nonetheless, wrap a towel around Fido's head Red Riding Hood-style so his ears are covered while you blow-dry his body.

Air-drying is the most convenient option at home. The only hard part is waiting for the dog to be bone-dry before adding the finishing touches. Feel for moisture at the skin level, throughout the coat and inside all the nooks and crannies to determine if Fido is completely moisture free. Drying may take a few hours, especially if Fido's coat is long or thick. While Fido is drying, keep him inside, away from drafts and in a temperate area.

A blow-dryer decreases drying time, fluffs up the coat, carries away any remaining loose and dead coat and helps release curls, but it's fraught with danger. Hot or even warm air can quickly burn Fido's sensitive skin, sometimes severely. To prevent injury, use the dryer's no-heat or warm setting and the lowest motor speed. Keep the airstream moving and position your hand so you can continually monitor the air temperature. The instant your hand remotely heats up, move the dryer along and hold it farther away. Moreover, never point the airstream directly into the ears, eyes, nose, mouth or rectum.

Dry the body first, starting at the base of the neck and working back toward the tail end. Then dry the head. A poorly managed airstream can tangle long coats. So aim the airstream with the grain of the coat while simultaneously running your free hand through the fur. Stop blow-drying if Fido is overheating, frightened or anxious. We want him to enjoy bathing and if that means a three-hour air dry, so be it. Remember, don't use the blow-dryer *in* the bathtub or if your dog is standing in a pool of water.

The Finishing Touches

If Fido is a Uniform Fur dog, attach his collar and present him with a treat and hug and send him on his merry way. If Fido is a Hair or Multilength Fur dog, a bit of brushing is in order. After all your effort, don't get lazy on me now—a postwash brush keeps the mats and tangles away. Before grabbing the brush, however, double-check that Fido is thoroughly dry. Brush Fido's body and then his head using your best Billy Brushing Technique. (See chapter 15, "Dirty Deeds Done Dirt Cheap . . . at Home.") Then, gently run a comb through his coat to verify that all tangles and mats are gone. Attach Fido's collar, give him a treat and kiss and release him. Reward yourself with a big box of bonbons; you worked hard!

17.
Dirt Emergencies

Your treat-loving pal is curious. He likes to sniff around and explore, which means you must be ready to handle any type of dirt he happens upon. Waiting until Fido's next grooming appointment to clean up a dirt emergency isn't wise, especially with irritating, stinky or potentially hazardous substances. In this chapter, I discuss the most common dirt emergencies I've encountered in my years as a professional groomer. If your dog stumbles upon something else, promptly seek help from your veterinarian or groomer.

Safety Rules for Combating Dirt Emergencies

1. If Fido comes in contact with or ingests a hazardous, flammable or chemical substance or has a severe reaction, immediately call your veterinarian or the ASPCA's Animal Poison Control Center (1-888-426-4435) for instructions. (See "First Aid for Poisoning" in chapter 6, "Keeping Fido Safe and Sound at Home.")

2. **Never** use chemical solvents, human products or household cleaners on your dog unless specifically directed by certified experts. "Certified expert" has a narrow definition: *your* veterinarian, *your* emergency veterinarian or the Animal Poison Control Center, *not* a dog owner, author or random pet-care Web site.

3. **Never** use gasoline, kerosene, turpentine, alcohol, acetone, nail polish remover, paint thinner or paint remover on your dog. They are caustic and can burn Fido's delicate skin or interact with the spilled substance.

4. Even if the spilled substance is nontoxic or easily removed, call the veterinarian if you're unsure of how to clean the mess or if it involves your dog's eyes, ears, nose, genitals or rectum.

5. If you're directed to clean with anything other than dog shampoo and water, keep the treatment away from the eyes, nose, mouth, genitals and rectum. As a precautionary measure, protect the eyes with ophthalmic ointment or mineral oil before applying the treatment.

6. Remove any contaminated item from your dog, such as the collar and leash, and discard in a securely covered trash can.

7. Don't be embarrassed to ask for help from Fido's professional staff. Your ego should never endanger your best friend's health and well-being. Occasionally, even the most innocent-looking dirt transforms into a problem.

||||||||||||||||||||||||||||||||||||||||||||||||||||||||||||||||||||||||||||||||||||||||||||||||||||||||||

Why I Use Dawn Only for My Dishes

Many books and Web sites recommend using Dawn dish-washing soap to remove grease and oil-based spills from a dog's coat. Twenty years ago, even I used it. There wasn't anything else! Today, however, scores of degreasing shampoos and specialty products are widely available to professionals and dog owners alike. These products are specifically formulated and pH balanced to protect canine skin while doing their job. So there's absolutely no excuse for using Dawn on a dog, other than a refusal to leave the past behind.

Yes, I'll admit Dawn is effective, but the price to Fido's skin, coat and eyes is *way* too high. While Dawn is cutting the grease from the salad dressing that spilled on your dog, it's also stripping his coat of natural oils and drying out his skin. Moreover, if one drop of dish soap accidentally finds its way into an eye, you can say hello to serious irritation and potentially grave and expensive eye damage. To make matters even worse, Dawn or any dish soap is concentrated and forms a massive amount of lather, which is extremely difficult and tremendously time-consuming to rinse out thoroughly—I'm talking thirty minutes *at a minimum*. Soap residue is irritating and incredibly uncomfortable and can quickly lead to a painful hot spot.

Twenty years ago, I had a man bring in a dog with severely inflamed skin after an accident with a can of motor oil. The owner, being the "bright, resourceful" type, decided to clean the pooch with Dawn after he "saw on the news that those people helping the ducks and geese clean up from an oil spill used Dawn." Unfortunately, removing the motor oil proved tricky, so the man washed the dog over and over and over again, but never thoroughly rinsed out the soap; the poor pooch had been so itchy that he chewed himself to pieces. After countless baths, I successfully removed all the soap residue, and thankfully, the dog's skin *eventually* cleared up.

So, leave the Dawn at the kitchen sink, where it belongs. Remove greasy goo from Fido's coat with a canine degreasing shampoo.

||||||||||||||||||||||||||||||||||||||||||||||||||||||||||||||||||||||||||||||||||||||||||||||||||||||

Handy Tools for Dirt Emergencies
- ✓ Bowl or container for mixing
- ✓ Canine degreasing shampoo
- ✓ Canine de-skunking shampoo
- ✓ Canine hypoallergenic shampoo
- ✓ Comb
- ✓ Disposable cups or containers
- ✓ Disposable and/or rubber gloves
- ✓ Hydrogen peroxide, three percent
- ✓ Magnifying glass
- ✓ Natural cotton balls and swabs
- ✓ Ophthalmic ointment or mineral oil and clean dropper
- ✓ Paper towels
- ✓ Pliers
- ✓ Slicker brush
- ✓ Sterile eyewash
- ✓ Tweezers
- ✓ Vegetable oil

Special Dirt-Removal Procedures

Problem	Solution
Blood	1. Determine why the dog is bleeding and if necessary call the veterinarian immediately and begin first aid. 2. Dab hydrogen peroxide onto the bloodstain with a cotton swab. 3. Spot wash the area with canine shampoo. **NOTE:** don't use hydrogen peroxide near the eyes, nose, mouth, genitals or rectum.
Food	1. If Fido cannot lick it off and it's not hazardous, allow the food to dry and then brush it off with your hand or a slicker brush. 2. If the food is dangerous (e.g., chocolate), immediately spot wash with canine shampoo. If the food spill is large, bathe the entire dog.
Glue	1. For *water-soluble* glue: bathe Fido in canine shampoo. Once Fido is dry, carefully brush out any residue with a slicker. 2. For *instant* glue (e.g., Superglue, Krazy Glue or any cyanoacrylate adhesive): **Never** use nail polish remover. Dab the area with vegetable oil, let the oil sit for a few minutes and wash with canine degreasing shampoo. 3. If any glue remains, cut it out if you can place the scissors between the skin and the affected fur. Otherwise, wait for the fur to grow out or shed.
Gum	1. Prevent Fido from ingesting the gum. 2. Rub ice on the gum to harden it. 3. Hold the hardened gum firmly so it won't pull the skin as you work. With a slicker brush or your fingers, carefully pull the individual strands of fur off the wad. 4. Alternatively, place your fingers between the skin and the scissors and cut out the gum.

Ink and Marker	1. Spot wash with canine shampoo to remove the stain.
	2. If unsuccessful, you have two options:
	  A. Carefully trim out the stain if you can place your fingers between the skin and the scissors.
	  B. Wait for the stained area to shed or grow long enough to safely trim out.

Mud	1. Systematically inspect the dog for mud, especially between the paw pads.
	2. Allow the mud to dry.
	3. Brush the mud off with your hand or a slicker brush.
	4. Spot wash to remove any muddy residue or wash the entire dog.
Oil and Grease	1. Systematically inspect the dog to determine the size and severity of the spill.
	2. If the skin is burned, call the vet immediately and begin first aid. Prevent the dog from ingesting the spilled substance.
	3. Otherwise, use paper towels to soak up the excess oil or grease.
	4. Bathe with a canine degreasing shampoo.
Paint	1. Systematically inspect the dog and prevent her from ingesting the paint.
	2. For *water-based* paint: immediately bathe the dog in canine shampoo.
	3. For *oil-based* paint: immediately bathe the dog in canine degreasing shampoo.
	4. If the paint is dry, try to brush it out with a slicker. Alternatively, trim it out if you can position your fingers between the skin and the scissors.
Tar, Asphalt, Pine Pitch and Tree Sap	1. Systematically inspect the dog and prevent her from ingesting the substance. If the skin is burned or the paw pads, eyes, ears, nose, mouth, genitals or rectum are involved, promptly call the vet and begin first aid.
	2. Otherwise, bathe the dog in canine degreasing shampoo.
	3. If the substance is stubborn, dab vegetable oil on the area and allow it to remain on the spot for several minutes.
	4. Bathe the dog in canine degreasing shampoo.
	5. If you can place your fingers between the skin and the scissors, trim out anything remaining in the coat.

Wax	1. Systematically inspect the dog and prevent her from ingesting the wax. If the skin is burned, contact the vet immediately and begin first aid.
	2. Allow the wax to harden.
	3. Use your fingers to carefully remove the fur from the dried wax strand by strand. Hold the wax firmly so you won't pull the skin as you work.
	4. Brush with a slicker to remove the stragglers, or trim them out if you can place your fingers between the skin and the scissors.
	5. Bathe the dog.

Burs, Hitchhikers, Grass and Seeds

Burs are the seeds of plants and weeds. Many people refer to smaller burs as prickers or hitchhikers. Although burs inspired the invention of Velcro, they're annoying and painful to your furry friend. Foxtail and other grasses have awns, which are sharp, dartlike fibers, or sharp barbed seeds that also adhere to fur.

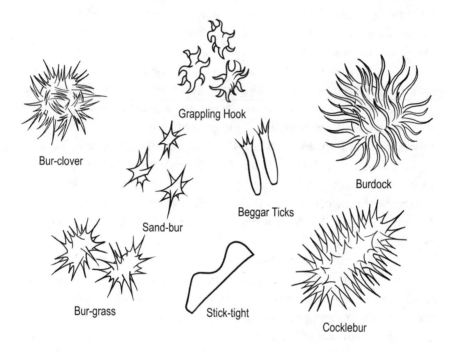

Bur-clover

Grappling Hook

Burdock

Sand-bur

Beggar Ticks

Bur-grass

Stick-tight

Cocklebur

The easiest way to prevent anything from clinging to Fido's coat is to avoid areas infested with burs, foxtails, tall grass and other such plants. This is easier said than done, since these plants grow everywhere, even on beaches and in vacant city lots. Outdoorsy dogs should wear a protective vest to shield their undercarriage when hiking, hunting or playing.

Remove all burs and awns ASAP! If left alone, they can embed themselves into Fido's skin and cause infections, abscesses and sores. Awns and seeds are especially dangerous because they can work their way *through* the skin and damage internal organs. In addition, fur can wrap around the plant material and form a nasty mat.

The moment you return home, systematically examine your pooch for any plant debris. Tweezers and a magnifying glass are helpful. The deerstalker hat, pipe and cape are optional. I always start at the back right leg and move counterclockwise around the dog, leaving the head for last. With long-haired dogs, use the divide-and-conquer method so you can actually see the skin. (See "Brushing Longer Fur" in chapter 15, "Dirty Deeds Done Dirt Cheap ... at Home.") As you inspect, play close attention to nooks and crannies where these annoying plant materials hide: between paw pads and toes; in armpits; under the tail; inside and around the nostrils, mouth, eyes and ears; inside wrinkles, folds and flaps and under the collar. Check closely around the genitals too.

To remove, hold the bur or awn still with one hand so you don't tug on the skin or fur. With your other hand, gently pull the fur off one strand at a time. Remove burs and awns as you uncover them, and place them directly into a cup or container. This prevents anyone from stepping on them and Fido from eating them. Crush large burs with pliers, but only if you can use your fingers as a barrier to protect the skin. Once you've removed everything you can find, brush the entire dog with a slicker brush, which should uncover any stragglers. Follow up with a comb, even on a Uniform Fur dog, to confirm that every last one of those little buggers is gone.

Watch for signs of trouble from embedded plant material, such as inflamed skin, bumps or abscesses, pain, swelling or discharge—especially around the eyes, ears or nose. Look for unusual behavior, including excessive sneezing, rubbing or pawing at the face, tilting or shaking the head, limping or maniacal scratching, licking or chewing. Fido might also gag, vomit or refuse to eat if a bur or awn made its way into his mouth or down his throat. If you observe any symptoms, call the veterinarian immediately and explain where Fido has been and the type of plant materials he may have encountered.

If the bur or awn infestation is excessive, ask your professional groomer or veterinarian for help. Removing these items from your pooch is difficult, but you must persevere. Ignoring them is too dangerous. A few years back, I received a hysterical phone call from one of my most beloved clients, who just so happens to be my witty and eloquent coauthor. Her pooch had a bad run-in at the doggy beach with a patch of three-lobe beggar-ticks. After removing over one hundred of them, neither she nor Filbert could stand it anymore. She rushed Filbert into my shop and I brushed him out for another twenty-five minutes until his coat was clear. Because Filbert's owner asked for help when the situation became overwhelming, Filbert avoided mats and infection.

Many "experts" recommend rubbing cornstarch in the area around a bur or awn to loosen the attached fur. Along with these words of "wisdom," the experts inevitably warn that cornstarch "may irritate canine eyes." Well, why would you risk hurting your dog when you can remove burs and awns without using any potentially harmful concoctions? Besides, the cornstarch is difficult to remove from the coat and the residue can irritate Fido's skin.

I Smell a Skunk

If Fido has been fraternizing with the neighborhood skunks, grab your hazmat suit and rubber gloves and rev up the decontamination lab. De-skunking is a smelly business and you'll want to be wearing old clothes or a disposable bodysuit. When a skunk attacks, it sprays the contents of its anal glands on the poor unsuspecting dog. (I know what you're thinking—this book has more content relating to anal glands than any other—but I'm telling it like it is.) As you might imagine, the smell is horrific. Your skunked dog's eyes will be irritated and he may be vomiting or rolling on the ground to remove the spray.

Skunk attacks can occur anywhere—I've recently come across two skunks in my residential city neighborhood. Unless the skunk attack occurs right outside the salon, you cannot wait for professional help. De-skunking is something you have to do yourself because the sooner you remove the spray, the less likely the stink will linger and the more comfortable your dog will be.

First, examine Fido for bites or scratches in case he actually fought with the skunk. If he has any wound, no matter how small, promptly contact the veterinarian. In zee wild, skunks aren't cute and cuddly like zee Pepe Le Pew. Rather, they can be vicious and carry rabies.

Next, begin the decontamination process. Water intensifies the stench, so don't put Fido in the bath until you have your de-skunking supplies in place. First, rinse Fido's irritated eyes with lots of sterile eyewash or clean, fresh tepid water. Then wash the dog. I use a commercial de-skunking shampoo. Follow the directions carefully. If you live in skunk territory, I suggest that you keep at least one bottle on hand to deploy in the event of a skunk emergency.

Alternatively, you may concoct your own skunk-odor remover. Don't make up the mixture and store it—it may explode if kept in a closed container. Always make a fresh batch and discard any leftovers. Keep extra ingredients on hand, since you may need a few batches. Do not allow Fido to ingest the mixture.

Admittedly this recipe violates my "no human products on dogs" rule. This *one* time, however, I'm deferring to the experts at the ASPCA's Animal Poison Control Center because they are the ultimate authority. The recommended mixture will harm a dog's eyes if it makes contact. I know you'll be extra careful, but as a precaution, treat Fido's eyes with ophthalmic ointment or mineral oil before you begin.

Homemade Skunk Odor Remover

- 1 quart unexpired 3% hydrogen peroxide
- ¼ cup baking soda
- 1 teaspoon liquid soap

Move away from an open flame or heat source and wear rubber gloves. Combine the ingredients in an open container and liberally apply the mixture, starting at the rear and ending with the head. Do not let Fido lick or swallow the mixture. Work the mixture through the coat down to the skin all over his body. Exercise extreme caution when in the eye area. Hold Fido's head in your hands facing you. Use your thumbs to control the mixture around the eyes. Allow the mixture to sit for several minutes and don't let Fido shake. Rinse *thoroughly* with clean, lukewarm water. Try to cover Fido's eyes with a washcloth while rinsing his head. If Fido still reeks, repeat until the smell is gone. Now bathe him with his regular hypoallergenic shampoo and conditioner. Call your veterinarian if your dog is vomiting or his eyes remain red, swollen or irritated. Discard his collar and leash if they were sprayed too.

Most de-skunking solutions, including this one, bleach fur. Don't fret; Fido's fur will grow back in the regular color. The skunk stench, however, may pop up for a while whenever Fido is wet. I have a client who stank up my whole shop every time I bathed him two years after he was sprayed.

18.
Yes, Virginia, Every Dog
Needs to Visit a
Professional Groomer

Picture me in a brown herringbone tweed sport coat, bespoke tailored at the finest Savile Row shop. A lustrous lavender silk handkerchief is folded and arranged into three symmetrical triangles in my breast pocket. My trousers are handcrafted from Super 180 wool, shorn from the scrotum of a reclusive mountain goat that resides on the highest peak of the Himalayas. Butter-soft cordovan leather loafers adorn my well-manicured feet. On my right is a burled walnut side table set with a newly lit antique mahogany pipe resting in a finely cut, handblown leaded crystal ashtray. I'm sitting in a supple, overstuffed russet leather club chair in a lovely library. The walls are lined with floor-to-ceiling shelves, which are overflowing with rare books. Zeke and Arthur are at my feet in front of the roaring fire.

"Welcome to *Master Groomer Theatre*," I remark in a posh South Side of Chicago accent as I open a gold embossed leather tome entitled *Billy's Excellent Grooming Adventures*. I gracefully thumb through the thick vellum pages and pause at a chapter entitled "A Tale of One Person Who Never Took Her Dog to a Professional Groomer." I delicately clear my throat and begin reading the sorrowful tale of Barbara, the two-year-old Labradoodle.

"Barbara and her owner came to my shop several years ago. Barbara was the size of a Labrador Retriever with a woolly, curly coat from her Poodle half. I examined Barbara and found that her coat was about eight inches long. The top four inches looked pretty and I nodded and smiled at the owner. As I continued my inspection, however, the smile slid off my face and rapidly morphed into a frown. The bottom four inches of Barbara's coat was a solid mat right down to the skin. When I inquired about her grooming routine, Barbara's owner replied, 'The breeder said that I should never take a Labradoodle to a professional groomer, that I should do it myself. I even looked at several Doodle Web sites that said that professional groomers don't know how to groom Doodles.'

"Barbara's owner had been dutifully washing her every few weeks for the last two years at a do-it-yourself dog wash. Clearly, however, the owner had been washing and brushing only the top four inches of the coat. (Had she read my book, of course, she would have known that it is imperative to get down to the skin.) I parted Barbara's coat and, with a well-practiced flourish of my hands, displayed the mats. The owner was truly flabbergasted. She had no clue whatsoever that Barbara's coat had any problems, let alone a webbing of mats covering her entire body.

"I tactfully informed the owner that Barbara required an immediate and complete shave down and a proper wash down to the skin level. Alas, Barbara didn't look like a Doodle or even a Poodle when she left my shop that day. With her new shave, she resembled an embarrassed Labrador Retriever for many months until her coat grew back. In the meantime, I showed Barbara's owner how to properly brush and wash her dog. Since that fateful day, Barbara has visited my shop every six weeks without fail and her owner correctly and frequently brushes and washes her at home. Now Barbara has a beautiful, healthy coat and a fashionable Doodle haircut."

Sighing, I gently close the book and break for a commercial.

So many lessons may be learned from this poignant tale. Let's discuss a few. Most importantly, *every dog* must visit a professional groomer periodically. Had Barbara's owner received accurate advice, she would have known that a Doodle is a Hair dog and, thus, requires professional grooming at least every four to six weeks *in addition* to frequent home grooming. Even a mediocre professional groomer would have discovered Barbara's mats well before they became severe and she would have been spared the humiliating shave down.

In addition, always independently confirm with a trusted professional *anything* that you read on the Internet. Recently, I found a Doodle owner posing a grooming question to a purported online expert. The owner wondered whether it was OK to let his Doodle's coat grow long for the winter, since the matting "doesn't seem to bother my dog." He complained that the groomers he visited all insisted that the dog must be shaved and the mats removed. *Of course* the groomers insisted! Mats, especially if covering the entire dog, are uncomfortable and painful and often harbor bacteria, dirt and infections.

So, dear reader, the answer is yes: *every* dog, even a Hairless breed, must visit a professional groomer pursuant to the schedule in chapter 11, "Planning Your Dog-Care Routine." Without a doubt, my answer remains the same even if you master and actually perform every single task and recommendation in this book. Here's why:

- A professional's eyes are practiced at inspecting a dog's skin and coat and often identify problems missed by a home groomer. Besides, it never hurts to have an additional set of eyes examining your pooch.
- A professional provides a thorough bath, intensive brushing and specialized skin and coat care.
- A professional can identify and remove mats safely. Eradicating a large number of mats or ones close to the skin is difficult and not a task for the home groomer.
- Correcting coat problems and performing complex coat maintenance, such as stripping or thinning a thick coat, are complicated, are potentially painful and require professional equipment and expertise.
- A professional has the experience, skill and tools to accurately and safely cut and style your dog's coat, including complex traditional breed clips.
- Nail clipping, ear-hair removal and anal-sac expression are safer when performed by a trained professional. Besides, would you want your anal sacs emptied by the same hands that prepared your dinner?

Remember, however, that even if your dog has a weekly or monthly standing appointment at the swankiest grooming salon in town, you *must* care for your dog at home. So, repeat after me: "Properly caring for a dog entails professional grooming *combined with* home grooming." Feel free to alter the balance between professional and home grooming depending on your personal taste, budget and dog's breed and personality.

How to Choose a Professional

Fido will be alone with the groomer for at least four hours. Accordingly, you must be 110 percent confident that your pooch will be safe and comfortable while out of your sight and control. Most states require neither a grooming license nor formal education. Moreover, many "groomers" advertise speed or low prices. Let's just say you get what you pay for!

Recently, one of my clients arrived at my salon distraught about what she had witnessed at a big-box pet store. A cute little white dog was shaking uncontrollably as the "groomer," and I use the term loosely, was roughly pulling his leg up like a wishbone in order to jam all his nails into a tub of styptic powder. Clearly, this "groomer" had carelessly cut the dog's nails and made *each* one bleed. Moreover, this little guy's fur was clipped so short that all the wounds from slapdash clipping were plainly visible. Obviously, this is NOT the type of groomer you want for your beloved pet. You heard it here first, folks: bargain grooming is no bargain at all if your dog comes back hurt and traumatized.

As long as I'm sharing horror stories, here's another one. Recently, I attended a grooming seminar and an adorable four-month-old yellow Labrador Retriever caught my eye. A novice groomer had rigged two grooming nooses to her table and to the dog so he could not move *at all* while he was being blow-dried. The poor pup was trembling like a motorboat, his little brown eyes oozed fear and his ears were flapping like a kite in a cyclone. Mind you, the groomer was not *technically* doing anything wrong—except not talking to the dog and blowing air too close to his ears. This groomer should have known better! Fact: a dog's ears are acutely sensitive to sound. Ergo, if you aim the dryer toward the ears, the poor pooch will undoubtedly think that a 747 is landing on his head.

My heart went out to this little guy. I walked over, cupped the dog's head in my hands and started talking to him. I kissed him on the forehead and whispered, "It's OK, little puppy—your groomer is not really trying to hurt you. She just doesn't understand that your ears are more sensitive than hers." Almost instantly the dog's tail went up and started wagging. He even stopped trembling. In less than a minute, using only a soothing voice and a light touch, I had transformed the dog's experience. Clearly, that groomer had a lot to learn.

Please, I beg you, do your research before choosing a groomer. Be cautious and bear in mind that bad experiences with a professional will make it harder for you to care for your dog at home. And I promise that no matter how often your pooch visits the groomer, you *will* have to bathe and care for your dog!

Word of mouth is an important resource for discovering both good and bad groomers. If you see a nicely groomed dog on the street, stop and ask the owner about his groomer. Also ask the owners of poorly groomed dogs, so you know which professionals to avoid. Your veterinarian and other dog people are also excellent sources. Check out the potential groomers on the Internet and contact the Better Business Bureau for information too.

Next, reconnoiter the shop of each groomer on your short list. There is no need for night-vision goggles or camouflage face paint, unless you like that sort of thing. Visit the shops in the afternoon after the fur has been flying for a few hours. Start your mission on the outside. Don't pay too much attention to the dogs arriving for their appointments because most are apprehensive on the way in. Instead, study the dogs that are leaving and look for signs of bad grooming, such as cuts, dull coats or uneven haircuts.

I'll admit that some breeds do have goofy-looking haircuts. Picture a Bedlington Terrier in a lamb clip or a Poodle in a show trim with a butt shave. In such cases, don't blame this on the groomer, as these clips are traditional for the breed. Instead, focus on whether the dogs look clean, evenly trimmed and happy. Study the owners too; do they seem pleased?

After concluding your outside reconnaissance, enter the salon and observe. Your mission is to ascertain whether the groomer (and his staff) is indeed *good with dogs*. That said, a groomer's people skills may not necessarily be an indicator of his dog skills. Sometimes, we groomers are not at our best with people—that's why we work with dogs. Instead, focus on the groomer's *dog* skills.

This brings to mind the most horrible grooming story I know.

The groomer—let's call her Darth Groomer—had as a client a disagreeable, crotchety old Poodle. Yes, the dog was feisty, but she nonetheless deserved respect and humane treatment. Darth Groomer fought with this poor Poodle during every appointment; she was even nastier and more bad-tempered than the dog. Clearly, when Darth Groomer was an Apprentice she had a vicious run-in with a Master Groomer on a volcanic Outer Rim planet.

One day, as Darth Groomer was trying to brush the Poodle, the dog kept biting at the brush. Rather than pausing to soothe and gently talk to the Poodle, Darth Groomer hit the dog with the brush several times. The dog became extremely agitated and had a heart attack and died right on the grooming table.

That's not even the worst part! Without exhibiting even a smidge of emotion, Darth Groomer removed the grooming noose, polished the Poodle's nails and fastened pink bows in her ears. When the owner arrived, Darth Groomer wouldn't return the Poodle until the owner paid.

Throughout my career as a groomer, competitor and judge, I have worked with and observed thousands of groomers. Thankfully, most are empathetic, caring people who have the dogs' best interests in mind. Unfortunately, however, I have come across a few Darth Groomers. With that in mind, study the potential groomer's interactions with the dogs. A groomer should handle dogs gently and compassionately—and I mean at *all times* and *especially* if the dog is scared, uncooperative or mean. It should be obvious to you that the groomer (and her staff) is concerned about the well-being of every dog in the shop. You have certainly found a bad groomer if you see him dragging a dog across the floor or screaming at or threatening a dog. If the groomer is behaving that way *in front of you*, imagine what he's doing after you leave. The same is true for the assistants and staff. No dog should ever be mishandled, neglected, mistreated or abused. Period. End of story.

As you inspect the salon, use all your senses. Take a deep breath. The predominant odor should be "dog," not feces, urine or any other foul stench. If you smell cigarette smoke, determine if anyone is lighting up near the dogs; if someone is, run, don't walk, to another groomer. Examine the cages, tools, floors and work surfaces and verify that they are clean and well maintained. Look for disinfectant and confirm that tools, brushes, towels, sponges and all work areas are properly cleaned between dogs. Moreover, visible signs of poop or urine are red flags unless the dog just deposited them and you see the groomer or an assistant rushing for a mop. Indeed, the shop should be clean and *relatively* fur free, even at the busiest time of day. If the shop is dirty, chances are your dog is not being properly washed.

Ask whether the groomer uses a cage dryer. A cage dryer is either a stand-alone metal box with glass doors and a blower inside or a separate machine that attaches to a regular cage and blows warm air inside. Unfortunately, cage dryers have caused numerous tragedies because the air temperature inside the cage or box builds rapidly and can cause a dog to overheat or worse. For this reason, most groomers, including me, have stopped using them entirely. If your groomer still utilizes a cage dryer, ensure that the machine has a timer, a thermostat and a safety shutoff. Better yet, find another groomer. In any event, confirm that someone will be vigilantly watching your dog the entire time she's under any type of dryer.

Once your examination is complete, chat with the groomer using my talking points as a guide. Remember that very few states require groomers to obtain professional certifications or attend grooming school. Unfortunately, this means that any Joe Schmo can, and often does, hang up a shingle and call himself a groomer. To be sure, certifications and education are no guarantee that you've found a good groomer. They do, however, indicate that the groomer is serious about his career and is voluntarily educating himself.

Whether or not your dog's nickname is Nervous Nellie, ask the groomer point-blank how he handles uncooperative or anxious dogs. The groomer must articulate a humane soothing strategy that clearly demonstrates patience and compassion. If you hear the word "tranquilizer," run for the hills and don't look back or you may turn into a pillar of salt. A dog should **never** receive any medication or herbal remedy without a doctor's order. Drugs are for groomers too lazy to devote time and effort to proper dog care.

Similarly, if your dog has any special needs or has a difficult or sensitive personality, discuss these issues with the groomer. Determine whether you agree with her policies and practices for working with your pooch's particular needs.

Review the groomer's muzzle policy and decide whether you agree. For dogs that are known biters or begin to bite while at the groomer, a properly fitted muzzle is necessary because it removes all biting risk. Remember, a bite can lead to government intervention and medical bills. The groomer shouldn't, however, use a muzzle merely to quiet barking dogs. Grooming shops are noisy, and the sound of barking is expected. After all, the shop is filled with *dogs*. It wouldn't be fair to muzzle an overly talkative person, so I wouldn't expect a groomer to muzzle a dog who is just expressing himself.

Next, ask the groomer if he offers any special services. Some groomers offer teeth brushing or a mini-grooming service consisting of a bath, brush out and trim. A good groomer will clip Fido's nails, express his anal sacs and remove ear hair between appointments.

Establish where your dog will stay while at the shop. Many clients ask me to forgo a cage and chain their dog to the wall while at my shop. In actuality, dogs truly prefer cages. After all, dogs are denning animals and they're more relaxed and calm in the enclosed environment. Dogs waiting out in the open are easily stressed; they pace, become tangled in their leash and are overstimulated each time someone enters or exits the shop.

Ascertain whether clean, fresh water is offered and establish Fido's bathroom arrangements. The groomer must be willing to let your dog relieve himself in an appropriate place. Just for the record, a cage is *not* an appropriate place. In addition, discuss the shop's first-aid protocol, safety precautions and emergency procedures.

How is the groomer's hygiene? Ask yourself whether you would want that person giving *your* undercarriage a "how's your father." If the groomer has dirty fingernails, looks or even smells like Pig Pen or has not bathed in a while, your dog's cleanliness is unlikely to be his primary concern. Establish who else will be handling your dog and observe them too. Ask the groomer to show you his dogs to see if they're well-groomed, clean and happy.

Finally, discuss fees and cancellation and payment policies and drop-off and pickup procedures. Decide whether they seem reasonable and convenient.

Your dog's welfare is involved. Therefore, **never** be shy about asking questions. The groomer's answers should be straightforward and he should be willing to answer all your queries. In the end, you must be comfortable with the people, the accommodations and the arrangements, since your dog will be at the shop for many hours at each visit.

Talking Points for Interviewing Professional Groomers

- Education
- Experience and job history
- References (Be sure to follow up.)
- Licensing and certifications (Verify they are current.)
- Grooming philosophy
- Staff: who they are and how, when and why they will handle your pooch
- Services offered
- Procedure for handling uncooperative or anxious dogs
- Product and equipment choices, e.g., no cage dryers
- Accommodations for dog: caged or chained to a wall
- Bathroom arrangements

- Water or snacks offered
- Your dog's special needs
- Cleaning protocol for tools, work areas, towels, etc.
- First-aid protocol, safety precautions and emergency procedures
- Fees, hours and policies for appointments, cancellations, payment, drop-off and pickup

Once you decide and make Fido's first appointment, remind the groomer about Fido's personality, health or special needs. For example, if your dog bites if he hears a loud noise, is deathly afraid of water or falls to pieces if he sees a person wearing green, tell the groomer. You are starting what we all hope will be a long, happy relationship. Open communication ensures a positive experience for your dog, for you and for the groomer. Indeed, at every appointment, alert the groomer about anything unusual going on in your dog's life. If your normally happy-go-lucky dog is having a bad day or suddenly develops a fear of Poodles, tell the groomer. That way, he'll know how to adjust his grooming routine to keep your dog relaxed and content.

Proper Drop-Off Etiquette

When dropping Fido off at the groomer, please be strong for his sake. Refrain from overly mollycoddling him at the first sign of nervousness. If you respond by melodramatically scooping him up while delivering kisses and using baby talk, your behavior validates and reinforces Fido's anxiety. Instead, as you walk into the shop, pat Fido on the head, smile and assure him everything is fine in a confident, *adult* voice. This strategy is useful at the vet's office too.

19.
Home Dog-Care Safety
and Basic First Aid

Please place your seats in the upright and locked position, stow your tray tables and direct your undivided attention to me. You can't miss me; I've slipped on my vintage Pucci Braniff International Airways air-hostess uniform. It's fabulous—a mini-length tunic, tights and a derby hat with an attached head scarf all in a matching harlequin pattern of absinthe green, soft lilac, lemon yellow and vibrant indigo. Drawings of stylized flags, Latin musical instruments and pre-Columbian art are randomly depicted within the diamonds, symbolizing the airline's ports of call. I've traded my sensible shoes for lime green ankle boots, which are accented with bold yellow stripes, and I am twirling my matching umbrella. We are now prepared to review safety in the event of a Grooming Emergency.

Home dog care is not all fun and games. You are wielding sharp objects around a living, breathing animal that probably has better things to do than sit perfectly still while you work. That said, if you are conscientious and patient and adhere to my recommendations, mishaps will rarely, if ever, occur. Follow my number one safety rule and you'll do just fine: **never leave your dog unattended at any time while grooming or caring for him.**

Advance preparation and practice will help keep *you* calm, capable and focused should an emergency arise. With no opposable thumbs and limited facility with human language, Fido will be of no assistance. Once again, my humorless and exceptionally irksome legal team requires me to "plainly and indisputably" state that, "although essential and valuable, my first-aid discussion is by no means comprehensive. Rather, it is meant to be an introduction to topics that should inspire additional study in a pet first-aid manual." When reading your manual, pay close attention to the techniques for transporting an injured dog, severe-blood-loss prevention, shock, canine CPR and the Heimlich maneuver.

Fortunately, most grooming injuries are minor. Nevertheless, even with minor injuries, I recommend calling your veterinarian to check in and obtain additional information and advice once you have helped your dog. If your pooch suffers a serious injury or you cannot control the situation, call the veterinarian IMMEDIATELY. The office will direct you and determine whether your dog requires urgent medical attention.

Muzzle 101

Even the sweetest dog can bite if she's injured or scared. A muzzle protects you while you are helping your pooch. If you do not have a ready-made muzzle handy, fashioning one from a long strip of cloth is not difficult if you practice *beforehand*. When you're in the midst of an emergency, you don't want to lose precious time fumbling with the instructions.

||||||||||||||||||||||||||||||||||||||||||||||||||||||||||||||||||||||||||||||||||||||||||||||||||||||

Making a Muzzle

1. Start with a long strip of clean cloth or gauze. Position it below the jaw and leave equal lengths on either side of the snout.
2. Bring the ends around to top of snout and tie a knot over the bridge of the nose. Avoid Fido's nostrils like the plague.
3–4. Bring the ends of the cloth under the jaw and cross them.
5–6. Pull the ends around the side of the head and behind the neck and knot firmly, but not so tight as to restrict airflow.

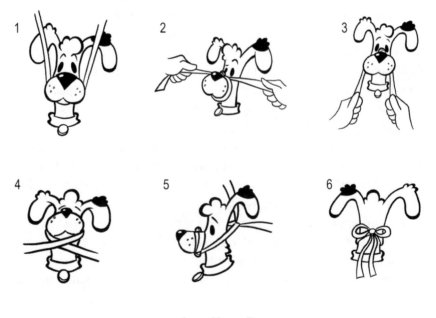

Never leave a muzzled dog unattended even for a moment. The muzzle can interfere with breathing if it slips into the wrong position.

DO NOT use a muzzle if the dog is suffering from any other serious condition, such as one of these:

- is unconscious
- is in shock
- is having a seizure
- has an obstructed airway
- is vomiting, coughing or gagging
- is having any trouble whatsoever breathing
- is suffering from heatstroke
- has a fractured skull
- has a severe chest wound

If in doubt, don't use a muzzle.

Nail-Clipping Injuries

If, despite my numerous warnings, you cut Fido's nails yourself, prepare for the inevitable injury. The moment you draw blood, immediately put down the nail clippers, raise your hands in the air and step away from the dog and toward your first-aid kit. Although it may sound that way, I'm *not* being patronizing—some people actually think that bleeding nails are no big deal and continue the pedicure. Believe me, Fido is in pain. Once the quick is cut, your main priority is to stop any bleeding ASAP!

First-Aid Procedure

- Remain calm and soothe your dog.
- Wash your hands with hot water and soap and/or put on disposable gloves.
- Restrain or muzzle the dog if necessary.
- Triage: assess the severity of the wound.
- Apply direct pressure to the end of the nail with a clean cloth,

towel, gauze pad or other sanitary material. Maintain pressure for five to ten minutes.

- Alternatively, apply a coagulating product, such as styptic gel or powder, to the end of the nail. Carefully follow the use instructions on the product's label.
- If the bleeding continues, contact the veterinarian immediately and transport your dog to the animal hospital.
- Monitor the injured area for signs of infection and contact your vet if you notice swelling or redness or if your dog is reluctant to bear weight on the injured nail.

Injury Triage Flowchart

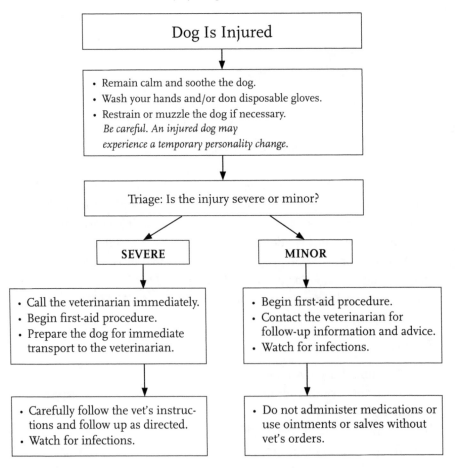

Bleeding from Cuts and Abrasions

Although it is rare, you may draw blood while grooming. Sometimes, cuts or abrasions seem minor at first, but the situation can go downhill quickly. Many people (maybe even you) are queasy around blood. Do your best to remain clearheaded so you can properly assess the situation and take appropriate steps to help your pet. The moment you see blood, STOP GROOMING IMMEDIATELY and begin first aid.

First-Aid Procedure

- Remain calm and soothe your dog.
- Wash your hands and/or don disposable gloves.
- Restrain or muzzle the dog if necessary.
- Triage: assess severity of the wound.

Severe Bleeding

- A wound is severe if it's spurting blood or bleeding profusely. **This situation is extremely serious and your dog needs immediate veterinary attention. Time is of the essence, since acute blood loss can result in shock or worse.** Your main priority is to stop any bleeding ASAP!
- **Do not** wash the wound, since this may remove crucial clots.
- Using a sterile gauze pad, sanitary napkin, clean towel or cleancloth, apply pressure directly to the wound to stop the bleeding. **Do not** move the material to check if bleeding has ceased. To maintain clots, as the material becomes soaked through, do not move it. Instead, place a new clean pad or cloth on top. Be patient; bleeding may not cease for five to ten minutes.
- As soon as possible, call the veterinarian and alert the office of your imminent arrival.
- If the dog has no broken bones, elevate the injured limb or body part.

- Continue to apply pressure to the wound as you transport your dog to the animal hospital.
- Review advanced blood-loss procedures including pressure-point and tourniquet techniques with your vet before an emergency strikes. They are difficult to perform properly and should be used only for life-threatening situations.

Minor Bleeding

- If possible, carefully trim away any fur that obstructs the wound, using your blunt-nosed scissors. Keep your fingers between the skin and the scissors.
- Gently clean the wound with hypoallergenic canine shampoo and rinse. (If the shampoo isn't handy, rather than risking infection, use a very small amount of mild hand soap. I know it's a human product, but this is a *medical* emergency, and a veterinary professional approved this instruction.) Lightly blot the area dry with a sterile gauze pad, clean towel or other unsoiled material.
- **Do not** wash the area again, as you will likely remove any clots and restart the bleeding.
- If the wound continues to bleed, apply pressure using a sterile gauze pad, clean towel or other unsoiled material.
- Once the bleeding stops, apply antibiotic ointment from your pet first-aid kit.
- Apply a clean sterile bandage. Never apply the bandage or adhesive tape directly to the fur. Removal is hazardous to *your* health. Fido will be furious if you rip off his fur while removing the bandage. If your dog licks the wound, consider an Elizabethan collar. These devices resemble a lampshade and prevents your pooch from reaching his wound.
- Call the veterinarian to discuss the injury and obtain further instructions. Inquire about administering medication, topical ointments or salves.
- Until the wound heals, change the bandage daily and reapply antibiotic ointment.
- Watch for signs of infection, including discharge, swelling, heat,

pain or redness. If the wound does not show signs of healing within a few days, contact the veterinarian.

Shock

Shock is an extremely grave condition that occurs when the body cannot maintain adequate blood flow. As the body attempts to counteract the inadequate circulation, it speeds up the heart, reduces urine output and constricts the blood vessels. The following are common signs of shock:

- Cold paws and legs
- Depressed mental state or unconsciousness
- Drop in body temperature or shivering
- Gray or white gums or lips
- Increased heart rate
- Pale skin
- Weak pulse

The moment your pooch experiences any injury that involves severe trauma, excessive blood loss, dehydration, heatstroke, frostbite or poisoning, contact the veterinarian and transport him to the animal hospital. Time *is* of the essence and can mean the difference between life and death.

Clipper Injuries

As I've said before, clippers are for professionals. Just for a moment, though, let's suspend disbelief and assume that you know how to use clippers. Have you considered that your dog naturally begins to lick when the area around his mouth is touched, which means that you can easily nick his tongue during a snout shave? While you're shaving his face, the clippers may slip and Fido may end up with a painful scratched cornea. But wait . . . there's more. While you remove the fur from his paw, the hot blade might burn Fido's paw pad. Any of these injuries is painful to your pooch and your budget.

Clipper burn is the most common clipper-induced injury. It occurs if you apply too much pressure or shave over the same spot too many times. The skin is pink, raw and covered in bumps. It's neither pretty nor comfortable. Clipper burns may not show up for twelve to twenty-four hours. Since you probably didn't notice the problem and kept clipping away, you'll be feeling awfully guilty then, won't you? Moreover, clippers can easily cut or abrade the skin and draw blood—lots of it. Truly, the most effective means to prevent clipper injuries is not to use them—ever (unless you're a trained professional).

First-Aid Procedure

- Remain calm and soothe your dog.
- Wash your hands and/or don disposable gloves.
- Restrain or muzzle the dog if necessary.
- Triage: assess the severity of the wound.
- If you've drawn blood with the clippers, follow the procedures for severe or minor bleeding on page 365–67.
- If your dog has clipper burn, turn off the clippers. Promptly contact the vet to obtain soothing medication. Do not apply anything to the skin—no homemade potions, herbal remedies or ointment from your medicine cabinet—until directed by a veterinarian
- Prevent the dog from licking, chewing or biting the affected area.
- Watch for signs of infection, including hot spots, discharge, redness, swelling, heat, and pain. If the affected area is not healing within a few days, contact the veterinarian immediately.

Burns From a Blow-dryer or Water

Although it is rare, the blow-dryer or hot water can burn Fido. Burns can singe fur and cause reddening of the skin, swelling, pain or tenderness in the affected area. If the burn is severe, blisters, charring, swelling under the skin and loss of skin are common. In some cases, your dog may exhibit no reaction even when the affected area is touched. If Fido is burned, stop grooming immediately and begin first aid.

First-Aid Procedure

- Remain calm and soothe your dog.
- Wash your hands and/or don disposable gloves.
- Restrain or muzzle the dog if necessary.
- Triage: assess the severity of the injury.
- If the burn is severe, if your dog is in pain or if he exhibits signs of shock, contact your veterinarian immediately for instructions and prepare for urgent transport to the animal hospital.
- If the burn is minor, begin first aid.
- Apply cold—not icy—water or a clean cold compress to the burned area.
- Do not apply butter, ointment, petroleum jelly or any other substance to the wound without prior veterinarian approval. Do not rub the area.
- Lightly place a sterile bandage or clean, moist cloth over the burned area for protection.
- Contact the veterinarian to discuss the injury and bring the dog to the animal hospital for examination.

Allergic Reactions

Food, environmental toxins and grooming products may cause an allergic reaction. Such reactions range from mild skin irritations to full-blown anaphylactic shock, a fancy name for severe allergic reactions. Although rare, anaphylactic shock is an extremely serious condition requiring immediate veterinary attention. Anaphylactic shock is not always instantaneous and, in fact, can develop over several hours. Often, the first signs are a change in pupils, hives, swelling, drooling, irritation, itchiness, redness or difficulty breathing, which are similar to symptoms of more run-of-the-mill allergic reactions. Believe it or not, I was grooming at a friend's shop years ago and a bee sneaked in and stung a dog sitting on the floor. The dog's face blew up like a Cabbage Patch doll in a matter of minutes. We called the veterinarian and he advised us to administer an antihistamine.

Fortunately, most allergic reactions involving grooming products are not severe. The moment your dog exhibits any sign of discomfort, itchiness, swelling, redness, skin irritation, bumps, hives, difficulty breathing or vomiting, stop using the product and begin first aid.

First-Aid Procedure

- Remain calm and soothe your pet.
- Wash your hands and/or don disposable gloves.
- Restrain or muzzle the dog if necessary.
- Triage: assess the severity of the reaction.
- If your dog's reaction is **severe**, contact the veterinarian or the ASPCA's Animal Poison Control Center at **1-888-426-4355** immediately. Prepare your dog for urgent transport to the animal hospital. Bring the offending item and any packaging with you for speedy and accurate diagnosis and treatment.
- If the allergic reaction is **mild**, thoroughly wash the dog with large amounts of clean, lukewarm water until the problematic product is completely removed.
- Apply a clean, cold (not icy) compress to the affected region.
- Contact the veterinarian for further instructions. Have the problematic item and packaging handy for reference during the call.
- Refrain from using any medication, ointment or salve until you are directed by the veterinarian.

Eye Injuries

Most grooming-related eye injuries involve either irritating the eye with a product or somehow injuring the eye itself, usually by scratching the cornea or poking it with a brush or scissors. If, despite your best efforts, Fido's eye is injured, stop grooming immediately and begin first aid.

First-Aid Procedure

- Remain calm and soothe the dog.
- Wash your hands and/or don disposable gloves.

- Restrain or muzzle the dog if necessary to prevent him from pawing at the injured eye.
- Triage: inspect the eye and assess the severity of the injury.
- If the injury is **severe**, such as if the eye is cut or abraded or large debris is embedded in or around the eye, immediately call the veterinarian and prepare to transport the dog to the animal hospital.
- If the injury is **minor**, such as if product or very small debris is in or around the eye, begin first aid.
- Carefully flush the eye with a large amount of unexpired sterile eyewash or clean tepid water. **Never** aim the water stream directly into the eye.
- **Do not** apply any ointment or salve to the eye or eye area unless directed by your veterinarian.
- Prevent the dog from pawing at the eye, which may require an Elizabethan collar or other restraint.
- Contact the veterinarian for further instructions.
- Watch for signs of infection, including discharge, redness, squinting or pawing at the eye.

Paw-Pad Perils

Although grooming shouldn't cause cracked pads, you may discover them while caring for your pooch. Debris often becomes lodged in the cracks and causes infection, tenderness and serious injury. If you discover deep cracks, infection or embedded debris, or if your pooch is limping, promptly contact the veterinarian.

Most cracks, thankfully, are minor. Moreover, many effective paw-pad moisturizers are available. Clean and dry the paws before applying any moisturizer and then follow the product's instructions.

Shockingly, I've seen "experts" recommend instant glue or adhesives to close up paw-pad cracks. To me, using a toxic chemical, especially one meant to permanently bond metal, plastic or wood, on an open wound is just plain foolish and downright dangerous. Your dog will lick his injured paw, ingest the glue and/or be permanently stuck to the floor.

Hanging, Falling and Drowning

Sorry to be melodramatic, but these horrible situations can (and unfortunately do) occur if you leave your dog unattended while grooming.

Injuries caused by hanging, falling and drowning require urgent veterinary attention. In addition, these serious and often deadly injuries require advanced first aid. Please review your pet first-aid manual and discuss appropriate techniques with your veterinarian.

Resources and
Additional Reading

Animal-Welfare Organizations

American Humane Association
www.americanhumane.org
63 Inverness Dr. E.
Englewood, CO 80112
303-792-9900

American Society for the Prevention of Cruelty to Animals (ASPCA)
www.aspca.org
424 E. 92nd St.
New York, NY 10128-6804
212-876-7700

Animal Poison Control Center, open 24 hours a day, 365 days a year,
1-888-426-4435
www.aspca.org/pet-care/poison-control/

Humane Society of the United States
www.hsus.org
2100 L St. NW
Washington, DC 20037
202-452-1100

Petfinder
www.petfinder.com
This Web site is a clearinghouse for more than twelve thousand shelters and rescues in North America and the Caribbean. My coauthor found her Miniature Poodle Shadow on this site.

U.S. Government Agencies and Regulators

Federal Trade Commission
www.ftc.gov
Consumer Response Center
600 Pennsylvania Ave. NW
Washington, DC 20580
1-877-382-4357

Food and Drug Administration (FDA)
www.fda.gov
5600 Fishers Lane
Rockville, MD 20857-0001
1-888-463-6332

FDA's Center for Veterinary Medicine
www.fda.gov/cvm
7519 Standish Place
Rockville, MD 20855-0001
240-276-9300 or 1-888-INFO-FDA

United States Department of Agriculture (USDA)
www.usda.gov
1400 Independence Ave. SW
Washington, DC 20250

Other Helpful Organizations

American Animal Hospital Association
www.healthypet.com
12575 W. Bayaud Ave.
Lakewood, CO 80228
303-986-2800

American Kennel Club
www.akc.org
8051 Arco Corporate Dr., Suite 100
Raleigh, NC 27617-3390
919-233-9767

The American Veterinary Medical Association
www.avma.org
1931 N. Meacham Rd., Suite 100
Schaumburg, IL 60173-4360
847-925-8070

Training and Obedience

Association of Pet Dog Trainers
www.apdt.com

Certification Council for Professional Dog Trainers
www.ccpdt.org
1350 Broadway, 17th Floor
New York, NY 10018
212-356-0682

Nutrition

Association of American Feed Control Officials
www.aafco.org

Food and Drug Administration
- Animal food (feed) product regulation information: www.fda.gov/cvm/prod-regulation.htm
- Pet-food recall information: www.accessdata.fda.gov/scripts/petfoodrecall

Toxic Plants

American Animal Hospital Association
- www.healthypet.com/library_view.aspx?id=133

ASPCA's Animal Poison Control Center
- www.aspca.org/site/PageServer?pagename=pro_apcc_toxicplants

Humane Society of the United States
- www.hsus.org/pets/pet_care/protect_your_pet_from_common_household_dangers/common_poisonous_plants.html

Going Green

Environmental Health Association of Nova Scotia
www.lesstoxicguide.ca
PO Box 31323, Halifax, Nova Scotia, B3K 5Y5
1-800-449-1995
- Recipes for homemade cleaning solutions: www.lesstoxicguide.ca/index.asp?fetch=household#airf

***Organic Gardening* magazine**
www.organicgardening.com

Sierra Club
www.sierraclub.org
85 Second St., 2nd Floor
San Francisco, CA 94105
415-977-5500
www.sierraclub.typepad.com/greenlife/2007/03/naturally_clean.html

First Aid and Disaster Preparedness

American Red Cross
www.redcross.org
2025 E St. NW
Washington, DC 20006
1-800-REDCROSS

ASPCA
• www.aspca.org/site/PageServer?pagename=pets_emergency

Federal Emergency Management Agency
www.fema.gov
PO Box 10055
Hyattsville, MD 20782-7055
1-800-621-3362
• www.fema.gov/plan/prepare/animals.shtm
• www.ready.gov/america/getakit/pets.html

Humane Society of the United States
• www.humanesociety.org/prepare

Legal Planning for Your Pets

Humane Society of the United States
• www.hsus.org/pets/pet_care/providing_for_your_pets_future_without_you

Michigan State University College of Law, Animal Legal and Historical Center
www.animallaw.info
Michigan State University College of Law
Shaw Lane
East Lansing, MI 48824-1300

Lost and Found Dogs and Pets

Find Toto
www.findtoto.com
For a fee, this company will call people in your neighborhood with an automated recorded message about your missing pet.

Pets 911
www.pets911.com
Gainey Ranch Financial Center
7377 E. Doubletree Ranch Rd., Suite 200
Scottsdale, AZ 85258
480-889-2640
Register and advertise a lost pet and find local shelters and veterinary clinics.

Traveling With Pets

Travel Web sites
- **Bark Buckle UP:** www.barkbuckleup.com
- **Dog Friendly:** www.dogfriendly.com
- **Pet Friendly Travel:** www.petfriendlytravel.com
- **Pet Travel:** www.pettravel.com
- **Pets Welcome:** www.petswelcome.com
- **Trips with Pets:** www.tripswithpets.com

Government and Animal-Welfare Groups
Federal Aviation Administration
www.faa.gov
800 Independence Ave. SW
Washington, DC 20591
1-866-835-5322
- Excellent information about flying with pets: www.faa.gov/passengers/fly_pets

Hawaii Department of Agriculture
www.hawaii.gov/hdoa/ai/aqs/info
Hawaii Department of Agriculture
1428 S. King St.
Honolulu, HI 96814
808-973-9560

International Air Transport Association
www.iata.org
Excellent information about flying with pets:
- www.iatatravelcentre.com/faq.php
- www.iata.org/whatwedo/cargo/live_animals/index.htm

United States Department of Agriculture
- www.aphis.usda.gov/animal_welfare/pet_travel/pet_travel.shtml

United States Department of State
www.state.gov
2201 C St. NW
Washington, DC 20520
202-647-4000
- Listing of foreign consular offices in the United States: www.state.gov/s/cpr/rls/fco

Traveling Without Pets

National Association of Professional Pet Sitters
www.petsitters.org
15000 Commerce Parkway, Suite C
Mt. Laurel, NJ 08054
856-439-0324

Pet Care Services Association
www.petcareservices.org
1702 East Pikes Peak Ave.
Colorado Springs, CO 80909
877-570-7788

Pet Sitters International
www.petsit.com
201 E. King St.
King, NC 27021
336-983-9222

Fun With Fido

General information:
- **Dog Play:** www.dog-play.com

Hiking:
- **Sierra Club:** www.sierraclub.org/e-files/dog_hiking.asp

Music and dancing with your dog:
- **Canine Freestyle Federation:** www.canine-freestyle.org
- **Musical Dog Sport Association:** www.musicaldogsport.org

Volunteering With Your Dog

Therapy-dog information, training and certification:
- **The Delta Society:** www.deltasociety.org
- **Love on a Leash:** www.loveonaleash.org
- **Therapy Dogs International:** www.tdi-dog.org
- **Therapy Dogs Inc.:** www.therapydogs.com

Search-and-rescue training and certification:
- California Rescue Dog Association: www.carda.org
- Disaster and Wilderness Ground Searchers, Inc.: www.dawgs.org

Community-service vacations:
- Best Friends Animal Society
  www.bestfriends.org
  5001 Angel Canyon Rd.
  Kanab, UT 84741-5000
- Green People: (435) 644-2001e
  www.greenpeople.org
  List of other sanctuaries: www.greenpeople.org/AnimalSanctuary.html

Pet-Loss Support

Many veterinary colleges and other organizations offer pet-loss and grief support. Here's a sampling.

Phone Hotlines
- ASPCA's Pet Loss Hotline: 1-877-474-3310
- Colorado State University (Argus Institute): 970-297-1242
- Cornell University: 607-253-3932
- Iowa State University: 1-888-478-7574
- Louisiana State University Best Friend Gone Project: 225-578-9547
- Michigan State University: 517-432-2696
- Ohio State University: 614-292-1823
- Tufts University: 508-839-7966
- University of California, Davis: 1-800-565-1526
- University of Illinois: 1-877-394-2273
- Virginia Tech University, Virginia–Maryland Regional College of Veterinary Medicine: 540-231-8038
- Washington State University: 509-335-5704

Web Sites
- American Veterinary Medical Association: www.avma.org/animal_health/brochures/pet_loss/pet_loss_brochure.asp
- Chance's Spot Pet Loss and Support Resources: www.chances spot.org
- Florida Animal Health Foundation: www.flahf.org/html/grief_support.htm
- University of Illinois College of Veterinary Medicine: www. vetmed.illinois.edu/CARE/

Parasites

The American Heartworm Society
www.heartwormsociety.org
PO Box 667
Batavia, IL 60510

American Lyme Disease Foundation
www.aldf.com
PO Box 466
Lyme, CT 06371

Centers for Disease Control and Prevention
www.cdc.gov
1600 Clifton Rd.
Atlanta, GA 30333
800-232-4636
- Pet information: www.cdc.gov/healthypets

The Companion Animal Parasite Council
www.capcvet.org and www.petsandparasites.org

Dogs and Ticks
www.dogsandticks.com

Natural Resources Defense Council
www.nrdc.org
40 W. 20th St.
New York, NY 10011
212-727-2700
- "Poisons on Pets: Health Hazards from Flea and Tick Products":
  www.nrdc.org/health/effects/pets/execsum.asp
- Information on chemicals used in pet products:
  www.greenpaws.org/products.php
- Information on pet-product safety:
  www.nrdc.org/health/effects/qpets.asp#products

University of Illinois College of Veterinary Medicine
- Information about West Nile virus: www.vetmed.illinois.edu/czr/
  wnvpets.html

United States Department of Agriculture
West Nile–virus disease map: diseasemaps.usgs.gov/

The Weather Channel
www.weather.com
Flea-season map: www.weather.com/activities/homeandgarden/pets/fleaactivity
.html

Dirt Emergencies

United States Department of Agriculture
Plant database includes illustrations and maps showing distribution: www.plants
.usda.gov

Books

- **Davis, Christine.** *For Every Dog an Angel.* **Portland, OR:** Lighthearted Press,
  2004.
- **Spira, Harold R.** *Canine Terminology.* **Wenatchee, WA:** Dogwise Publishing,
  2002.
- **Tack, Karen, and Alan Richardson.** *Hello Cupcake.* **Boston:** Houghton Mifflin
  Co., 2008.

Photograph Credits

All photographs by Michael Vistia, Vistia Designs unless otherwise indicated.

Cover: L–R, Bailey Fergus, proudly spoiled, owned and loved by Bill and Anna Fergus; Baxter, David Malkin's best friend; Rafa, loved by John J. Lanzendorf; Lily, loved and cherished by Rosemary Withaeger; Walter Little Touch of Satan, owned and loved by John Sattelmaier; K. B., loved by Rolli Grayson. Cover photo by Sheri Berliner, www.petraits.com.

p. ii: Top row L–R, Shadow, Ian Danger Cahr's best buddy and favorite Woo. Molly, the happy girl loved by Dave and Joann Reed. Rufus, the bouncing baby boy loved by Jim, Shelley, Jimmy and Kathleen Rafferty. Middle row L–R, Lola, loved forever by Lisa, Bill, Darienne and Jenna. Rudy, baby of the family loved by Pat, Dreama, Sarah, Patrick and Katie Rafferty. Duke, the big ol' teddy bear loved by Bobby Moore and Crystal Rafferty. Bottom row L–R, Betty, loved by Kate, Isabel, Claire and Rob Levin. Allie, loved by Taylor and Nicole Golub. Murphy Margaret Wattman, loved by ML and Brian.

p. 1: L–R, Zeke and Arthur Rafferty, loved by Billy Rafferty.

p. 11: L–R, Lily and Louis Erspamer: the puppy loves of my life.

p. 29: L–R, Sophie and Solomon, loved and missed by Oprah Winfrey. Photo Copyright: 1999 Harpo Print, LLC/All Rights Reserved/Photographer: George Burns.

p. 49: L–R, Buster and Clancy Roffe, beloved sheepdogs of the Roffe Family.

p. 65: L–R, Link, Cochon and Tron, loved and cherished by Chef Art Smith and Artist Partner Jesus Salgueiro.

p. 89: Bella, loved by Sheri Salata.

p. 115: L–R, Rafa and Louis, loved by John J. Lanzendorf.

p.127: L–R, Gooey Timmers, the happiest dog I ever met. Trio, loved by Sue Naiden, the power of three will set you free!

p. 153: Shadow, Ian Danger Cahr's best buddy and favorite Woo.

p. 181: Bottom row L–R, Moby Dick McMillan. Jesse, loved by Alan and Judy Yale. Chewbacca McMillan. Middle row L–R, Tower Daisy Sunshine, loved by the McKeever-Larry Family: Jeffery, Susan, Lester-Malik, Chad Amir and Alana Sahara. Zeke Rafferty, loved by Billy Rafferty. K.B., loved by Rolli Grayson. Back row, Keela, loved by Rolli Grayson.

p. 203: L–R, Chloé Connolly, sent by Coco for Trudye to help heal her broken heart. Cagney and Bogart Damon, loved by Alexa, Dana, Jimmy, Marilyn, Antonio and the fish Trentadue. Lily Harris. Huckleberry Pollack.

p. 215: Walter Little Touch of Satan, owned and loved by John Sattelmaier. Photo by Sheri Berliner, www.petraits.com.

p. 229: L–R, Oscar, loved by Tamron Hall, News Anchor MSNBC. Charlie "the lover," loved by Bill Heffernan.

p. 255 L–R, Zander and Zoe Quick, loved by Steve and Melissa Quick.

p. 269: L–R, Stuart the Rascal and Lily the Romantic, loved by Dan Smith and Noel Shaw.

p. 313: L–R, Baxter, David Malkin's best friend. Lola, loved forever by Lisa, Bill, Darienne and Jenna. Sammy, loved by Jackie, Joseph, Jackson and Justin Petree.

p. 333: L–R, Maro, the stinkiest dog in the world! Loved by Simona Iosif and Paul Payton. Spike and Lily, loved by Dylan and Miles Burke. Princess Poppy Rose, loved by Fran and Eric Abramovitz.

p. 347: Sebastian Arial Flounder Vistia, the biggest little dog you'll ever meet.

p. 359: L–R, Charlie and Tophie, loved by Emmett and Nancy Peck. Lexie and Nicole Povsher, my two Uptown Girls.

INDEX

ABOUT THE AUTHORS

Billy Rafferty is a nationally recognized, multicertified and award-winning pet stylist and dog care expert who has been working with dogs for over twenty-five years. In addition to being a Certified Master Groomer, Dermatech Specialist and Companion Animal Hygienist, Billy is a sanctioned grooming show judge and a highly regarded speaker and lecturer. Billy is the owner and principal stylist at Doggy Dooz Pet Styling Salon in Chicago, Illinois. His clients include Oprah Winfrey, NBC News' Tamron Hall and Chef Art Smith. Billy shares his life (and sofa!) with Zeke, a Portuguese Water Dog, and Arthur, a Cocker Spaniel.

Jill Cahr is an accomplished writer and has been involved with Chicago animal shelters and rescues for over a decade. In her former life as a litigation and intellectual property attorney, she earned a prestigious clerkship for a United States District Court judge. She has lived her whole life with dogs and is as obsessed with them as you are—and she has done the research to prove it. Jill and her family share their home with Shadow, a rescued Poodle.

Visit the authors at www.happydogland.com.